T0163095

# THE TREASURES AND
# PLEASURES OF TURKEY

# By Ron and Caryl Krannich, Ph.Ds

## TRAVEL AND INTERNATIONAL BOOKS

*Best Resumes and CVs for International Jobs*
*Directory of Websites for International Jobs*
*International Jobs Directory*
*Jobs for Travel Lovers*
*Mayors and Managers in Thailand*
*Politics of Family Planning Policy in Thailand*
*Shopping and Traveling in Exotic Asia*
*Shopping in Exotic Places*
*Shopping the Exotic South Pacific*
*Travel Planning on the Internet*
*Treasures and Pleasures of Australia*
*Treasures and Pleasures of China*
*Treasures and Pleasures of Egypt*
*Treasures and Pleasures of Hong Kong*
*Treasures and Pleasures of India*
*Treasures and Pleasures of Indonesia*
*Treasures and Pleasures of Italy*
*Treasures and Pleasures of Morocco and Tunisia*
*Treasures and Pleasures of Mexico*
*Treasures and Pleasures of Paris and the French Riviera*
*Treasures and Pleasures of the Philippines*
*Treasures and Pleasures of Rio and São Paulo*
*Treasures and Pleasures of Singapore and Bali*
*Treasures and Pleasures of Singapore and Malaysia*
*Treasures and Pleasures of Southern Africa*
*Treasures and Pleasures of Thailand*
*Treasures and Pleasures of Turkey*
*Treasures and Pleasures of Vietnam and Cambodia*

## BUSINESS AND CAREER BOOKS AND SOFTWARE

*101 Dynamite Answers to Interview Questions*
*101 Secrets of Highly Effective Speakers*
*201 Dynamite Job Search Letters*
*America's Top Internet Job Sites*
*Best Jobs for the 21st Century*
*Change Your Job, Change Your Life*
*The Complete Guide to International Jobs and Careers*
*The Complete Guide to Public Employment*
*The Directory of Federal Jobs and Employers*
*Discover the Best Jobs for You!*
*Dynamite Cover Letters*
*Dynamite Networking for Dynamite Jobs*
*Dynamite Resumes*
*Dynamite Salary Negotiations*
*Dynamite Tele-Search*
*The Educator's Guide to Alternative Jobs and Careers*
*Find a Federal Job Fast!*
*From Air Force Blue to Corporate Gray*
*From Army Green to Corporate Gray*
*From Navy Blue to Corporate Gray*
*Get a Raise in 7 Days*
*High Impact Resumes and Letters*
*No One Will Hire Me!*
*Interview for Success*
*Job Hunting Guide*
*Job-Power Source* and *Ultimate Job Source* (software)
*Jobs and Careers With Nonprofit Organizations*
*Military Resumes and Cover Letters*
*Moving Out of Education*
*Moving Out of Government*
*Re-Careering in Turbulent Times*
*Resumes & Job Search Letters for Transitioning Military Personnel*
*Savvy Interviewing*
*Savvy Networker*
*Savvy Resume Writer*

# THE TREASURES AND PLEASURES OF

# Turkey

## BEST OF THE BEST IN TRAVEL AND SHOPPING

RON AND CARYL KRANNICH, PH.DS

IMPACT PUBLICATIONS
MANASSAS PARK, VA

# THE TREASURES AND PLEASURES OF TURKEY

**Photos:** Cover photos and those on pages 67, 133, 173, and 201 courtesy of the Ministry of Tourism, Turkey. All remaining photos were taken by Ron and Caryl Krannich.

### Library of Congress Cataloguing-in-Publication Data

Krannich, Ronald L.
    The treasures and pleasures of Turkey: best of the best in travel and shopping / Ronald L. Krannich,
Caryl Rae Krannich
        p. cm. – (Impact guides)
    Includes bibliographical references and index.
    ISBN 1-57023-180-X
    1. Shopping – Turkey – Guidebooks. 2. Turkey –
Guidebooks. I. Krannich, Caryl Rae.
II. Title. III. Series.
                               2002109077

**Publisher:** For information on Impact Publications, including current and forthcoming publications, authors, press kits, related websites, online bookstore, and submission requirements, visit Impact's website: www.impactpublications.com. For additional information on this and other books in the series, see these related websites: www.ishoparoundtheworld.com and www.contentfortravel.com.

**Publicity/Rights:** For information on publicity, author interviews, and subsidiary rights, contact the Media Relations Department: Tel. 703-361-7300, Fax 703-335-9486, or email info@impactpub lications.com.

**Sales/Distribution:** Bookstore sales are handled through Impact's trade distributor: National Book Network, 15200 NBN Way, Blue Ridge Summit, PA 17214, Tel. 1-800-462-6420. All other sales and distribution inquiries should be directed to the publisher: Sales Department, IMPACT PUBLICATIONS, 9104 Manassas Drive, Suite N, Manassas Park, VA 20111-5211, Tel. 703-361-7300, Fax 703-335-9486, or e-mail: info@impactpublications.com.

# Contents

# Liabilities and Warranties

WHILE THE AUTHORS HAVE ATTEMPTED to provide accurate information, please remember that names, addresses, phone and fax numbers, e-mail addresses, and website URLs do change, and shops, restaurants, and hotels do move, go out of business, or change ownership and management. Such changes are a constant fact of life in ever-changing Turkey. We regret any inconvenience such changes may cause to your travel and shopping plans.

Inclusion of shops, restaurants, hotels, and other hospitality providers in this book in no way implies guarantees nor endorsements by either the authors or publisher. Recommendations are provided solely for your reference. The honesty and reliability of shops can best be ensured by **you**. It's okay to be a little paranoid when travel-shopping. Indeed, always ask the right questions, request proper receipts and documents, use credit cards, take photos, and observe several other shopping rules we outline in Chapter 3 (pages 34-64) as well as on our companion website: www.ishoparoundtheworld.com.

*The Treasures and Pleasures of Turkey* provides numerous tips on how you can best experience a trouble-free adventure. As in any unfamiliar place or situation, and regardless of how trustworthy strangers may appear, the watchwords are always the same – *"watch your wallet!"* If it seems too good to be true, it probably is. Any *"unbelievable deals"* should be treated as such. In Turkey, as elsewhere in the world, there simply is no such thing as a free lunch. Everything has a cost. Just make sure you don't pay dearly by making unnecessary shopping mistakes!

# Preface

WELCOME TO ANOTHER IMPACT GUIDE that explores the many unique treasures and pleasures of shopping and traveling in one of the most fascinating destinations in Europe, Asia, and the Middle East – Turkey. Join us as we explore this country's many treasures and pleasures, from great shops and top restaurants to fine hotels, sightseeing, and entertainment. We'll put you in touch with the best of the best these places have to offer visitors. We'll take you to popular tourist destinations, but we won't linger long, since *lifestyle shopping* is our travel passion – combining great shopping with terrific dining and sightseeing. If you follow us to the end, you'll discover a whole new dimension to both travel and shopping. Indeed, as the following pages unfold, you'll learn there is a lot more to Turkey, and travel in general, than taking tours, visiting popular sites, and acquiring an unwelcome weight gain attendant with new on-the-road dining habits.

Exciting Turkey offers wonderful travel-shopping experiences for those who know what to look for, where to go, and how to properly travel and shop major destinations in this fascinating country. While this country is a popular place for visiting mosques, museums, monuments, ancient ruins, beaches, and obscure historical sites that often characterize Turkey's travel image, for us Turkey is an important shopping destination that yields unique carpets, textiles, ceramics, art, antiques, leather goods, and handicrafts as well as excellent restaurants, hotels, and sightseeing. Their people, products, sights, and sounds have truly enriched our lives.

If you are familiar with our other *Impact Guides*, you know this will not be another standard travel guide to history, culture, and sightseeing in Turkey. Our approach to travel is very different. We operate from a particular perspective, and we frequently show our attitude rather than just present you with the sterile "travel facts." While we seek good travel value, we're not budget travelers who are interested in taking you along the low road to Turkey. We've been there, done that at one stage in our lives, and found it to be an interesting learning experience. If that's the way you want to go, you'll find several guidebooks on budget travel to Turkey as well as a whole travel industry geared toward servicing budget travelers and backpackers with everything from cheap guest houses to Internet cafés. At the same time, we're not obsessed with local history, culture, and sightseeing. We get just enough history and sightseeing to make our travels interesting rather than obsessive. Accordingly, we include very little on history and sightseeing, because they are not our main focus; we also assume you have that information covered from other resources. When we discuss history and sightseeing, we do so in abbreviated form, highlighting what we consider to be the essentials. As you'll quickly discover, we're very focused – we're in search of quality shopping and travel. Rather than spend eight hours a day sightseeing, we may only devote two hours to sightseeing and another six hours learning about the local shopping scene. As such, we're very people- and product-oriented. Through shopping, we meet many interesting and talented people and learn a great deal about their country.

> ❏ Our approach to travel is very different from most guidebooks – we offer a unique travel perspective and we frequently show our attitude.
>
> ❏ We're not obsessed with local history, culture, and sightseeing. We get just enough history and sightseeing to make our travels interesting rather than obsessive.
>
> ❏ Through shopping, we meet many interesting and talented people and learn a great deal about their country.
>
> ❏ We're street people who love "the chase" and the serendipity that comes with our style of travel.

What we really enjoy doing, and think we do it well, is shop. For us, shopping makes for great travel adventure and contributes to local development. Indeed, we're street people who love "the chase" and the serendipity that comes with our style of travel. We especially enjoy discovering quality products; meeting local artists and craftspeople; unraveling new travel-shopping rules; forming friendships with local business people;

staying in fine places; and dining in great restaurants where we often meet talented chefs and visit their fascinating kitchens. In the case of Turkey, we seek the best quality carpets, art, antiques, textiles, crafts, apparel, and jewelry as well as discover some of the best artists and craftspeople. In so doing, we learn a great deal about Turkey and its very talented and entrepreneurial people.

The chapters that follow represent a particular travel perspective of Turkey. We purposefully decided to write more than just another travel guide with a few pages on shopping. While some travel guides include a brief section on the "what's" and "where's" of shopping, we saw a need to also explain the "how-to's" of shopping in Turkey (Chapter 3). Such a book would both educate and guide you through this country's shopping mazes – from finding great carpets, ceramics, antiques, and handicrafts and navigating numerous bazaars to getting the best deals and arranging for the shipping of large items – as well as put you in contact with the best of the best in restaurants, accommodations, and sightseeing. It would be a combination travel-shopping guide designed for people in search of quality travel experiences.

The perspective we develop throughout this book is based on our belief that traveling should be more than just another adventure in eating, sleeping, sightseeing, and taking pictures of unfamiliar places. Whenever possible, we attempt to bring to life the fact that Turkey has real people and interesting products that you, the visitor, will find exciting. This is a country with very talented artists, craftspeople, traders, and entrepreneurs. When you leave Turkey, you will take with you not only some unique experiences and memories but also quality products that you will certainly appreciate for years to come.

We have not hesitated to make qualitative judgments about the best of the best in Turkey. If we just presented you with travel and shopping information, we would do you a disservice by not sharing our discoveries, both good and bad. While we know that our judgments may not be valid for everyone, we offer them as **reference points** from which you can make your own decisions. Our major emphasis is on quality shopping, dining, accommodations, sightseeing, and entertainment, and in that order. We look for shops which offer excellent quality and styles. If you share our concern for quality shopping, as well as fine restaurants and hotels, you will find many of our recommendations useful to planning and implementing your Turkey adventure. Best of all, you'll engage in what has become a favorite pastime for many of today's discerning travelers – lifestyle shopping!

Throughout this book we have included "tried and tested" shopping information. We make judgments based upon our experience – not on judgments or sales pitches from others. Our research method was quite simple: we did a great deal of shopping and we looked for quality products. We acquired some fabulous items, and gained valuable knowledge in the process. However, we could not make purchases in every shop, nor do we have any guarantee that your experiences will be the same as ours. Shops close, ownership or management changes, and the shop you visit may not be the same as the one we shopped. So use this information as a starting point, but ask questions and make your own judgments before you buy. For related information on shopping in Turkey, including many of our recommended shops, please visit our companion website: www.ishoparoundtheworld.com.

Whatever you do, enjoy Turkey. While you need not *"shop 'til you drop,"* at least shop it well and with the confidence that you are getting good quality and value. Don't just limit yourself to small items that will fit into your suitcase or pass up something you love because of shipping concerns. Consider acquiring larger items that can be safely and conveniently shipped back home. Indeed, shipping is something that needs to be *arranged* rather than lamented or avoided.

We wish to thank the many people who contributed to this book. They include shop owners, hotel personnel, tourism officials, and others who took time to educate us about the local shopping, dining, and travel scenes. A special thanks goes to Turkish Airlines and the Ministry of Tourism for assisting us with various phases of the project. We especially wish to thank Nedim Kurtuluş and Serkan Taner who served as our guide and driver for this unusual approach to travel in Turkey. They cheerfully tolerated our many hours of interviews and shopping.

We wish you well as you prepare for Turkey's many treasures and pleasures. The book is designed to be used in the streets of Turkey. If you **plan** your journey according to the first three chapters and **navigate** our major destinations based on the next six chapters, you should have an absolutely marvelous time. You'll discover some exciting places, acquire some choice items, and return home with many fond memories of a terrific adventure. If you put this book to use, it will indeed become your best friend – and passport – to the many unique treasures and pleasures of Turkey. Enjoy!

Ron and Caryl Krannich
krannich@impactpublications.com

# THE TREASURES AND
# PLEASURES OF TURKEY

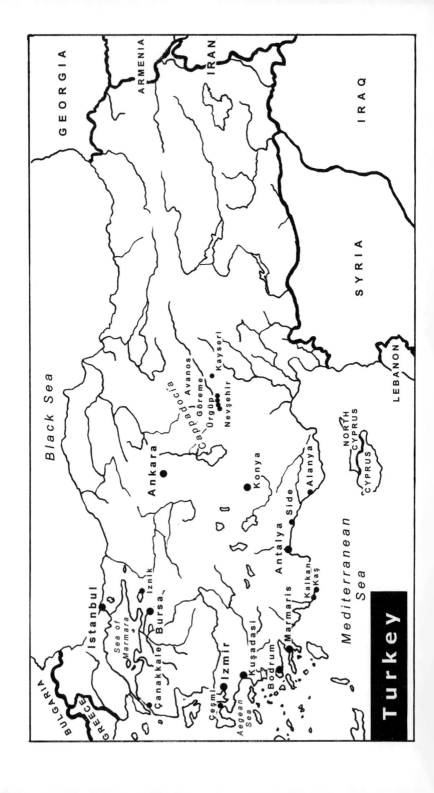

# Welcome to
# Surprising Turkey

W ELCOME TO ONE OF THE WORLD'S MOST
fascinating destinations for both travel and shopping. Geographically part of Europe, but also
very Middle Eastern and Asian, Turkey lies at
the crossroads of Europe, Asia, and the Middle
East. It was once known as Asia Minor. In fact, today Turkey
often defies geographic classification – Is it part of Europe, Asia,
or the Middle East? Even the Turks are uncertain where they
belong, with many feeling they are more Asian than European!
For now, many people are content to place Turkey with Europe
in the hope that it will eventually become a member of the EU
(European Union).

## AN EXCITING DESTINATION

Turkey is a country of great history, beauty, charm, and exotic
sights and sounds. From energetic, crowded, and architecturally
impressive Istanbul on the delightful Bosphorus Straits to the
fairy chimneys of Cappodocia to the emerald seas of the Mediterranean and the many mountains and lakes elsewhere in the
country, Turkey is a visual feast beckoning visitors to sample its
many unique treasures and pleasures. It's one of the few countries that truly excite first-time visitors who often want to come

back again and again. Indeed, more so than most countries we visit, we often hear the same comments from visitors – *"fabulous trip," "best-ever trip," "gorgeous country and really wonderful people,"* or *"I'm ready to go back again, and for much longer this time!"* It's a country that will touch you in many positive ways.

## COMPELLING TURKEY

Within the past decade Turkey has attracted numerous visitors who have discovered its many fascinating treasures and pleasures. Being a relatively inexpensive destination, Turkey offers good value to most travelers. Food, accommodations, and transportation are amazingly cheap compared to nearby European destinations. In fact, Europeans now crowd Turkey's many Mediterranean coastal towns and beaches precisely because it is such a good value compared to elsewhere in Europe and around the Mediterranean. With over 7,000 kilometers of picturesque coastline, Turkey continues to draw numerous beach lovers, water enthusiasts, sailors, and resort-oriented tourists.

❏ This is one of the few countries that truly excite first-time visitors.

❏ Being a relatively inexpensive destination, Turkey offers good value to most travelers.

❏ Turkey's 5,000 miles of lovely coastline draws numerous beach lovers, water enthusiasts, sailors, and resort-oriented tourists.

❏ Turkish hospitality is truly exceptional – warm and generous, like meeting a long-lost friend.

But it's the people who make this such a delightful place to visit. Turkish hospitality is truly exceptional – warm and generous, like meeting a long-lost friend. Visitors usually leave this country with fond memories of the wonderful people they met, individuals who were genuinely pleased visitors came so far to see their country, and who helped facilitate the visitor's stay. Friendly, helpful, and colorful, the Turkish people are the highlight of any visit to this compelling country.

## A GRAND HISTORY FOR THE BOOKS

But there is much more to Turkey than beaches and resorts. This is a country of great history, sightseeing, and shopping. Its history of mankind dates nearly 10,000 years and encompasses many famous civilizations, cities, and empires. The heartland of modern Turkey, the Anatolia, hosted many great civilizations from the Bronze Age to the 20<sup>th</sup> century. Step into Ankara's impressive Anatolian Civilizations Museum and you'll come away with a renewed appreciation of Turkey's ancient and modern history. This was the homeland of the powerful Hittite Empire (1900 - 1250 BC) which was centered near Konya and encompassed Anatolia and parts of present-day Syria. At various times the Greeks and Romans controlled much of coastal Turkey and left in their aftermath great cities and eternal stone monuments throughout modern-day Turkey – Troy, Ephesus, Halicarnassus (Bodrum), Lydia, Van, Izmir, Iznik, Aspendos, Perge, Side, and Pergamum, For nearly 1,000 years the Byzantine Empire ruled from Constantinople, or today's Istanbul.

Modern Turkish history encompasses the Ottoman Empire centered in Istanbul. Capturing Constantinople in 1453, the Ottoman Turks created one of the world's great empires. From the 15th century until the defeat of the Turks in World War I, the Ottoman Empire variously ruled parts of Europe, the Middle East, and North Africa. During the 16th century, under the rule of Sulan Süleyman the Magnificent (1520-1566), the Ottoman Empire reached its zenith in power, wealth, and ethnic diversity. Indeed, in Istanbul you can see much of the art and architecture, especially in mosques and palaces, created during this flourishing period which also found the Ottomans engaged in constant warfare.

*Few countries in the world can claim to have been shaped so fundamentally by one very determined and powerful man – Kemal Atatürk.*

With the collapse of the Ottoman Empire and its impending dismemberment by the Allies immediately following World War I came the rise to power of the Turk's war hero, Mustafa Kemal, who united Turkey in the War for Independence. Rising to the occasion with great leadership and political skills, he amazingly defeated the occupying Greeks and nearly drove them into the sea near Izmir. Most important of all for Turkey's future, Mustafa Kemal renegotiated the terms of the Ottoman Empire's defeat in World War I and declared the Turkish Republic in 1923. A constitution was adopted in 1924, and thereafter Mustafa Kemal inaugurated numerous radical political, economic, and social reforms that fundamentally transformed Turkey into a Western nation, including all the trappings of Western-style democracy. Indeed, the modern history of Turkey is all about the indelible stamp of Mustafa Kemal on what became a new Turkish nation stretching from Europe to Asia,

Few countries in the world can claim to have been shaped so fundamentally by one very determined and powerful man whose vision of a modern Turkish nation was such a major departure from the past history of the Turks. In many respects Mustafa Kemal is Turkey's single Founding Father. He remains omnipresent in Turkey, as his many imposing photos, paintings, and sculptures will constantly remind you wherever you travel in Turkey. In fact, he was declared "Father Turk," or Atatürk, by the Parliament and thereafter became known as Kemal Atatürk. He is responsible for creating new institutions and political principles that today characterize Turkey as a secular Western democratic – although at times heavy-handed by Western standards – state that shares very little with its nearby Islamic and Arab states, even though 99 percent of Turkey's population is Muslim. In Turkey under Kemal Atatürk, Western legal codes were instituted. Strict separation of church and state took place as Islam lost its much-coveted position as the state religion and the power of its religious leaders was serious eroded. The Turkish Arabic alphabet was replaced with a mostly Romanized alphabet modified with special phonetic symbols. The fez, considered by Kemal Atatürk as a subversive and backward symbol, was outlawed. Civil, as opposed to religious, marriages, were required. In the 1930s women were given the right to vote and hold elective office. Avoiding the mistakes of World War I, Kemal Atatürk and his successor saw to it that Turkey remained neutral during World War II. After his death in 1938, his heavy hand in the evolution of the modern Turkish state was lifted as Turkey moved more and more in the direction of a Western democracy.

Today, Turkey is the only Islamic country with a secular government and a functioning Western-style democracy. Surrounded to the south and east by a sea of radical Islamic states (Syria, Iraq, and Iran) and to the west by a not-so-receptive Europe, Turkey remains a staunch ally of the United States and an active member of NATO. While it continues to seek, but is denied, admission to the European Union (EU), its fate is more closely tied to the United States than Europe. Turkey seems to be the odd country out in Europe – a continent of governments that ostensibly despise the Turks after over 1,000 years of often bitter history and negative stereotypes. While European tourists flock to Turkey's attractive and inexpensive seaside resorts, their governments are often viewed in the eyes of Turks as anti-Turk. Surprising to some, the Turks are more friendly with Americans and feel much closer to the United States than to any European country.

# TURKEY, TERRORISM, AND TOURISM

Since Turkey is 99 percent Muslim, many potential visitors who know little about Turkey are concerned about safety there, especially the potential for political violence and terrorism, given Turkey's close proximity to the radical Islamic states of Iraq, Iran, and Syria. In fact, immediately following the September 11th terrorist events in the United States, tourism basically collapsed throughout Turkey, except in a few resort areas frequented by European tourists. But very few Americans traveled to Turkey because of perceived terrorism threats. Accordingly, locals asked us this question: *"Why aren't the Americans coming? After all, we're sending our troops to help fight the war on terrorism and we have American troops stationed in Turkey?"*

While difficult to answer, the question itself says a lot about safety in Turkey and Turkish friendship. Except for the traffic, safety doesn't get much better than in Turkey. A fiercely secular state with a strong police and military presence, the government doesn't tolerate outbreaks of religious fundamentalism or political violence. At the same time, the Turks are what some observers might call "good Muslims." Peaceful and religious, they confine their religious activities to their mosques and homes, and religious leaders in Turkey are reluctant to cross the secular line strictly laid down by the state. As you'll frequently be reminded during your stay, this is still Kemal Atatürk's Turkey of limited political freedom, where crossing that line will get one into big trouble. It's a country obsessed with maintaining stability, order, and secularism in a region noted for instability, disorder, and religious fundamentalism.

❑ Turkey is the only Islamic country with a secular government and a functioning Western-style democracy.

❑ The Turks feel much closer to the United States than to any European country.

❑ Except for the traffic, safety doesn't get much better than in Turkey.

❑ Turkey is a country obsessed with maintaining stability, order, and secularism in a region noted for instability, disorder, and religious fundamentalism.

Except for the political violence associated with the Kurdish conflict in southeast Turkey, which has all but ended in recent years, Turkey is a very open and safe country to travel in. Most people genuinely welcome visitors and try to be helpful to their "guests." In large part this is what Turkish hospitality is all about – treating you warmly as their guests. It's this hospitality that truly impresses many visitors who feel so comfortable in what is a seemingly chaotic and exotic country.

## SHOPPING TREASURES

While Turkey has a grand history represented by many monuments as well as numerous appealing seaside resorts to enjoy the sun, surf, and turquoise seas, it also is a shopper's paradise. From the Grand Bazaar, chic boutiques, and dazzling jewelry shops of Istanbul to the antique, ceramic, rug, and leather shops of Bursa, Ankara, Cappadocia, Konya, Antalya, Marmaris, Bodrum, Kuşadasi, Izmir, and Çeşme, Turkey has a great deal to offer travel-shoppers. You can easily spend weeks treasure hunting for many unique products at bargain prices. Indeed, one of the most enjoyable ways to experience Turkey is to go shopping in its many bazaars, markets, and shops. There you will discover some wonderful products, experience exotic sights and sounds, meet interesting people, and hopefully walk away with many unique treasures which also were good buys.

But shopping can be a tricky business in Turkey, as is the case in most countries that boast colorful bazaars, markets, and shops that primarily cater to the tourist trade. Knowing where to go for good quality and prices is often a mystery, and especially if you are with a tour guide who leads you into so-called "recommended" shops that invariably give kickbacks (commissions) to guides for stopping by with their clients.

*One of the most enjoyable ways to experience Turkey is to go shopping in its many bazaars, markets, and shops.*

As you will quickly discover, this book is especially designed for travel-shoppers who want to have a wonderful time discovering many of Turkey's unique treasures. We have attempted to cut through the shopping clutter to identify some of the best shops in several key destinations in Turkey. At the same time, we identify important aspects of the local shopping culture – from bargaining to "reading" shops – which should be useful to you as you make your sojourns into bazaars and shops.

But this book is about more than just shopping. As travel-shoppers, we're into "lifestyle shopping," which means we enjoy combining shopping with great restaurants, hotels, and sightseeing. To just go shopping without taking in these other complementary aspects of travel to Turkey would be to miss the many joys of traveling through this fabulous land.

# DISCOVERING OUR TURKEY

The chapters that follow take you on a well worn path through the many highlight destinations of Turkey. We take you on what could well be a fast-paced two- to four-week trip to several popular and varied places.

The heart of our journey is **Istanbul**. Strategically located on the Borphorus, with breathtaking architecture and crowded streets, markets, and bazaars, it's an energetic, exciting, exotic, and vibrant city with lots to see and do. A melting pot of European, Asian, and Arabic forces, Istanbul is unlike any other city you have visited. As might be expected, it boasts some of the best shops, restaurants, hotels, and sights in the country. Plan to spend at least four days here, although a week would be much better and more rewarding. The city constantly unfolds with numerous travel and shopping surprises. Like many other visitors to Turkey, you may fall in love with this city of great character.

**Bursa** to the south of Istanbul is an old city with many delightful surprises. Often bypassed by tour groups, it's a "must see" destination on our list of travel-shopping destinations. It boasts many interesting antique shops and a fun market and bazaar, making this an especially rewarding place to visit. The nearby town of **Iznik**, once Turkey's most famous ceramic center, still produces some lovely treasures you won't want to miss.

**Ankara**, Turkey's capital and center for diplomatic activities, is usually bypassed by tour groups on their way to ostensibly more interesting places in Anatolia. Many visitors, who don't know better, view Ankara as "unTurkish" – a somewhat boring modern Western city. That's unfortunate, if you are on one of those tours. It's good news if you want to avoid the tourist crowds. The real winners here are the diplomatic personnel who understand the shopping treasures of Ankara. The city boasts a wonderful market (Copper Alley) and many excellent shops that offer quality products at good non-tourist prices. Ankara also houses the country's best museum – Anatolian Civilizations Museum – and offers many fine restaurants and hotels. Whatever you do, make sure you budget a couple of days in Ankara. If you follow our recommendations, you'll find many unique treasures and pleasures in this city.

**Cappadocia** is everyone's favorite area with its unusual fairy chimneys, subterranean cities, delightful small but intriguing towns, and one of the world's most exciting hot air balloon trips. Centered on the communities of Urgüp, Ortahiser, and Avanos, shopping in this area is full of interesting surprises ranging from antiques and ceramics to rugs and paintings. Plan to spend two to four days exploring this fascinating area. Be sure to bring lots of film since this whole area is a photographer's paradise.

**Konya** is a conservative religious center best known for the famous whirling dervishes and the Mevlâna Museum and mosque. The city boasts a few interesting shops well worth visiting. However, given the conservative nature of this community, there's not much to do here. A three- to four-hour drive through Konya may be sufficient to take in its many sites and shops. In fact, if you drive from Cappadocia to Antalya, you can't miss Konya since it's on the main highway.

Located in the south of Turkey on the Mediterranean Sea, **Antalya** and **Side** are especially popular destinations for beach-loving German tourists and budget travelers. Being resort cities, they boast many aggressive tourist shops and vendor stalls (*"Can I help you spend your money?"*) which offer jewelry, carpets, clothing, ceramics, and leather goods. At the same time, the surrounding area is rich with Roman ruins, especially well preserved amphitheaters in Side, Perge, and Aspendos. A visit to this delightful and varied area combines appealing beach and water activities with shopping and historic sightseeing.

Farther west, along the road to Marmaris and Bodrum (the Turquoise Coast), are the charming Mediterranean coastal fishing villages of **Kaş** and **Kalkan**. These are two of Turkey's most delightful travel and shopping destinations. Small but catering to upscale travelers and yachtsmen, the two villages with their cobblestone streets offer numerous quality shops and restaurants – the ultimate in lifestyle shopping. They are pleasant departures from the often crowded packaged tourist centers of Antalya and Side. Kaş and Kalkan are great places to just kill time and enjoy the lovely settings.

Located along the Mediterranean, the port of **Marmaris** is a popular destination for day-trippers from the nearby Greek island of Rhodes, cruise ships, and yachtsmen. Its attractive marina with many million-dollar-plus yachts, bazaars, and restaurants make this an appealing day stop along the way to Bodrum and other destinations to the northwest.

**Bodrum** is everyone's favorite resort destination. Popular with European yachtsmen, jet setters, and well-heeled travelers in search of Turkey's best resort pleasures, Bodrum seems to have it all – a gorgeous oceanfront setting surrounded by white-cubed houses in the hills and lots of fine restaurants, hotels, shops, and entertainment venues.

**Kuşadasi**, Turkey's gateway port city to the famous nearby

Roman ruins of Ephesus, is located halfway between Bodrum and Izmir. It's a city of shops and restaurants that heavily depends on regular cruise ship traffic that disembarks hundreds of passengers each day into the downtown area. The city's huge market area, boasting a high concentration of jewelry, carpet, leather, and ceramic shops, beckons visitors to shop 'til they drop!

The small but exclusive coastal town of **Çeşme** is a pleasant surprise. Especially popular with upscale French tourists and locals from Izmir and Istanbul, Çeşme is connected to Izmir by a surprising six-lane toll road which was built in response to NATO's war efforts in Bosnia during the 1990s. Located only a half hour west of Izmir, Çeşme offers some excellent shopping along with many resort amenities.

Nearby **Izmir** is Turkey's second largest port and its third largest city. Situated on a large ringed gulf with mountains in the background, this is a major business center and a pleasant city for shopping, dining, and sightseeing. Its tree-lined boulevards, upscale shopping, and interesting bazaars make Izmir one of the most interesting stops in Turkey.

## A UNIQUE PEOPLE PERSPECTIVE

The pages that follow are not your typical treatment of travel in Turkey. While we recognize the importance of background information for developing a travel-friendly perspective, this book is not big on history, culture, and sightseeing. Indeed, there are numerous general guidebooks available on Turkey that basically focus on similar themes – history and culture – and we encourage you to acquire one or more of these guides as a companion to the focus on this book. Many of these books are heavy on history, monuments, and museums to the near exclusion of contemporary Turkey and its many talented people. Numerous budget guides, touting the oft repeated *"I'm a traveler, not a tourist"* philosophy, outline how to experience inexpensive Turkey on your own. They provide a generous offering of cheap restaurants, hotels, and transportation for extremely budget-conscious travelers. If this is your primary

*We learned long ago that one of the best ways to meet the local people and experience another culture is to shop!*

interest and style of travel, you will find several guidebooks that offer this approach to Turkey.

Like other volumes in the ***Impact Guides*** series (see the order form on pages 252-253), this book focuses on quality travel-shopping in Turkey. Yes, shopping. Contrary to what some travelers may think, shopping is not a sin. It can and does change lives for the better. We learned long ago that one of the most enjoyable aspects of travel – and one of the best ways to meet people, experience another culture, and contribute to local economies – is to seek out the best shops, markets, factories, and galleries – and shop! In so doing, we explore the fascinating worlds of artisans, craftspeople, and shopkeepers and discover quality products, outstanding buys, and talented, interesting, and friendly people. We also help support the continuing development of local arts and crafts. As many of our enthusiastic readers testify (see the introductory four pages of this book), our approach to travel changes lives. Our approach is all about talented people and what they have to offer discerning visitors in search of such talent.

## A TRAVEL-SHOPPING EMPHASIS

Much of *The Treasures and Pleasures of Turkey* is designed to provide you with the necessary **knowledge and skills** to become an effective travel-shopper. We especially created the book with three major considerations in mind:

- Focus on quality shopping.
- Emphasis on finding unique items.
- Inclusion of travel highlights, from top hotels and restaurants to major sightseeing attractions, that especially appeal to discerning travelers.

Throughout this book we attempt to identify the **best quality shopping** in Turkey. This does not mean we have discovered the cheapest shopping or best bargains, although we have attempted to do so when opportunities for comparative shopping arose within and between communities. Our focus is primarily on shopping for **unique and quality items** that will retain their value in the long run and can be appreciated for years to come. This means many of our recommended shops may initially appear expensive. But they offer top quality and value that you will not find in many other shops. For example, when we discover a unique piece of jewelry in Istanbul, we acknowledge the fact that the work is expensive, but it is very beautiful and unique, so much so that you quickly forget the price after you acquire and continue to admire the workmanship. At the same time, we identify what we consider to be the best buys for various items, especially carpets, silk, ceramics, leather goods, antiques, and handicrafts.

We also include many of the top travel amenities and attractions in our selected cities. As with other volumes in the *Impact Guides* series, many of our readers appreciate quality travel. When they visit a country, they prefer discovering the best a country has to offer in accommodations, restaurants, sightseeing, and entertainment. While they expect good value for their travel dollar, they are not budget travelers in search of the cheapest hotels, restaurants, and transportation. With limited time, careful budgeting, and a good plan, they approach Turkey as a once-in-a-lifetime travel experience – one that will yield fond memories for many years to come. By focusing on the best Turkey has to offer, we believe you will have a terrific time in this delightful country. You'll acquire some great products, meet many wonderful people, and return home with fond memories of an exciting travel-shopping adventure.

## APPROACHING THE SUBJECT

The chapters that follow take you on a whirlwind travel-shopping adventure of Turkey with a decided emphasis on quality shopping, dining, and sightseeing. We literally put a shopping face on this place – one we believe you will thoroughly enjoy as you explore Turkey's many other pleasures.

We've given a great deal of attention to constructing a complete **user-friendly book** that focuses on the shopping process, offers extensive details on the "how," "what," and "where" of shopping, and includes a sufficient level of redundancy to be informative, useful, and usable. The chapters, for example, are organized like one would organize and implement a travel and shopping adventure. Each chapter incorporates sufficient details, including names and addresses, to get you started in some of the best shopping areas and shops in each city.

**Indexes and table of contents** are especially important to us and others who believe a travel book is first and foremost a guide to unfamiliar places. Therefore, our index includes both subjects and shops, with shops printed in bold for ease of reference; the table of contents is elaborate in detail so it, too, can be used as another handy reference index for subjects and products. If, for example, you are interested in "what to buy" or "where to shop" in Istanbul, the best reference will be the table of contents. If you are interested in carpets in Istanbul, look under "Carpets" in the index. And if you are interested in learning where you can find good quality ceramics, then look under "Ceramics" in the index. By using the table of contents and index together, you can access most any information from this book.

The remainder of this book is divided into two parts and eight additional chapters which look at both the process and content of traveling and shopping in Turkey. Part I – **"Smart Traveling and Shopping"** – assists you in preparing for your adventure by focusing on the how-to's of traveling and shopping. Chapter 2, **"Know Before You Go,"** takes you through the basics of getting to and enjoying your stay in Turkey. It includes advice on when to go, what to pack, required documents, currency, business hours, transportation, tipping, tour groups, insurance, safety, tax refunds, and useful websites. Chapter 3, **"The Shopping Treasures and Rules For Success,"** examines Turkey's major shopping strengths, from jewelry and ceramics to carpets and antiques. It also includes lots of advice on comparative shopping, shopping tips, bargaining rules, and shipping strategies for shopping at its very best.

The eight chapters in Part II – **"Great Destinations"** – examine the how, what, and where of traveling and shopping in and around several of Turkey's major cities, towns, and villages. We start where most of the action is – Istanbul – and then travel south to Bursa and Iznik in Western Anatolia. From there we head east and go clockwise through Central Anatolia, the Eastern Mediterranean, the Western Mediterranean, the South Aegean, and the North Aegean before returning to Istanbul via Çanakkale and the Dardanelles:

| | |
|---|---|
| Northwest: | Istanbul |
| Western Anatolia: | Bursa and Iznik |
| Central Anatolia: | Ankara, Cappadocia, Konya |
| Eastern Mediterranean: | Side and Antalya |
| Western Mediterranean: | Kalkan, Kaş, and Marmaris |
| South Aegean: | Bodrum and Kuşadasi |
| North Aegean: | Izmir and Çeşme |

In each place we identify major shopping strengths; detail the how, what, and where of shopping; and share information on some of the best hotels, restaurants, and sightseeing for each community and surrounding area. If you decide to cover all of our destinations, you could easily do so in four weeks by driving our circular route from Istanbul and back. But be sure to rent a car with a big trunk, or a van, since you'll most likely fill it up with many treasures you acquire along the way. As you'll quickly discover, this is a very fun and rewarding trip if you enjoy the adventure of driving in Turkey, which we highly recommend. There's no better way to really see the country, meet the people, and haul away your treasures than by car.

## OUR RECOMMENDATIONS

We hesitate to recommend specific shops, restaurants, hotels, and sites since we know the pitfalls of doing so. Shops that offered excellent products and service during one of our visits, for example, may change ownership, personnel, and policies from one year to another, or they may suddenly move to another location or go out of business. In addition, our shopping preferences may not be the same as your preferences. The same is true for restaurants, hotels, and some tourist sites.

Since we put shopping up front in our travels to Turkey, our major concern is to outline your shopping options, show you where to locate the best shopping areas, and share some useful shopping strategies that you can use anywhere in Turkey, regardless of particular shops or markets we or others may recommend. Armed with this knowledge and some basic shopping skills, you will be better prepared to locate your own shops and determine which ones offer the best products and service in relation to your own shopping and travel goals.

However, we also recognize the "need to know" when shopping in unfamiliar places. Therefore, throughout this book we list the names and locations of various shops we have found to offer good quality products. In some cases we have purchased items in these shops and can also recommend them for service and reliability. But in most cases we surveyed shops to determine the quality of products offered without making purchases. To buy in every shop would be beyond our budget, as well as our home storage capabilities! Whatever you do, treat our names and addresses as **orientation points** from which to identify your own products and shops. If you rely solely on our listings, you will miss out on one of the great adventures in Turkey – discovering your own special shops that offer unique items and exceptional value and service.

The same holds true for our recommendations for hotels, restaurants, sites, and entertainment. We sought out the best of the best in these major "travel pleasure" areas. You should find most of our recommendations useful in organizing your own special Turkey adventures.

## EXPECT A REWARDING ADVENTURE

Whatever you do, enjoy your Turkey adventure as you open yourself to a fascinating world of travel-shopping. We're confident you'll discover some very special treasures and pleasures that will also make Turkey one of your favorite destinations.

So arrange your flights and accommodations, pack your credit cards and traveler's checks, and head for this delightful destination. Two to four weeks later you should return home with much more than a set of photos and travel brochures. You will have some wonderful purchases and travel tales that can be enjoyed and relived for a lifetime.

*As a travel-shopper, you are a very treasured guest rather than just another tourist or traveler.*

Shopping and traveling in Turkey only takes time, money, and a sense of adventure. Take the time, be willing to part with some of your money, and open yourself to a whole new world of travel. If you are like us, the treasures and pleasures outlined in this book will introduce you to an exciting world of quality products, friendly people, and interesting places that you might have otherwise missed had you just passed through these countries to eat, sleep, see sites, and take pictures. When you travel our Turkey, you are not just another tourist or traveler. You are a special kind of visitor who discovers quality and learns about places through the people and products that continue to define their culture. Best of all, you support quality arts, crafts, and design as well as promote local talent, encourage entrepreneurism, and contribute to the development of local economies. As a travel-shopper, you are a very treasured guest rather than just another tourist or traveler. You'll leave Turkey with very special memories and quality products that will remind you of the wonderful time you had in a very special place called Turkey.

# PART I

# Smart
# Travel-Shopping

# Know Before You Go

T HERE ARE A FEW THINGS YOU SHOULD KNOW about Turkey before visiting this intriguing country. When, for example, is the best time of the year to visit? How should you pack? Are you likely to encounter many language problems? Should you join a tour group or travel on your own? Is it advisable to drive? What kind of documents do you need? How safe is the country? What can you legally take out of the country? Are there any particular websites that can help you plan your trip to Turkey?

Answers to these and many other basic travel questions can help you better prepare for your travel-shopping adventure.

## LOCATION AND GEOGRAPHY

Turkey occupies an area of 814,578 square kilometers, which makes it the world's 36$^{th}$ largest country. A rectangular-shaped country that is 1,660 kilometers wide, Turkey is approximately the size of Chile or Pakistan and about half the size of neighboring Iran or Alaska in the United States.

Turkey is somewhat of a geographic anomaly because of its strategic location at the crossroads of Europe, Asia, and the Middle East and Africa. Historically the great Silk Road and its legion of traders crossed this area, which is also known as Asia

Minor. The area has been a center for several ancient civilizations as well as the Roman, Greek, Byzantine, and Ottoman. In fact, there are more ancient Roman ruins in Turkey than any other country in the world. Most of Turkey is part of the far western Asian land mass, the Anatolian plain, with only three percent of the country lying within the geographic confines of Europe. However, politically, economically, and socially it has more in common with Europe and the West than with Asia and the Middle East. At the same time, Turkey has many exotic Middle Eastern and Asian elements to challenge it as being primarily a European country. Indeed, just visit the Grand Bazaar on the European side of Istanbul and you may feel as if you are in a large Middle Eastern or Asian market. As a result, Turkey is best viewed as being simultaneously European, Asian, and Middle Eastern. From a geographic and cultural perspective, it can be whatever you want it to be!

Turkey has long (7,000+ kilometers) and beautiful coastlines which it shares with the Aegean Sea in the west, the Mediterranean Sea in the south, and the Black Sea in the north. The country is a critical gateway for Russia, Ukraine, and Romania to the Mediterranean Sea via the Bosphorus Straits, Sea of Marmara, and the Dardanelles. It borders Greece and Bulgaria to the northwest; Syria, Iraq, and Iran in the south and southeast; and Georgia and Armenia in the east. It's situated adjacent to some of the world's most intriguing, if not politically controversial and unstable, countries which seem to have little effect on Turkey other than scaring away some tourists who may be geographically and politically challenged.

Turkey thus is best approached in terms of seven distinct geographic, economic, and cultural regions: Black Sea, Marmara, Aegean, Mediterranean, Central Anatolia, East Anatolia, and Southeast Anatolia. Istanbul in the Marmara region is a world unto its own. Straddling both Europe and Asia along the Bosphorus Straits and Sea of Marmara in the northwest corner of the country, this cosmopolitan yet exotic city is three times larger than the next largest city in Turkey, Ankara. Near the southeastern shore of the Sea of Marmara lies the old city of Bursa and the nearby historic town of Iznik. Ankara lies in Central Anatolia, which stretches into the fascinating region of Cappadocia. More adventuresome, politically unstable, and less developed eastern and southeastern Turkey sees few tourists. The popular Mediterranean coastal region in the south and southwest includes numerous resort cities and villages, such as Side, Antalya, Kalkan, Kaş, and Marmaris. The Aegean coastal region, which is often subdivided into the south, central, and north Aegean, encompasses the western coastal area of Turkey.

It includes such cities and towns as Bodrum, Kuşadasi, Izmir, Çeşme, and Çanakkale.

Overall, Turkey is a strikingly beautiful and geographically varied country boasting gorgeous coastlines comparable to the French and Italian Rivieras, beaches, pine forests, mountains, arid plains, and the unusual outcrops and "fairy chimneys" of Cappadocia that beg to be explored and enjoyed by car, boat, and air. You can enjoy seaside resorts in the south and south-west while, at the same time, go snow skiing in nearby mountains or sightseeing among ancient Roman ruins that lie within close proximity of your resort.

## CLIMATE AND WHEN TO GO

Depending on where you plan to visit, Turkey can be enjoyed year round. It has a varied climate influenced by its varied typography. The Mediterranean and Aegean coastal regions are known for hot summers and mild winters – a typical Mediterranean climate. The Black Sea coast tends to have warm summers, mild winters, and rain. Central Anatolia boasts hot and dry summers and cold winters. Eastern Anatolia is known for its mild summers and long cold and snowy winters. Southeastern Anatolia has hot summers and mild, although rainy, winters.

While the high tourist season tends to be in August, because of vacationing Europeans, in terms of weather and crowds, spring (April and May) and fall (September and October) are ideal times to visit several regions simultaneously in Turkey.

## WHAT TO PACK AND WEAR

Light, cotton summer clothing is appropriate for most coastal areas during the spring, summer, and fall seasons. Since evenings can get cool in the interior, you may want to pack a sweater or light jacket for those months. During the winter, pack accordingly for cold days and nights in the central and eastern part of the country.

You need not pack formal attire since even the best restaurants do not require dresses, suits, or coats or ties. Indeed, don't waste packing space with such items, which will probably never get worn on this trip. Smart casual is the best you'll ever have to dress. Resort wear is acceptable in the resort areas.

Since women are expected to cover their heads when visiting mosques, they may want to pack a scarf for such occasions.

During the summer months, sunglasses and sun hats come in handy. Be sure to wear comfortable shoes since you will most likely walk a lot as you shop and explore archaeological sites.

We recommend carrying a small compass. It will come in handy since you may frequently become disoriented by streets, maps, and bazaars which often lack important details. Indeed, signage is a problem in Turkey. Our compass usually keeps us on track and helps us get to our destinations.

## REQUIRED DOCUMENTS

You may or may not require a tourist visa, depending on your country of origin. For example, citizens of Australia, Canada, France, Germany, and Singapore can enter Turkey with a valid passport and stay up to three months. Citizens of the United States, Italy, Spain, and the United Kingdom need a visa, which can be acquired at a Turkish embassy or consulate or at the port of entry. U.S. citizens pay a US$65 visa fee (exact amount paid in U.S. currency at entry point). However, if you need a business visa, you must acquire it before arriving in Turkey.

For visa requirements and forms, go to these websites:

- Tourism Turkey          http://tourismturkey.org
- Turkey Visa             www.turkey.be/En/visa.htm
- Turkish Consulates      www.turkishconsulates.net
- Travel Docs             www.traveldocs.com/tr
- Visatogoabroad.com      http://visatogoabroad.com

## POPULATION, RELIGION, AND LANGUAGE

Turkey's total population is approximately 68 million. Nearly 40 percent of the people live in rural areas. The major cities are Istanbul, Ankara, Izmir, Adana, Antalya, and Bursa.

Ninety-nine percent of the population are Muslim. A strictly secular state, religion plays no major political role in Turkey.

While English is widely spoken in tourist areas, especially Istanbul, you may encounter language difficulties elsewhere in Turkey. But you won't get lost for long. Chances are someone who speaks some English will come along and help you.

## TIME

Turkey is two hours ahead of Greenwich Mean Time (GMT). When it's 1pm in London, it's 3pm in Istanbul. If you are from New York, Turkey will be seven hours ahead – 1pm on Tuesday in New York will be 8pm the same day in Istanbul. If you have difficulty figuring out the time differences in reference to your time zone, you may want to visit these two websites:

www.timezoneconverter.com
www.worldtimeserver.com

## SAFETY AND SECURITY

Turkey is a relatively safe place to visit, assuming you take basic travel precautions such as always securing your valuables and being leery of strangers who approach you for anything. The major safety hazard is the traffic. If you drive, do so defensively and avoid driving at night. Assume drivers do not think about other drivers on the road. Indeed, many Turkish drivers fail to signal their intentions, drive very slowly, take unexpected actions, and may stop in the middle of the road to talk to someone. You should expect the unexpected. As a pedestrian, assume you have no rights since vehicles do not feel obliged to stop for you. Be careful when crossing streets and roads as well as in choosing a safe mode of transportation. Istanbul has a very high rate of traffic-related pedestrian deaths.

Like anywhere you travel, including New York City, you should take normal safety precautions by securing your valuables. It's okay to be somewhat paranoid about your possessions, especially your passport, money, and camera – and yourself. Be very cautious with your purse and wallet – hold them very close and with a firm grip. Keep your valuables, including your money and passport, in safe places, such as your hotel safe or in a money belt. It's always a good idea to carry a photocopy of essential passport information – front info and stamped visa page – as well as traveler's check receipts separate from the originals.

If you need reassurance about travel safety to Turkey, check out the U.S. State Department's online travel advisories and tips for these countries:

travel.state.gov/travel_warnings.html

You may also want to review their pamphlet, *A Safe Trip Abroad*, which is available online (travel.state.gov), by autofax (202-647-3000), or through the U.S. Government Printing Office (Superintendent of Documents, Washington, DC 20402). It includes several useful safety tips, which many travelers often forget. It's well worth reviewing in preparation for your trip and before you pack your bags!

## GETTING THERE

Turkey is easily accessible by air, sea, rail, and land. If you are flying from the United States, the most convenient air link is Turkish Airlines which flies nonstop from New York City to Istanbul. Several other carriers fly nonstop from major European cities to Istanbul, Ankara, Izmir, and Antalya. To check on flight schedules and carriers, visit these websites:

- **Turkish Airlines**      www.turkishairlines.com
- **Expedia**                    www.expedia.com
- **Travelocity**              www.travelocity.com
- **Orbitz**                      www.orbitz.com

Turkish Airlines also maintains an extensive network of domestic routes, with frequent daily flights to and from the major cities.

Numerous cruise ships make regular stops at the ports of Istanbul, Izmir, Çeşme, Kuşadasi, Bodrum, Marmaris, and Antalya. Private yachts can enter Turkey at 40 ports along the Mediterranean and Aegean coasts.

You also can enter Turkey by train and car. Istanbul is the main rail hub for trains coming from Europe. Vehicles can enter Turkey from several border crossings. If you are driving, you'll need the following documents at the border: your passport, an international driving license, car license, and an international green card (insurance card).

## GETTING AROUND WITH EASE

If you have limited time and wish to travel comfortably and safely, we recommend taking taxis and/or hiring a car, driver, and guide to get around in the cities, especially in the cases of Istanbul, Ankara, and Izmir. Avoid driving in Istanbul since it's inconvenient to park and the traffic can be very congested.

Outside the cities, Turkey's extensive network of well maintained roads makes it easy to get around by yourself as long as you have a good map, a sense of adventure, carry a compass, don't mind occasionally stopping and asking directions, and drive defensively. Numerous rental car companies, such as Avis, Budget, Ekan, Europcar, Hertz, and Surf, are found in the major cities of Istanbul, Ankara, Antalya, and Izmir. Most other cities also will have rental car companies or travel agencies that can arrange transportation and tours. At the same time, the major cities are served by Turkish Airlines, regular bus and coach service, and first- and second-class trains operated by Turkish State Railways.

## INTERNATIONAL TOUR GROUPS

Many visitors to Turkey come with an organized tour group. Several companies offer a wide variety of interesting package tours that may focus on a particular aspect of Turkey, from history, culture, religion and textiles to sailing, bicycling, golfing, diving, or hiking. Many of these groups offer excellent value and good service. Best of all, they take out the hassles attendant with arranging your own travel details, especially local transportation, hotels, and guides. You'll find such tour groups through your local travel agent, or search for them online by using our favorite search engine for travel planning – google.com. Just enter the keywords "Travel Turkey" or "Tour Groups Turkey" and you'll pull up several relevant websites of groups specializing in travel to Turkey. You may want to check out the ads for Turkey in *International Travel News*. The names, addresses, and websites (hotlinks) of their advertisers are included in ITN's website: www.intltravelnews.com. Experienced tour operators such as San Francisco-based Cultural Folk Tours run by the energetic Bora Özkök (www.boraozkok.com) have an enthusiastic following of travelers who find his personalized approach to Turkey fascinating. You'll see Bora's big tour buses on the roads in Turkey. He also recently opened a wonderful boutique hotel in Göreme, the Cappadocia Cave Suites (see Chapter 7).

For information on travel agencies and tour operators specializing in Turkey from a variety of countries around the world, visit the Ministry of Tourism's revealing "Tour Operators" page:

www.turizmgov.tr/turizm.tb?app=diger&diger-20&Ing-eng

In the case of the United States, the list of 99 tour operators includes such familiar names as Abercrombie & Kent, Blue Heart Tours, Collette Tours, General Tours, Globus & Cosmos, Grand Circle Travel, Mountain Travel Sobek, Pacha Tours, Tauck World Discovery, Trafalgar Tours, and Travcoa. You are well advised to explore this website since it also includes the websites and e-mail addresses of the tour operators. You can learn a great deal about travel to Turkey by just exploring the websites of the tour operators. For example, the first company with a website is A.T.C. Anadolu Travel and Tours: www.atc-anadolu.com. This site includes a wealth of information on discounted international airfares, domestic and regional flights, independent travel, custom travel, package tours, blue cruises, mini tours, daily tours, car rentals, hotels, frequently asked questions, weather, and news.

## LOCAL TRAVEL ASSISTANCE

If you arrive in Turkey as an independent traveler, you can easily find local travel agencies and tour operators that offer a variety of group and customized travel services: half- to full-day city tours, car and driver, English-speaking guide, hotel reservations, train and airline ticketing, cruises, and regional tours. Just check with your hotel or the local Tourist Information Office (operated by the Ministry of Tourism) for names, addresses, and phone numbers of reputable groups. Most cities have at least one Tourist Information Office that promotes tourism and provides assistance to visitors. Large cities, such as Istanbal, Ankara, and Izmir, have several such offices. In Chapter 7 on Cappadocia, we include the names and phone numbers of the major tour operators in this area since you may find it's easier to cover this rather dispersed area with the assistance of such groups rather than on your own.

## ONLINE TRAVEL DEALS

If you use the Internet, you can easily make airline, hotel, and car rental reservations online by using several online booking groups. The five major reservation services are:

www.expedia.com           www.priceline.com
www.travelocity.com        www.hotwire.com
www.orbitz.com

Other popular online reservation services, with many claiming discount pricing, include:

www.air4less.com           www.moments-notice.com
www.airdeals.com           www.onetravel.com
www.air-fare.com           www.site59.com
www.bestfares.com          www.smarterliving.com
www.biztravel.com          www.thetrip.com
www.cheaptickets.com       www.travelhub.com
www.concierge.com          www.travelscape.com
www.lowestfare.com         www.travelzoo.com

However, while these online booking operations may appear to be convenient, we've found many of them can be more expensive than using a travel agent. This is especially true in the case of airline tickets. You'll often get the best airline rates through consolidators, which may be 30 to 40 percent less than the major online ticketing operations. Consolidators usually have small box ads in the Sunday travel sections of the *New York Times*, *Washington Post*, *Los Angeles Times*, and other major newspapers. Some of them, such as International Discount Travel, also provide price quotes on the Internet: www.idt travel.com. Other popular consolidators specializing in discount ticketing include TicketPlanet (1-800-799-8888, www.ticket planet.com), Airtreks.com (1-800-350-0612, www.airtreks. com), Air Brokers International (1-800-883-3273, www.air brokers.com), Airline Consolidator (1-800-468-5385, www.air consolidator.com), and World Travellers' Club (1-800-693-0411). If you're in a gambling mood, try these two "reverse auction" sites that allow you to set the price in the hopes that the company will make your dream price come true: www. priceline.com and www.hotwire.com. Make certain you are aware of any restrictions, such as departure and return dates, before you book.

## PASSING U.S. CUSTOMS

It's always good to know your country's Customs regulations before leaving home. If, for example, you are a U.S. citizen planning to travel abroad, the United States Customs Service provides several helpful publications which are available free of charge from your nearest U.S. Customs Office. Several also are available in the "Traveler Information" section of the U.S. Customs website, www.customs.ustreas.gov/travel/travel.htm.

- *Know Before You Go* (Publication #512): Outlines facts about exemptions, mailing gifts, duty-free articles, as well as prohibited and restricted articles. Includes duty-free exemptions and duty rates.

- *International Mail Imports* answers many questions regarding mailing items from foreign countries back to the U.S. The U.S. Postal Service sends packages to Customs for examination and assessment of duty before they are delivered to the addressee. Some items are free of duty and some are dutiable. The rules have changed on mail imports, so do check on this before you leave the U.S.

- *GSP and the Traveler* itemizes goods from particular countries that can enter the U.S. duty-free. GSP regulations, which are designed to promote the economic development of certain Third World countries, permit many products, especially arts and handicrafts, to enter the United States duty-free, but only if GSP is in effect at the time of your re-entry to the U.S. Each time GSP expires, Congress must pass a bill to extend it, and often there is a lag between GSP's expiration and re-passage. GSP duty exemptions are tied to particular beneficial countries (currently a total of 140 such countries).

U.S. citizens may bring into the U.S. $400 worth of goods free of U.S. taxes every 30 days; the next $1,000 is subject to a flat 3 percent tax (effective as of January 1, 2002). Goods beyond $1,400 are assessed duty at varying rates applied to different classes of goods.

---

## CURRENCY AND EXCHANGE RATES

The Turkish unit of currency is the lira (TL). As we went to press in August 2002, the exchange rate between the U.S. dollar and the Turkish lira was US$1 to 1,665,010TL. You may get a false sense of wealth with such large numbers! To check on the latest exchange rates for various currencies relating to the Turkish lira, visit these two currency converter websites:

www.oanda.com
www.xe.net/ucc

The lira is issued in banknotes of 100,000, 500,000, 1,000,000, and 5,000,000. Coins are issued in dominations of 10,000, 25,000, 50,000, and 100,000.

You can exchange your money at banks, hotels, and exchange booths. Most places prefer dollars over traveler's checks. Exchange booths give the best exchange rates. Since exchange rates tend to fluctuate and many shops give a better exchange rate on purchases paid for with U.S. dollars, you may want to be conservative in terms of how much money you exchange.

**ATM machines** are widely available throughout Turkey. They tend to give better exchange rates than for traveler's checks. However, be aware that there may be special fees involved in using ATMs abroad.

**Credit cards** are increasingly accepted by even small shops in Turkey, though all prefer and some will only accept cash.

Visa and MasterCard tend to be preferred over American Express and other cards.

## TIPPING

Tips are expected by service personnel who generally receive low wages. Consequently, you are well advised to carry lots of small bills for tips. While most restaurants add a 10-15 percent service charge to the bill, which does not necessarily get shared with waiters, they expect you to leave another 10 percent tip. Hotel porters expect to receive US$.75 to US$1 per bag. Taxi drivers appreciate having the fare rounded up by US$.10 or US$.25. Give your masseur or masseuse a US$2 or US$3 tip. Reward your tour guide with a generous tip.

## TAX REFUNDS

Tourists may receive a refund on the Value Added Tax (katma değer vergisi or KDV) they pay on goods in Turkey. Included in the price of all goods and services, the KDV runs from 15 to 17 percent. In order to claim a refund, you must shop with retailers who are authorized to give such refunds. In most cases you'll have to ask the retailer for a special KDV refund receipt (you should get three copies). You take this receipt with you and have it stamped at the airport Customs Office as you depart with your goods. If the bank in the Customs area is open, you can receive a cash refund by presenting them with the stamped receipt. Alternatively, you can mail the stamped receipt to the shop and request that you receive a refund check. This could take a few months to arrive, if it arrives at all!

## ELECTRICITY AND WATER

Electricity in Turkey is 220 volts, 50 cycles alternating currency (AC). Most outlets take a rounded two-prong plug.

While tap water is supposed to be safe in most cities and resorts, it's best to play it safe and stay with bottled water, which is readily available in restaurants and stores.

## HEALTH AND INSURANCE

You should consider taking out a special insurance policy when traveling to cover situations not covered by your medical, home, auto, and personal insurance back home. For example, many insurance policies do not cover treatment for illnesses or accidents while traveling outside your home country. Check whether your medical insurance will cover treatment abroad, and consider acquiring evacuation insurance in case serious illness or injuries would require that you be evacuated for medical treatment in a nearby country or home through special transportation and health care arrangements. Many companies offer this insurance. One of the best kept travel secrets for acquiring inexpensive evacuation insurance is to join DAN (Divers Alert Network). In the U.S., call 1-800-446-2671 (The Peter B. Bennett Center, 6 West Colony Place, Durham, NC 27705; website: www.diversalertnetwork.org). Without this insurance, special evacuation arrangements could cost from US$20,000 to US$50,000 or more! Their yearly rates are the best we have encountered. American Express has recently begun offering yearly insurance coverage at special rates as an option to its card holders. Whether or not you are into adventure travel and plan to engage in physically challenging and risky activities, health and evacuation insurance should be on your "must do" list before departing for your international adventure.

When considering special travel insurance, first check your current insurance policies to see if you have any coverage when traveling abroad. Also contact a travel agent to find out what he or she recommends for special coverage. The following websites will connect you to several companies that offer special insurance for travelers:

www.worldtravelcenter.com
www.globaltravelinsurance.com
www.travelinsurance.com
www.travelex.com
www.etravelprotection.com
www.travelguard.com
www.travelsecure.com
www.travelprotect.com
www.globalcover.com

## BUSINESS HOURS

Most **shops** are open Monday through Saturday from 9:30am to 1pm and from 2pm to 7pm or later. **Government offices** are open Monday through Friday from 8:30am to 12noon and from 1:30pm to 5:30pm. **Banks** are open Monday through Friday

8:30am to 12noon and from 1:30pm to 5pm. **Museums** are open Tuesday through Sunday (closed Mondays) from 9:30am to 5 or 5:30pm. **Palaces** keep the same hours as museums but usually close on Tuesdays and Thursdays rather than Mondays.

## USEFUL WEBSITES

Several websites provide useful information on Turkey. You should start exploring Turkey through these gateway websites:

- **Turizm** — www.turizm.gov.tr
- **Tourism Turkey** — www.tourismturkey.org
- **Turkish Embassy (US)** — www.turkey.org
- **The Turkey Guide** — www.turkeyguide.com
- **Explore Turkey** — www.exploreturkey.com
- **Turkiye Online** — www.turkiye_online.com
- **Anatolia** — www.anatolia.com
- **Info Exchange** — www.infoexchange.com/ Turkey/Turkey.html

- **Turk Travel** — www.turktravel.net
- **Lets Go Turkey** — www.letsgoturkey.com
- **Turkish Hotels** — www.turkishhotels.com
- **Turkish Daily News** — www.turkishdailynews.com

We identify several other useful websites in this and other chapters on everything from buying carpets to exploring the treasures and pleasures of Antalya, Marmaris, and Bodrum.

For useful online travel guidebook treatments of Turkey, visit the websites of Fodor's, Lonely Planet, and Rough Guides:

- **Fodors** — www.fodors.com
- **Lonely Planet** — www.lonelyplanet.com
- **Rough Guides** — www.roughguides.com

For travel-shopping information related to this guidebook as well as several other countries, visit our iShopAroundTheWorld website:

www.ishoparoundtheworld.com

# Shopping Treasures and Rules For Success

WHILE SHOPPING IN TURKEY MAY INITIAL-
ly appear familiar to you, there are certain things
you need to know about acquiring treasures in
Turkey that will make your shopping experience
more rewarding. From encountering new people,
discovering unique products, bargaining, and paying for items,
to packing, shipping, and handling customs, you should find
shopping to be one of the highlights of your adventure to
Turkey. You'll encounter an extremely enjoyable and rewarding
shopping culture that will yield many cherished treasures to
grace your home and wardrobe.

## DISCOVER UNIQUE TREASURES

Each destination we examine in subsequent chapters yields its
own unique mix of products and shopping rules. In **Istanbul**,
for example, you will be exposed to the full range of Turkish
products, from carpets, arts, and antiques to jewelry, ceramics,
leather goods, clothing, home furnishings, and souvenirs. As
might be expected, the best shopping is found in cosmopolitan
Istanbul, which is three times larger than the next largest city,

lection, quality, and design. While prices in Istanbul may be higher on such items as carpets, leather goods, and jewelry, on the other hand, the selections and designs of most Turkish products – as well as imported items – are the best in Istanbul. In fact, if you only have time to shop in one place in Turkey, make sure it's Istanbul. It is the closest Turkey has to a shopper's paradise.

You also are well advised to start and end your Turkish sojourn in Istanbul. This city offers the ultimate lifestyle travel-shopping adventure. Visiting the many places we recommend in Chapter 4 will give you a good idea of what's available in Istanbul, including quality and prices, before venturing into other areas of Turkey. Indeed, many people mistakenly believe the best shopping can be found outside the major cities when, in fact, most of the "good stuff" has already found its way into discerning shops in the major cities. While buying at a production source in the country-side may seem to make good sense and result in an interesting travel-shopping adventure, it seldom results in the expected – better quality purchases than in the cities. After all, the city dealers have most likely already acquired the best products from the sources with whom they have long-term buying relationships.

> ❑ The best shopping in Turkey is found in cosmopolitan Istanbul.
>
> ❑ Istanbul offers the ultimate lifestyle travel-shopping adventure.
>
> ❑ Bursa is especially well known for its antique and collectible shops as well as silk and textile production facilities.
>
> ❑ Ankara, with its Copper Alley and antique shops, is one of the best kept shopping secrets in Turkey.
>
> ❑ Ürgüp and Avanos in Cappadocia are noted for their carpet, antique, and pottery shops.

On the other hand, **Bursa and Iznik** (Chapter 5) offer a few shopping surprises which are not readily found in Istanbul. Bursa is especially well known for its antique and collectible shops as well as silk and textile production facilities. If you enjoy collecting antiques or just browsing through junk shops, Bursa is the place to go. Bursa's silks appeal to many visitors, but its other textiles are probably best left to local buyers who appreciate the rather bland designs and colors. Several studios in Iznik now produce attractive ceramics not found in other places in Turkey.

**Ankara**, which is famous for its Copper Alley and adjacent bazaar-style street shops, offers a few surprises for visitors interested in arts, antiques, carpets, and handicrafts. In fact, Ankara is one of the best kept shopping secrets in Turkey. The quality of shopping here also reflects the nature of Ankara's clientele –

diplomatic personnel interested in good quality arts, antiques, and collectibles. You just might find several porcelain German stoves, antique silver from Iraq, and Russian icons left over from the diplomatic community that is not above trading their wares. Merchants here are less aggressive and also less willing to bargain on what they already consider to be good prices.

While the Anatolian region of **Cappadocia** is primarily an adventure and sightseeing destination, it also yields a few shopping surprises. Some of the major towns in this area, especially Ürgüp and Avanos, are noted for their carpet, antique, and pottery shops. The famous whirling dervish town of **Konya** also has a few shops that offer some unique carpets and antiques. A brief stop in Konya should be in your travel plans.

Both the **Mediterranean and Aegean** coastal areas, from Side in the south to Çanakkale in the northwest, are primarily major resort and sightseeing destinations especially noted for their beaches, cruises, ancient ruins, restaurants, and lively nightlife. Major resorts and cruise destinations, such as Antalya, Marmaris, Bodrum, and Kuşadasi, also offer lots of shopping opportunities for jewelry, clothing, carpets, and souvenirs. Most items in the shops and markets are brought in from their production sources in Istanbul and Izmir. You'll occasionally find a unique shop that offers items not readily available in Istanbul.

# BEST BUYS

Turkey is a relatively inexpensive travel destination. Food is cheap by most world standards. Indeed, dining out is usually a real bargain. Shopping also is a bargain if you know where to go and how to bargain properly. Some shops primarily cater to tourists and their guides who receive anywhere from 10 to 30 percent commission on everything their clients purchase. If you shop in such places, expect to pay 10 to 30 percent above retail.

## CARPETS, KILIMS, AND TEXTILES

Real bargains can be found on Turkish **carpets, kilims, and textiles,** for which Turkey is world famous. In fact, nowhere else in the world will you find so many rugs available in such a range of colors and designs. Some visitors quickly become overwhelmed with the range of choices and the sheer number of rug shops both inside and outside the bazaars. Other visitors snap up three, five, or 10 rugs at incredibly inexpensive prices. Carpet and kilim prices can run anywhere from US$50 to

US$25,000, depending on the size, color, quality, and source of the rug. Before being tempted by such products, you are well advised to know something about Turkish rugs as well as the buying culture, which we will share with you in this chapter.

## CERAMICS AND POTTERY

Turkey also is well noted for its **ceramics** in the forms of tiles, plates, bowls, and other items produced in classic Iznik designs. The traditional centers for Turkish ceramic production, especially in the 17th and 18th centuries, were Iznik (east of Bursa) and Kütahya (southeast of Bursa). While ceramic tile production is being slowly revived in Iznik, most ceramics production is now done in Kütahya. Some of the best quality ceramics are found in Istanbul. The town of Avanos (in the Cappadocia area) is the center for **red clay pottery**.

## ANTIQUES AND COLLECTIBLES

You'll find many unique antiques and collectibles throughout Turkey. Look for antique furniture, prints, glassware, ceramics, lamps, and home decorative items in Istanbul's many antique shops, emporiums, and auction houses. Keep in mind that antiques over 100 years old may not be exported from Turkey. However, there are many attractive treasures in Turkey that are under 100 years old, especially old copper pots, lamps, and lanterns, that can be excellent buys. Anyone who offers antiquities or old coins at archaeological sites is selling fakes.

Some of the best places to buy antiques and collectibles are in Istanbul, Bursa, Ankara, Cappadocia, Konya, and Bodrum. Many places also offer old textiles, lacquerware, carved boxes, silver, and jewelry from neighboring countries such as Iraq, Uzbekistan, Turkmenistan, and Afghanistan.

## JEWELRY

Turkey has several top jewelers who offer unique designs that appeal to visitors. Other jewelers are very talented in copying designs from major international jewelers, such as Tiffany's and Cartier, as well as reproducing jewelry from Hellenistic, Egyptian, Roman, Byzantine, or Ottoman times. Most of the top jewelers are found in Istanbul with shops in the major five-star hotels. Many bazaars throughout Turkey include a jewelry section that offers lots of gold and silver jewelry designed for local consumption.

## LEATHER GOODS

Turkey is famous for its leather products, especially coats, jackets, shoes, belts, wallets, handbags, and luggage. While the quality is by no means comparable to similar products found in Italy or France, the prices can be very good. However, the best designers and shops in Turkey import top quality leather hides from Italy and design and fabricate their products in Turkey. Both Istanbul and Izmir are major centers for leather production. Most leather items in Turkey are ready-made, although some places will do made-to-order.

## SOUVENIRS AND GIFTS

Turkey's many markets and tourist sites offer a wide range of souvenir and gift items. Look for copper pots, folding lanterns, meerschaum pipes, ceramics, embroidery, wood carvings, prints, glassware, inlaid boxes, baskets, "evil eyes," Turkish delights (sweets), apple tea, and spices.

# TAKE KEY SHOPPING INFORMATION

Depending on what you plan to buy, you should take all the necessary information you need to make informed shopping decisions. Do your shopping research and documentation *before* you leave home. Shops in Turkey are not good places to get an expensive education, especially when it comes to purchasing carpets and jewelry. If you are looking for carpets, art, antiques, and home furnishings, include with your "wish list" room measurements to help you determine if particular items will fit into your home. Without floor and wall measurements, you may have to guess whether or not a interesting item will work in your home. Consider bringing along photographs of rooms you hope to furnish or add to.

❑ Take measurements and photographs of rooms that could become candidates for home decorative items.

❑ Be sure to take with you information on any clothes, accessories, or jewelry (sizes, colors, comparative prices) to look for or have made when in Turkey.

❑ Half the fun of shopping is the serendipity of discovering the unique and exotic.

If you plan to shop for clothes and accessories, your homework should include taking an inventory of your closets and identifying specific colors, fabrics, and designs you wish to acquire to complement and enlarge your present wardrobe. Be sure you know what colors work best for your wardrobe.

## Do Comparative Shopping

You should do comparative shopping both at home and within Turkey in order to get a good idea of what is or is not a good buy. Our rule of thumb is that if a comparable item is available at home, and it is not at least 20 percent cheaper buying it abroad, it's probably not worth the effort of buying it abroad for such a small savings. This is especially true in the case of carpets and jewelry where it's usually "buyer beware" when dealing with such issues as authenticity, quality, and pricing. After all, back home you most likely will have return privileges, and you may be protected by consumer protection regulations or you can take legal action should such items be misrepresented.

However, many items in Turkey are unique, especially carpets, kilims, ceramics, antiques, leather products, and handicrafts. These are the type of items one has to see, feel, and fall in love with – they must "speak" to you.

The first step in doing comparative shopping starts at home. Determine exactly what you want and need. Make lists. As you compile your lists, spend some time "window shopping" in the local stores, examining catalogs, telephoning for information, and checking Internet shopping sites such as www.novica.com and www.eziba.com.

Once you arrive in Turkey, your shopping plans will probably change considerably as you encounter many new items you had not planned to purchase but which attract your interest and buying attention. Indeed, half the fun of shopping while traveling in Turkey is the serendipity of discovering the unique and exotic – a beautiful carpet, a gorgeous piece of jewelry, an old copper pot with lots of character, a nice ceramic tile, a lovely intricate carved wood box from Uzbekistan, an appealing CD or tape of Turkish music, a beautifully tailored leather jacket, or a collectible meerschaum pipe – things you could not have anticipated encountering but which you now see, feel, and judge as possible acquisitions for your home or wardrobe. These are the great shopping moments that require local knowledge about differences in quality and pricing. Many products, such as carpets, embroidery, ceramics, or jewelry, may be unique one-of-a-kind items that are difficult to compare. You must judge them in terms of their designs, colors, and intrinsic value. Other items, such as jewelry, ready-made clothing, and souvenir items, will beg comparative shopping because the same or similar quality items are widely available in numerous shops and bazaars.

You'll have plenty of opportunities to do comparison shopping in the shops and bazaars of the largest and most touristed cities – Istanbul, Ankara, Izmir, Kuşadasi, and Antalya. Many of the shops in these cities offer similar items that beg to be compared for prices and quality. You are well advised to visit several shops soon after your arrival in these cities in order to get some sense of market prices for various items you are likely to frequently encounter. Many of these items can be quickly surveyed in bazaars.

## KEEP TRACK OF RECEIPTS

It's important to keep track of all of your purchases for making an accurate Customs declaration. Be sure to ask for receipts wherever you shop. If a shop doesn't issue receipts, ask them to create a receipt by writing the information on a piece of paper, include the shop's name and address, and sign it.

Since it's so easy to misplace receipts, you might want to organize your receipts using a form such as this:

CUSTOMS DECLARATION RECORD FORM

| | Receipt # | Item | Price (lira) | Price (US$) |
|---|---|---|---|---|
| 1. | 4179 | Carpet | 650,000,000 | $400.00 |
| 2. | | | | |
| 3. | | | | |
| 4. | | | | |

This can be especially useful when receipts are written in a language you cannot read. Staple a sheet or two of notebook or accountant's paper to the front of a large manila envelope and number down the left side of the page. Draw one or two vertical columns down the right side. Each evening, sort through that day's purchases, write a description including style and color of the purchase on the accompanying receipt, and enter that item on your receipt record. Record the receipt so later you'll know exactly which item belongs to the receipt. Put the receipts in the manila envelope and pack the purchases away. If you're missing a receipt, make a note beside the appropriate entry.

# Key Shopping Rules For Success

Wherever you shop in Turkey, keep these basic shopping rules in mind. They may serve you well in identifying the best quality shops and in avoiding many mistakes frequently reported by visitors to Turkey:

1.  **Expect to shop in two very different shopping cultures which require different shopping skills.** The first world is the most familiar one for visitors – shopping centers, department stores, and hotel shopping arcades. Shops in this culture tend to have window displays, well organized interiors, and fixed prices which may or may not be all that fixed, depending on your ability to persuade shops to discount prices. The second shopping culture consists of traditional street shops, bazaars, vendor stalls, and touts which tend to be somewhat chaotic and involve price uncertainty and bargaining skills. You will most likely be able to directly transfer your shopping skills to the first culture, but you may have difficulty navigating in the second shopping culture which at times can be intimidating but often fun.

2.  **Be prepared for "in-your-face" retailing.** Turkish merchants, especially those found in the bazaars, can be very aggressive. Used to maintaining close personal space, many of these people will get up close to you – even breathe on you – and thus may make you feel uncomfortable as they try to persuade you to enter their shops and buy their products. If you're not interested, don't maintain eye contact nor engage in a conversation with such individuals. Doing so only encourages them to be even more aggressive!

3.  **Don't be surprised to establish a close friendship with a merchant.** Turkish hospitality tends to extend to all types of relationships. It's also surprising how it often unexpectedly evolves. Everyone seems to have a friend in Turkey. Even before you leave home, for example, a friend may recommend that you contact his Turkish friend in Istanbul, who, in turn, puts you in contact with a friend or relative who is a merchant. The merchant, in turn, may take you to dinner and develop a very warm and friendly relationship with you that lasts for years. Later back home you meet a friend who plans to visit Turkey. Guess what

you do? You recommend that he contact your friend in Istanbul. Turkey is a real friendly country!

4. **Expect to find the best quality shopping at the best quality locations.** Quality shops tend to go where the money congregates. Therefore, it should come as no surprise that the best quality shopping is usually found in the shopping arcades of top quality hotels, which tend to screen the quality of shops that are allowed to rent their shop space. These shops tend to cater to the tastes of upscale visitors who stay there. And it should come as no surprise that the best quality shopping will be found in the top hotel shopping arcades and the upscale neighborhoods of Istanbul. With the exception of several well-established shops in and around Istanbul's Grand Bazaar, don't expect to do your best quality shopping in the bazaars. These are fun and exotic places to acquire "bargains" and encounter a variety of interesting cultural experiences. When in doubt where to shop for quality items, head for the major hotels. If the hotel does not have a shopping arcade, ask the concierge or front desk for shopping recommendations. They usually know the best places to shop based upon the experiences of their hotel guests.

5. **Focus your initial shopping on the major shopping areas.** Most shopping areas are very well defined – hotel shopping arcades, shopping centers, bazaars, factories, major streets, and vendor stalls and touts at tourist sites.

6. **Remember to seek out the best shops by checking with people "in the know."** The concierges and front desk personnel in most five-star hotels know where the best shopping can be found. Knowledgeable about their community and frequently in communication with guests, shops, and fellow concierges, they usually have a good sense of the best shops to visit for quality, pricing, and reliability. They often know where their best guests shop for such popular items as carpets, jewelry, clothes, art, handicrafts, and antiques. They also know which shops generate complaints because of high prices, poor quality and service, and problems with shipping. Ask for their top three recommendations in different product categories. However, not all concierges are necessarily knowledgeable or objective about shopping. Some may get "kick-backs" on recommending you to particular shops. It depends on

the hotel and the services it provides for its guests. Some concierges may essentially function as bell boys. In Istanbul, for example, concierges who really know the "ins" and "outs" of the city are found at the Four Seasons Hotel and the Çirağan Palace Hotel. The worst people to ask for shopping recommendations are tour guides, drivers, touts, and general service personnel. They are either on "on the take" or have no sense of quality shopping. You'll pay dearly for their advice!

7. **Be sure to comparative shop for many items.** Many shops carry similar items, and prices can vary considerably from one shop to another on carpets, jewelry, clothes, leather goods, copper ware, and handicrafts. Be sure to survey your shopping options by visiting various shops offering such products. You'll quickly get some idea as to how to best value these items.

8. **Bargain for most items you purchase in the bazaars.** The tourist bazaars are fun places to practice your bargaining skills. Here, discounts can run from 20 to 70 percent, depending on the merchant and your haggling skills. Most will extend a discount if you ask the simple question, *"Is it possible to do any better on this price?"* Doing better often means a 20-percent discount. If you do comparison shopping, spend some time with the merchant, and persist. Chances are you can get a 40- to 50-percent discount on many items in the bazaars. However, there are no hard and fast rules on bargaining – only whatever you can achieve with particular merchants.

9. **Don't assume you can bargain everywhere you shop in Turkey.** Bargaining is best done in tourist bazaars where you are expected to haggle over prices. But once outside the bazaars, shops may give very little discounts on what they consider to be fixed prices. In fact, many shops don't discount, whereas others may give you a five- or 10-percent discount for cash. Just because you successfully bargain for discounts in the bazaars is no reason to assume that you can do the same in shops outside the bazaars. When in doubt, probe for a discount by nicely asking our "possibility" question, *"Is it possible to do any better on this price?"* As you may quickly discover, life is full of possibilities in Turkey. Many merchants respond to this question with a discount, especially if you are purchasing expensive items in carpet, jewelry, art, or antique

shops. The worst thing that can happen to you is to be told "no," but "maybe" or "yes" is a more likely outcome.

10. **Expect to spend more time shopping than you initially planned.** Especially in bazaars and carpet shops, your shopping plan can easily go awry as many merchants invite you to join them for coffee, tea, conversation, and a demonstration. You may find it difficult to disengage from such situations. Be careful not to accept too many invitations to come into their shops. Once in, you may feel like a captive for 10 to 30 minutes!

11. **Ask for directions whenever you feel you need it.** Signage is often a problem when looking for particular streets and shops. At times, especially in bazaars, you may feel lost and have difficulty finding specific shops or products. Whenever this happens, just ask for assistance from your hotel, shopkeepers, and others. Turks are very friendly and will help you if they can. Hopefully you won't accidentally meet a friendly tout who claims he's taking you to his brother's shop where prices are real cheap. This is not the friend you want to make for more than a minute!

12. **Be sure to check out all the rooms in a shop.** Some shops keep their best items in the back rooms or upstairs or downstairs – for serious buyers and dealers. If a shop has a window display, don't assume what's on display represents the best inventory. If a shop catches your interest, go inside and check it out thoroughly. Ask about other rooms, especially what is upstairs and downstairs.

13. **Be sure to ask for assistance and background information.** One of the great pleasures of shopping in Turkey is learning about various products and craftspeople. Since you may be unfamiliar with many Turkish-produced items, such as rugs, kilims, embroidery, and leather goods, be sure to ask questions about the various selections. Shopkeepers tend to be very friendly and informative. They can quickly educate you about their products and artisans. In so doing, you will probably gain a new appreciation for "Made in Turkey" products as well as the history and culture of this fascinating country.

14. **Use your credit cards whenever possible.** Many shops, including those in the bazaars, accept major credit cards.

Many also will accept U.S. dollars. However, consider charging your purchase just in case you later have a problem with authenticity or shipping. Your credit card company may be able to assist you in resolving such problems. Credit card purchases usually receive the best exchange rates.

15. **Collect receipts for everything you purchase.** You may need the receipt for Customs or as documentation for contacting the merchant. Make sure you have essential information on the receipt – shop name, address, and telephone and fax numbers as well as the salesperson you dealt with.

16. **Take photos of all your purchases.** It's always good to have a visual record of your purchases, and especially with the merchant holding your item. This photo may make a great memento of your shopping adventure as well as serve as documentation for where you purchased the item.

17. **Don't believe everything you're told about carpets, antiques, and jewelry.** Many merchants make exaggerated claims about quality, authenticity, and savings. Do your homework before arriving in Turkey as well as do comparative shopping in Turkey.

18. **Be suspicious of street touts and tour guides who want to take you shopping.** Beware of shopping in major tourist shops and factories frequented by tour buses and taxis. Like elsewhere in the world, these places tend to be patronized by clients of tour guides who get commissions – often in the 10 to 40 percent range – on everything their clients purchase. The quality of products in these places is usually mediocre and the prices are often high. Expect to pay a real premium for shopping in such places that are highly recommended by tour guides and drivers. Whatever you do, don't ask your tour guide or driver to help you bargain for an item – a frequent request of naive tourists. Your guide is not your friend in these places. He or she instead is the problem – leading you to the shopping slaughter where you are likely to pay 20 to 50 percent above retail! A percentage of what you pay for each item will go directly into the pocket of your guide or driver. If you are taken to such a place, take advantage of the "freebies" (drinks and snacks) but be careful what you buy; you can find better places to shop.

19. **Expect most shops to arrange packing and shipping.** Don't be afraid to purchase large or delicate items that you may not want to take with you. Most shops have experience in packing and shipping since they regularly deal with international visitors. However, if you decide to have items shipped, it's always a good idea to get a receipt describing the item and stating who is doing what and for how much. If an item is considered an antique or piece of art, the receipt should specify the age or state "original work of art" – important issues with U.S. Customs and its GSP exemptions.

20. **In some cases, plan to do your own packing and re-packing.** Some small shops claim to do packing, but chances are you will not be happy with the result. Either closely supervise the packing process by instructing the shop how to pack things securely or do your own packing and re-packing by acquiring packing material, especially bubble wrap and cardboard. Don't trust even the best hotels to do an adequate packing job.

21. **Take photos of all items being shipped.** We always take pictures just in case we have a shipment problem, which occasionally occurs. Better still, take a photo of the item with the merchant and/or shipper standing next to it. Such visual documentation may later come in handy and it's always a nice memorable photo of interesting people you met and did business with in Turkey. The photo also helps in later clearing Customs, especially if they are not sure how to classify and assess a particular item.

22. **Take items with you whenever possible.** While many shops can pack and ship, especially tourist shops selling large and heavy carpets, you may want to take smaller items with you. Don't just take a shop's word that they can ship with no problem. You may discover the cost of shipping a small item can be very expensive, especially when it arrives "collect" by international courier service!

23. **Take your purchases with you as part of your carry-on or check-through luggage.** While shipping from Turkey is relatively easy to arrange, it also can be very expensive. We usually try to take our purchases with us whether they be small or large. In preparation, we usually limit ourselves to one check-through piece of luggage on our flight to Turkey. For the two of us, this allows us

three more check-through pieces of luggage on our international flight back home. Our advice: take very little luggage with you on your way to Turkey in anticipation of accumulating purchases along the way that you will want to take with you. Alternatively, if two people are traveling together, take two pieces of luggage and fill the second one primarily with bubble wrap and packing materials. You still can have two boxes made for larger pieces and bring them home at no additional costs. You'll save a great deal of time and money by planning in this manner. If you purchase an item that can be checked through as luggage, such as a piece of pottery or rug, ask the shop to pack the item well so it can be checked through with your airline as a piece of luggage. Be sure to check with your airline on the dimensions of allowable check-through items. Most shops can do such packing or they can arrange for expert packing to protect delicate purchases. Even large pieces of pottery can be well packed (packer builds a sturdy wood box) to be shipped through as an extra piece of luggage. Make sure the size of such boxes are within the dimensions allowed by the airline.

24. **Be very careful when buying rugs, jewelry, and so-called antiquities.** If you're unfamiliar with such items, you need to get a quick education before making any serious purchases. In the case of jewelry, patronize the top jewelry shops and ask lots of questions about their products – gold and silver content, origin and quality of gems, craftsmanship, and designers. Do they basically copy designs or create their own unique designs? A good shop will make a special effort to educate its potential clients. Beware of antiquities. They cannot be exported from Turkey without special government permission. Since reproductions of antiquities – both good and bad – abound in Turkey, it's safe to assume that most antiquities for sales in Turkey are fakes. And be especially cautious when buying rugs. Carpets and kilims are everywhere, including the prices. If you shop around for rugs and ask lots of questions (see our rug buying tips on pages 55-59), you should be able to learn a great deal about what to look for when buying rugs, especially desirable colors, designs, sizes, fabrics, and quality of weaves. Turkish rug merchants are like rug dealers elsewhere in the world – very entrepreneurial and at times creative in their storytelling. Potential carpet owners need to become savvy buyers by sitting through several rug demonstra-

tions, comparing products, asking questions, and focusing on exactly what they need rather than be tempted to buy any rug just because it seems to be a "good deal" at the time. Remember, most rug merchants want to quickly sell you on the "deal" (it's cheap, it's a good investment, it's very rare, will ship free) rather than understand and respond to your home or office decorative needs (room size, color scheme, style of furnishings). Our shopping rule of thumb: Be cautious of rug merchants who appear to have fallen in love with their rugs . . . and with you! Don't mistake Turkish rug hospitality, and seemingly instant carpet shop friendship, with Turkish hospitality in general.

> *Be cautious of rug merchants who appear to have fallen in love with their rugs . . . and with you!*

## BARGAINING TIPS AND SKILLS

If you're not used to bargaining when shopping, you will be at a price disadvantage in Turkey's many bazaars and rug shops. If you consider yourself a good bargainer in other countries, you may quickly discover your bargaining skills need to be upgraded for the Turkish shopping culture. This isn't China, Indonesia, India, or Brazil.

### BARGAINING AND PRICE UNCERTAINTY

Bargaining can be great fun and result in excellent buys. But for the uninitiated, bargaining can be very intimidating; it seems to be a waste of precious shopping and travel time. Individuals from fixed price cultures would rather see a price sticker and make a decision of whether or not to purchase without someone haggling with them over the price. But if everything were fixed prices, you would really miss out on a terrific cultural experience in Turkey. So let's take a look at some basic bargaining rules to put you on the road to shopper's heaven.

Not knowing the price of an item, many shoppers from fixed-price cultures face a problem. *"What is the actual value of the item? How much should I pay? At what point do I know I'm getting a fair price?"* After all, you don't want to be "taken" by an unscrupulous merchant who preys on naive tourists. These questions can be answered in several ways. First, you should have some idea of the **value** of the item, because you already did comparative shopping at home by examining catalogs and visiting discount houses, department stores, and specialty shops. If you are interested in an emerald ring, for example, you should know what similar quality jewelry sells for back home.

Second, you have done comparative shopping among the various shops you've encountered in Turkey in order to **establish a price range** for positioning yourself in the bargaining process. You've visited shops in Istanbul's major shopping centers to research how much a similar item is selling for at a fixed price. You've checked with a shop in your hotel and compared prices there. In your hotel you might ask *"How much is this item?"* and then act a little surprised that it appears so expensive. Tell them that you are a hotel guest and thus you want their *"very best price."* At this point the price may decrease by 10 to 20 percent as you are told this is *"our very special price for hotel guests."*

Once you initially receive a special price from your first price inquiry, you may get another 10 to 20 percent through further negotiation. But at this point do not negotiate any more. Take the shop's business card and record on the back the item, the original price, and the first discount price; thank the shopkeeper, and tell him or her that you may return. Repeat this same scenario in a few other shops. After doing three or four comparisons, you will establish a price range for particular items. This range will give you a fairly accurate idea of the going discount price. At this point you should be prepared to do some serious haggling, playing one shop off against another until you get the best price.

## THE EFFECTIVE SHOPPER

Effective shoppers in Turkey quickly learn how to comparative shop and negotiate the best deal. In learning to be effective, you don't need to be timid, aggressive, or obnoxious – extreme behaviors frequently exhibited by first-time practitioners of the art of bargaining. Although you may feel bargaining is a defensive measure to avoid being ripped off by unscrupulous merchants, it is an acceptable way of doing business in many cultures. Merchants merely adjust their profit margins to the customer, depending on how they feel about the situation as well as their current cash flow needs. It is up to you to adapt to such a pricing culture.

Chances are you will deal with a merchant who is a seasoned businessman. As soon as you walk through the door, most merchants will want to sell you items then and there.

**The best deal you will get is when you have a personal relationship with the merchant**. Contrary to what others may tell you about bargains for tourists, you often can get as good a deal – sometimes even better – than someone from the local community. It is simply a myth that tourists can't do as well on prices as the locals. Indeed, we often do better than the locals because we have done our comparative shopping and we know well the art of bargaining – something locals are often lax in doing. In addition, some merchants may give you a better price than the locals because you are *"here today and gone tomorrow."* After all, you won't be around to tell their regular customers about your very special price.

More often than not, the pricing system operates like this: **If the shopkeeper likes you, you are a friend of a friend or relative, or he is in need of cash flow that day, you can expect to get a good price**. Whenever possible, drop names of individuals who referred you to the shop; the shopkeeper may think you are a friend and thus you are entitled to a special discount. But if you do not have such a relationship and you present yourself as a typical tourist who is here today and gone tomorrow, you need to bargain hard.

### PRACTICE **12** RULES OF BARGAINING

The art of bargaining in Turkey can take on several different forms. In general, you want to achieve two goals in this haggling process: **establish the value of an item** and **get the best possible price**. The following bargaining rules work well in most negotiable shopping situations.

1. **Do your research before talking about prices and initiating the bargaining process.**

   Compare the prices among various shops, starting with the fixed-price items in department stores. Spot-check price ranges among shops in and around your hotel. Also, refer to your research done with catalogs and discount houses back home to determine if the discount is sufficient to warrant purchasing the item abroad.

2. **Determine the exact item you want to buy, but don't express excessive interest.**

   Select the particular item you want and then focus your bargaining around that one item without expressing excessive interest. Even though you may be excited by the item and want it very badly, once the merchant knows you are committed to buying it, you weaken your bargaining position. Express a passing interest; indicate through eye contact with other items in the shop that you are not necessarily committed to the one item. As you ask about the other items, you should get some sense concerning the willingness of the merchant to discount prices.

3. **Set a ceiling price you're willing to pay – and buy now!**

Before engaging in serious negotiations, set in your mind the maximum amount you are willing to pay, which may be 20 percent more than you figured the item should sell for based on your research. However, if you find something you love that is really unique, be prepared to pay more if you can afford it. In many situations you will find unique items not available anywhere else. Consider buying **now** since the item may be gone when you return. Bargain as hard as you can and then pay what you have to – even though it may seem painful – for the privilege of owning a unique item. Remember, it's only money and it only hurts once. You can always make more money, and after returning home you will most likely enjoy your wonderful purchase and forget how painful it seemed at the time to buy it at less than your expected discount. Above all, do not pass up an item you really love just because the bargaining process does not fall in your favor. It is very easy to be *"penny wise but pound foolish"* in Turkey simply because the bargaining process is such an ego-involved activity. You may return home forever regretting that you didn't buy a lovely item just because you were too cheap to "give" on the last US$5 of haggling. In the end, put your ego aside, give in, and buy what you really want. Only you and the merchant will know who really won this game, and once you return home the US$5 will seem to be such an insignificant amount. Chances are you still got a good bargain compared to what you would pay elsewhere if, indeed, you could even find a similar item!

4. **Play the role of an intelligent buyer in search of good quality and value.**

Shopping in Turkey involves playing the roles of buyer and seller with lots of expressive drama. It's one of the best shows in town. Turkish merchants, especially those in the bazaars, are terrific role players. When you encounter a Turkish merchant, you are often meeting a very refined and sophisticated role player. Therefore, it is to your advantage to play a complementary role by carefully structuring your personality and behavior to play the role of buyer. If you approach sellers by just "being yourself" – open, honest, somewhat naive, and with your own unique personality – you may be quickly walked over by a seasoned seller. Once you enter a shop, think of yourself as an actor walking onstage to play the lead role as a shrewd buyer, bargainer, and trader. Take, for example, this common scenario. Merchants will kindly invite you into their shop, ask you to sit down, pour you coffee or tea, and try to become your friend. Then they will abuse your wallet in very dramatic ways. Now that your guard is supposedly down because of their hospitality, they may quote you a high initial price for an item that interests you – not exactly what a friend should do to another! You may counter with a low price and they will respond by becoming very animated – as if you just insulted a good friend: *"Oh, my God! I'll lose money."* They will tell you what an absurd price you're offering, that they can't lose money, and that you'll have to pay a lot more to do business with them. At this point you may feel overwhelmed with the drama. Don't worry. It's all part of the role-playing game. Stick in there and continue with another absurd counter offer. Better still, become equally animated. Hit your forehead with the palm of your hand and counter by loudly saying *"How can you expect me to pay such a high price!"* This role reversal will often catch the merchant off-guard as he tries to top your drama.

5. **Establish good will and a personal relationship.**

A shrewd buyer also is charming, polite, personable, and friendly. You should have a sense of humor, smile, and be light-hearted during the bargaining process. But be careful about eye contact, which can be threatening. Keep it to a minimum. Sellers prefer to establish a personal relationship so that the bargaining process can take place on a friendly, face-saving basis. In the end, both the buyer and seller should come out as winners. This cannot be done if you approach the buyer in very serious and harsh terms. You should start by exchanging pleasantries concerning the weather, your trip, the city, or the nice items in the shop. After exchanging business cards or determining your status, the shopkeeper will know what roles should be played in the coming transaction.

6. **Let the seller make the first offer.**

If the merchant starts by asking you *"How much do you want to pay?,"* always avoid answering this rather danger- ous set-up question. He who reveals his hand first is likely to lose in the end. Immediately turn the question around: *"How much are you asking?"* Remember, many merchants try to get you to pay as much as you are willing and able to pay – not what the value of the item is or what he or she is willing to take. You should never reveal your ability or willingness to pay a certain price. Keep the seller guess- ing, thinking that you may lose interest or not buy the item because it appears too expensive. Always get the mer- chant to initiate the bargaining process. In so doing, the merchant must take the defensive as you shift to the offensive.

7. **Take your time, being deliberately slow in order to get the merchant to invest his or her time in you.**

The more you indicate that you are impatient and in a hurry, the more you are likely to pay. When negotiating a price, **time** is usually in your favor. Many shopkeepers also see time as a positive force in the bargaining process. Some try to keep you in their shop by serving you tea while negotiating the price. Be careful; this nice little ritual may soften you somewhat on the bargaining process as you begin establishing a more personal relationship with the merchant. The longer you stay in control pro- longing the negotiation, the better the price should be. Although some merchants may deserve it, **never** insult them. Merchants need to "keep face" as much as you do in the process of giving and getting the very best price.

8. **Use odd numbers in offering the merchant 40 percent to 60 percent less than what he or she initially offers.**

Avoid stating round numbers, such as 700, 1,800, or 1,000. Instead, offer 62, 173, or 817. Such numbers im- press upon others that you may be a seasoned haggler who knows value and expects to do well in this negotia- tion. Your offer will probably be 20 percent less than the value you determined for the item. For example, if the merchant asks US$100, offer US$40, knowing the final price should probably be US$60. The merchant will probably counter with only a 20-percent discount – US$80. At this point you will need to go back and forth with another two or three offers and counter-offers. In some cases you want to initially offer 75 percent less than the asking price, depending on the item and seller. Bus stop tourist shops often have extremely inflated prices; a 75-percent discount in these places might be a fair price!

9. **Appear a little disappointed and then take your time again.**

Never appear upset or angry with the seller. Keep your cool at all times by slowly sitting down and carefully examining the item. Shake your head a little and say, *"Gee, that's too bad. That's much more than I had planned to spend. I like it, but I really can't go that high."* Appear to be a sympathetic listener as the seller attempts to explain why he or she cannot budge more on the price. Make sure you do not accuse the merchant of being a thief! Use a little charm, if you can, for the way you conduct the bargaining process will affect the final price. This should be a civil negotiation in which you nicely bring the price down, the seller "saves face," and everyone goes away feeling good about the deal.

10. **Counter with a new offer at a 35-percent discount.**

Punch several keys on your calculator, which indicates you are doing some serious thinking. Then say something like *"This is really the best I can do. It's a lovely item, but US$162 is really all I can pay."* At this point the merchant will most likely counter with a 20-percent discount – US$200. He may say that's the best he can do. But don't believe him. There's still more room to negotiate, if you become somewhat creative.

11. **Be patient, persistent, and take your time again by carefully examining the item.**

Respond by saying *"That's a little better, but it's still too much. I want to look around a little more."* Then start to get up and look toward the door. At this point the merchant has invested some time in this exchange, and he or she is getting close to a possible sale. The merchant will either let you walk out the door or try to stop you with another counter-offer. If you walk out the door, you can always return to get the US$200 price. But most likely the merchant will try to stop you, if there is still some bargaining room. The merchant is likely to say: *"You don't want to waste your time looking elsewhere. I'll give you the best price anywhere – just for you. Okay, US$190. That's my final price."*

## 12. Be creative for the final negotiation.

You could try for US$180, but chances are US$190 will be the final price with this merchant. Yet, there may still be some room for negotiating "extras." At this point, get up and walk around the shop and examine other items; try to appear as if you are losing interest in the item you were bargaining for. While walking around, identify a US$10 item you like which might make a nice gift for a friend or relative, which you could possibly include in the final deal. Wander back to the US$10 item and look as if your interest is waning and perhaps you need to leave. Then start to probe the possibility of including extras while agreeing on the US$190: *"Okay, I might go US$190, but only if you include this with it."* The "this" is the US$10 item you eyed. You also might negotiate with your credit card. Chances are the merchant is expecting cash on the US$190 discounted price and will add a 2- to 6-percent "commission" if you want to use your credit card. In this case, you might respond to the US$190 by saying, *"Okay, I'll go with the US$190, but only if I can use my credit card."* You may get your way, your bank will float you a loan in the meantime, and your credit card company may help you resolve the problem in case you later learn your purchase was misrepresented. Finally, you may want to negotiate packing and delivery processes. If it is a fragile item, insist that it be packed well so you can take it with you on the airplane or have it shipped. If your purchase is large, insist that the shop deliver it to your hotel or to your shipper. If the shop is shipping it by air or sea, try to get them to agree to absorb some of the freight and insurance costs.

This very slow, civil, methodical, and sometimes charming approach to bargaining works well in most cases. However, Turkish merchants do differ in how they respond to situations, and many of them are unpredictable, depending on whether or not they like you. In some cases, your timing may be right: the merchant is in need of cash flow that day and thus he or she is willing to give you the price you want, with little or no bargaining. Others will not give more than a 10- to 20-percent discount unless you are a friend of a friend who is then eligible for the special "family discount." And others are not good businessmen, are unpredictable, lack motivation, or are just moody; they refuse to budge on their prices even though your offer is fair compared to the going prices in other shops. In these situations it is best to leave the shop and find one which is more receptive to the traditional haggling process.

This bargaining process often takes on additional drama in the bazaars and factories frequented by tourists. In some bazaars you may encounter merchants who play "bait and switch": they urge you to come into their shop where you can buy a particular item for the cheap price of US$10, but once you enter the shop, the price mysteriously goes to US$50. His objective is to get you to come into his shop where he believes he will be in control of the negotiation process. As noted earlier, he'll probably soften you up by offering you apple tea. We discovered four additional rules that work well in such situations – the "8 Foot Rule," "Oh, My God! Rule," "Never Ask Your Tour Guide to Negotiate for You Rule," and "The Best Deal is After Everyone Leaves the Place Rule." They go like this:

13. **Observe the "8 Foot Rule" for negotiating your best deal:** Turks like to maintain close personal space – at times they are literally in your face. Merchants maintain control by bringing customers into as well as keeping them in their shops. If you stand outside the shop to bargain (stay 8 feet from the merchant and his goods), you'll be in a much stronger bargaining position. However, if you're already in the shop, it may be time to make a "10 percent exit" – your exit could be worth another 10 percent discount! Do the following. Once you get near a final negotiated figure, walk 8 feet outside the shop. Yes, 8 feet and the price drops again. Tell the merchant his final price is too much and that you need to think about it as well as look elsewhere. Say goodbye, turn around, and literally walk 8 feet from the entrance of the shop and stop. Turn around and look at the shop and merchant and then look up and down the street. Look as if you are trying to decide where to go next. Chances are your new friend will still be talking to you, trying to persuade you that he offered you an excellent price and asking you to please come back into the shop

and talk. Shake your head and say *"It's too expensive. I really need to look some more."* Whatever you do, do not go back into the shop at this point; you'll be at a disadvantage if you do. You should now be in control of the situation. Make the merchant come to you in the street – that's your turf. Take your time and don't move from your position for at least three minutes. There's a high probability (70 percent or better) the merchant will come out and agree to give you the item at the final price you offered. For some unexplained reason, 8 feet seems to be the perfect distance for this final negotiation (we literally count our steps to make sure our final exit stops at 8 feet!); inside the shop the merchant may be within 6 inches of your face which may make you feel uncomfortable. By going into the street, you take final control of the negotiation. The merchant knows once you turn to leave, you'll probably be gone forever. The wise merchant knows it's better take less or lose out forever.

14. **Be just as expressive as the merchant by repeating the *"Oh, my God!"* phrase.** Many merchants in the bazaars have a flair for the dramatic. Indeed, the whole buying and selling transaction at times is high drama. Merchants often respond to your counter-offer by exclaiming *"Oh, my God"* as if you've just insulted them. This is part of their game. Don't be intimidated by such an extreme expression. Dish it back to the merchant by saying *"Oh, my God"* (add a little more drama by hitting your forehead with the palm of your hand as you make this exclamation) when they quote you a price. This often puts you on an even playing field – they perceive that you understand their psychology. You can now cut through the dramatics and get down to the real business of determining the final price.

15. **If you're with a tour group, bargain hard on your own.** Do not ask your tour guide or driver to help you negotiate a price. Since most of these service personnel are being paid commissions on everything you buy at their recommended shop, don't expect them to be an enthusiastic participant in helping you bargain for a good deal which cuts into their commission! Many will tell you the prices are fixed, which indeed they are . . . and you are the recipient of the "fix"!

16. **If you're visiting a bus stop shop or factory, don't buy where the crowds congregate, or be the last one out.** Remember, the herd never gets a good deal – it only gets taken to the slaughter. And he who buys early in the crowd tends to pay a high price. After all, the salesperson has no incentive to discount when he knows lots of naive tourists are willing to pay the full asking price. At this point, it's to your advantage to survey the competition next door or across the street. There are often similar shops nearby that do not have a busload of tourists shopping inside. If you visit these places, you may discover similar items are one-half to one-third the prices being asked at the other shop. If there are no comparable shops around, it's best to wait until everyone leaves the shop to get back on the bus. Being the last one out, chances are you can negotiate a good deal. After all, once you're gone, there will probably be little or no business until another bus comes. The one exception is if you find an item, one of a kind, that you absolutely must have. In this case, bargain as much as you can and then buy. If you walk out, you may return to find that someone from the bus has already purchased "your" item.

Whatever you do, have lots of fun bargaining for your loot. If you follow our rules, you'll approach such situations with confidence, and you'll walk away with a good deal. Some locals may even compliment you on your ability to bargain so well. Indeed, you'll probably be a much better bargainer than most locals! But make sure you really want something before you go through this whole process.

## BARGAIN FOR NEEDS, NOT GREED

One word of caution for those who are just learning the fine art of bargaining. **Be sure you really want an item before you initiate the bargaining process**. Many tourists quickly learn to bargain effectively, and then get carried away with their new skill. Rather than use this skill to get what they want, they enjoy the process of bargaining so much that they buy many unnecessary items. After all, they got such "a good deal" and thus could not resist buying the item. Be very careful in getting carried away with your new-found competency. You do not need to fill your suitcases with junk in demonstrating this ego-gratifying skill. If used properly, your bargaining skills will lead to some excellent buys on items you really need and want.

# TIPS ON BUYING CARPETS

The carpet shops are so ubiquitous to Istanbul and throughout Turkey, the rugs so beautiful and varied, and the rug salesmen so polished, that few travelers resist totally. Even if you are determined you will not buy a carpet, chances are you will buy at least one! So you better prepare for the inevitable.

Buying a rug as you travel can be a wonderful adventure that gives you a useful addition for your home as well as memories of the trip that can be re-lived as you enjoy the carpet and perhaps even the satisfaction of believing that you got a great deal! Many rug buyers take home carpets they love and enjoy for many years to come. Other rug buyers return home to find the carpet is too large for their room; the colors or patterns don't fit well with the decor of their home; or they realize they paid more than they should have. They succumbed to the euphoria of the moment in the carpet shop or to the polished sales pitch of the rug salesman.

The carpet shops of Turkey abound with wonderful carpets old or new; hand woven or machine made; dyed with vegetable dyes or chemical dyes; using bright colors or muted tones; bold tribal patterns or subdued patterns with a "European" look; flat weaves (kilim), pile rugs, or sumakh (a brocading technique). As the rug salesman says, *"There is a carpet for everyone. It is up to you to find it."*

In order to have the best chance to find a rug you love and that will fit into your home, you need to follow a few tips on how to prepare before you leave home as well as how to handle your encounters with the many rug sellers who will find you as you travel Turkey. The first two tips are the two traps you should avoid. Follow the suggestions in these as well as the remaining tips on things you can do to greatly increase the likelihood that if you do buy a carpet it will be a purchase you will love rather than regret.

1. **Don't buy a rug you have no place for.** Many travelers get carried away by the smooth sales pitch and euphoria of the moment. Here you are in exciting Turkey, sitting in a shop with more carpets than you have ever seen in one place. As you sip your tea – the third cup – the shop assistants pile ever more carpets on the floor before you. *"Just look."* the salesman says, *"No pressure to buy."* There are so many beautiful carpets. And soon you find your resolve not to buy a carpet melting away. The carpet salesmen are pros. You are not. You are no match for them! They have

met tourists like you before and encountered sales resistance, and they are pros at softening your resistance until you succumb and make the purchase.

Avoid this trap. Before you travel, survey your home. Take photos and measurements of any room that might be a candidate for a rug. (Measure the area for the carpet, not just the total room size.) If you have color swatches of fabrics in the room, take those as well. If you don't have actual fabric swatches, visit a paint store and get sample paint chips that match the shade and clarity (degree of brightness) of the predominate colors in the room. Buying a carpet that will fit in your home and that you will love for years to come is possible if you prepare well before you meet the "carpet you cannot live without."

2. **Don't buy a carpet as an investment.** Unless you are very savvy about rugs, don't expect to make money anytime soon on a carpet you buy. Despite what merchants may want you to believe, carpets are not liquid investments. Although any carpet may appreciate over time, it will most likely basically keep pace with inflation. Just because a carpet is old does not necessarily mean it is valuable. Some carpets were poorly made a hundred years ago just as they are today. The quality of the antique carpet, its scarcity, and its condition will all factor into its value. The person selling the carpet probably knows its value, and it is unlikely he will sell it to you for a great deal less than it is worth. You may pay less than you would for the same carpet if you bought it at home – if you could even find it – but the price difference is not likely to be enough to justify your carrying/shipping it home and perhaps paying duty on it as well. And once you get it home, though it may have cost you less than what you could buy it for in your hometown, that doesn't mean you can sell it for that greater amount.

Avoid this trap. Buy a carpet because you truly love it and have a place for it in your home. If you find out your rug is worth a lot more than you paid you have a bonus – a carpet you love and a great deal!

3. **Before you travel, check carpet stores in your area or travel to a big city near your home.** See the range of what is available and check prices. It is true that you won't find the exact carpet in the store at home that you may fall in love with in Turkey. So your comparisons will be general, but having a sense of what is available at home and

the price range for various carpets is better than having no idea at all. Many carpet shops in the United States sell carpets like mattresses – always on sale! Few people ever buy a carpet at full retail price.

4. **Look at examples of great rugs.** You may be able to do this before you leave home if you have a museum of textiles near you (Washington, DC, for example, has the Textile Museum). Two of Istanbul's museums, the Vakiflar and The Turkish and Islamic Art Museum show examples of masterpieces. No you won't be buying historic museum pieces, but surveying some of the best will help educate your eye to quality.

5. **Visit a lot of carpet shops and look at as many carpets as you can before they all start to blur in your mind's eye.** Listen to the carpet sellers; the best of them can give you a basic education in types of carpets, various weaves, and typical designs from various parts of Turkey. As you listen and learn, don't worry about gaining encyclopedic knowledge; rather, try to learn what carpets you like best or you believe will work best in your home. You can begin narrowing the field and start asking to see those in the future.

6. **Determine what you might be serious about buying:** You need to consider several factors when purchasing a rug: pile rug or flat woven kilim; vegetable or chemical dyes; bright or muted colors; formal or tribal design; contemporary or antique. Remember that just because a carpet is old, doesn't necessarily make it valuable. A poor quality carpet is still poor quality after decades. You may prefer the price, look and condition of contemporary hand-woven rugs using vegetable dyes.

7. **Look at more shops, now zeroing in on what you have determined you like, want, or need.** It takes stamina to go into rug shop after rug shop ostensibly starting the process over again each time. But if you are comfortable with the parameters you have set and only want to look at a narrow range of rugs, you can shorten the time spent in each shop.

8. **However, once you are ready to get serious you will need to fit your style to better mesh with that of the seller** which generally means much "small talk" and much

tea drinking. To get a good price on the carpet you buy, you must invest some time in the deal. The more time you spend on making a deal, the better should be the final price. Taking time, being patient, and schmoozing over tea should result in a final price favorable to you.

9. **Bargain hard.** Of course you will be told that you would pay twice (or several times) as much at home. Perhaps true, but you don't want to pay any more than you must pay to get it in Turkey. Don't expect to pay New York City or London prices in Istanbul or Santa Fe and Cannes prices in Cappadocia. Bargain, bargain, bargain. Before making a final decision, leave the shop (this may lower the price some more) and think it over or look at more carpets.

10. **Pay with a credit card – if you can.** Some shops take only cash, but most will take a credit card though they would prefer cash. Don't indicate you want to pay by credit card until you have bargained what seems to be the lowest price you can get. Only then, hesitantly indicate, *"Well, I might buy at that price, but only if I can use my credit card."* Use of your credit card may give you some recourse if the dealer never ships the rug or you determine it was misrepresented.

11. **Carry your carpet purchase with you if at all possible.** Avoid having it shipped to you later. Some carpet shops have waterproofed bags with handles so you can carry the carpet like a suitcase. We brought an 8x10 carpet home with us in this manner and it counted as one of our check-through bags so there were no shipping costs. A larger carpet can be rolled and wrapped in burlap and plastic sheeting and shipped through with your checked luggage. Tip the porters and let them handle it for you.

12. **Once you have made the purchase, don't continue shopping for that same carpet.** Shop for another one if you wish, but don't worry about whether you got the lowest price you could have on the carpet you bought. You bargained as hard as you could, and bought at a price you were willing to pay. Don't set yourself up for disappointment by playing this post-buying comparison game. You did the best you could at the time, so take your carpet home and enjoy it!

For additional tips on purchasing Turkish carpets – including information on different types of rugs, regional variations, colors, designs, and technical details on what to look for in carpets – visit the following websites:

www.about-turkey.com/carpet
www.tourarium.com/info/carpets
www.awildorchid.com/carpets.htm
www.turkishnews.com/DiscoverTurkey/culture/carpets
www.kilim.com

## EXAMINE YOUR GOODS CAREFULLY

Before you commence the bargaining process, carefully examine the item, being sure that you understand the quality of the item for which you are negotiating. Then, after you settle on a final price, make sure you are getting the goods you agreed upon. At this point, do two things:

1. Take a photo of your purchase, ideally with the merchant posing with the item.

2. Ask for an official receipt that states what you bought, for how much, and when. Make sure the shop includes its name, address, phone, and/or fax and e-mail address.

You should carefully observe the handling of items, including the actual packing process. If you bought several items, make sure you count and recount exactly what you bought. It's often easy to get distracted at the end and forget to account for everything. Use your receipt as a final checklist before you leave the shop. If at all possible, take the items with you when you leave. If you later discover you were victimized by a switch or misrepresentation, contact the tourist authorities as well as your credit card company if you charged your purchase. You may be able to resolve the problem through these channels. However, the responsibility is on you, the buyer, to know what you are buying.

## BEWARE OF POSSIBLE SCAMS

Although one hopes this will never happen, you may encounter unscrupulous merchants who take advantage of you. The most frequent scams to watch out for include:

1. **Switching the goods.** You negotiate for a particular item, such as a piece of jewelry or a rug, but in the process of packing it, the merchant substitutes an inferior product.

2. **Misrepresenting quality goods.** Be especially cautious in rug and jewelry shops. Rugs may not be the quality presented to you. Precious stones may not be as precious as they appear. Some merchants may try to sell "new antiques" at "old antique" prices.

3. **Goods not included in the package(s) you carry with you.** You purchase several items in one shop. The seller wraps them and presents them to you, but "forgot" to include one of the items you paid for.

4. **Goods not shipped.** The shop may agree to ship your goods home, but once you leave, they conveniently forget to do so. You wait and wait, write letters of inquiry, fax, make phone calls, and e-mail the shop; no one can give you a satisfactory response. Unless you have shipping and insurance documents, which is unlikely, and proper receipts, you may not receive the goods you paid for.

Your best line of defense against these and other possible scams is to be very careful wherever you go and whatever you do in relation to handling money. A few simple precautions will help avoid some of these problems:

1. **Do not trust anyone with your money** unless you have proper assurances they are giving you exactly what you agreed upon. Trust is something that should be earned – not automatically given to friendly strangers you may like.

2. **Do your homework** so you can determine quality and value as well as anticipate certain types of scams.

3. **Examine the goods carefully,** assuming something may be or will go wrong.

4. **Watch very carefully how the merchant handles items** from the moment they leave your hands until they get wrapped and into a bag.

5. **Request receipts** that list specific items and the prices you paid. Although most shops are willing to "give you a receipt" specifying whatever price you want them to write for purposes of deceiving Customs, be careful in doing so. While you may or may not deceive Customs, your custom-designed receipt may become a double-edged sword, especially if you later need a receipt with the real price to claim your goods or a refund. If the shop is to ship, be sure you have a shipping receipt which also includes insurance against both loss and damage.

6. **Take photos of your purchases.** We strongly recommend taking photos of your major purchases, especially anything that is being entrusted to someone else to be packed and shipped. Better still, take a photo of the seller holding the item, just in case you later need to identify the person with whom you dealt. This photo will give you a visual record of your purchase should you later have problems receiving your shipment, whether one of loss or damage. You'll also have a photo to show Customs should they have any questions about the contents of your shipment.

7. **Protect yourself against scams by using credit cards** for payment, especially for big ticket items which could present problems, even though using them may cost you a little more. Although your credit card company is not obligated to do so, most will ask the merchant for documentation, and if not satisfactorily received, will remove the charge from your bill.

If you are victimized, all is not necessarily lost. You should report the problem immediately to the local Tourist Information Office, the police, your credit card company, or insurance company. While inconvenient and time consuming, nonetheless, in many cases you will eventually get satisfactory results.

## Ship With Ease

Shipping can be a problem in Turkey since many shops are not experienced with international shipping. You should not pass up buying lovely items because you feel reluctant to ship them home. Indeed, some travelers only buy items that will fit into their suitcase because they are not sure how to ship larger items. We seldom let shipping considerations affect our buying decisions. For us, *shipping is one of those things that must be arranged*. You have numerous shipping alternatives, from hiring a professional shipping company to hand-carrying your goods on board the plane. Shipping may or may not be costly, depending on how much you plan to ship and by which means.

Before leaving home, you should identify the best point of entry for goods returning home by air or sea. Once abroad, you generally have five shipping alternatives:

1. Take everything with you.

2. Do your own packing and shipping through the local post office (for small packages only).

3. Have each shop ship your purchases.

4. Arrange to have one shop consolidate all of your purchases into a single shipment.

5. Hire a local shipper to make all arrangements.

Taking everything with you is fine if you don't have much and if you don't mind absorbing excess baggage charges. If you are within your allowable baggage allowance, you can have large items packed to qualify as part of your luggage. If you have more items than what is allowable, ask about the difference between "Excess Baggage" and "Unaccompanied Baggage." Excess baggage is very expensive, while unaccompanied baggage is less expensive, although by no means cheap.

If items are small enough and we don't mind waiting six to eight weeks, we may send them through the local post office by parcel post; depending on the weight, sometimes air mail is relatively inexpensive through local post offices.

Doing your own packing and shipping may be cheaper, but it is a pain and thus no savings in the long run. You waste valuable time waiting in lines and trying to figure out the local rules and regulations concerning permits, packing, materials, sizes, and weights.

On the other hand, many shops, especially art galleries, can ship goods for customers. They often pack the items free and only charge you for the actual postage or freight. If you choose to have a shop ship for you, insist on a receipt specifying they will ship the item. Also, stress the importance of packing the item well to avoid possible damage. If they cannot insure the item against breakage or loss, do not ship through them. Invariably a version of Murphy's Law operates when shipping:

*"If it is not insured and has the potential to break or get lost, it will surely break or get lost!"* At this point, seek some alternative means of shipping. If you are shipping only one or two items, it is best to let a reputable shop take care of your shipping.

If you have several large purchases – at least one cubic meter – consider using a local shipping company, since it is cheaper and safer to consolidate many separate purchases into one shipment which is well packed and insured. Sea freight charges are usually figured by volume or the container. There is a minimum charge – usually you will pay for at least one cubic meter whether you are shipping that much or less. Air freight is calculated using both weight and volume, and usually there is no minimum. You pay only for the actual amount you ship. One normally does not air freight large, heavy items, but for a small light shipment, air freight could actually cost you less and you'll get your items much faster. However, many shops in Turkey prefer shipping everything by air freight rather than sea. Since this can be very expensive, make sure you understand the costs before deciding to purchase a large item. When using air freight, use an established and reliable airline, even though in the end you may not know who will actually transport your shipment. In the case of sea freight, choose a local company which has an excellent reputation among expatriates for shipping goods. Ask your hotel concierge or front desk personnel about reliable shippers. For small shipments, try to have charges computed both ways – for sea and for air freight. Sea shipments incur port charges that can further add to your costs. Port charges at the shipment's point of entry will not normally be included in the price quoted by the local shipping agent. They have no way of knowing what these charges will be. If you have figures for both means of shipping, you can make an informed choice.

We have tried all five shipping alternatives with various results. Indeed, we tend to use these alternatives in combination. For example, we take everything we can with us until we reach the point where the inconvenience and cost of excess baggage requires some other shipping arrangements. We consolidate our shipments with one key shop in a major city early in our trip and have shipments from other cities in that country sent to our shop for consolidation.

When you use a shipper, be sure to examine alternative shipping arrangements and prices. The type of delivery you specify at your end can make a significant difference in the overall shipping price. If you don't specify the type of delivery you want, you may be charged the all-inclusive door-to-door rate. For example, if you choose door-to-door delivery with unpacking services, you will pay a premium to have your shipment clear Customs, moved through the port, transported to your door, and unpacked by local movers. On the other hand, it is cheaper for you to designate port to port. When the shipment arrives, you arrange for a broker to clear the shipment through Customs and arrange for transport to your home. You do your own unpacking and dispose of the trash. It will take a little more of your time to make the arrangements and unpack. If you live near a port of entry, you may clear the shipment at Customs and pick up the shipment yourself.

We simply cannot over-stress the importance of finding and establishing a personal relationship with a good local shipper in the country you visit, who will provide you with services which may go beyond your immediate shipping needs. A good local shipping contact will enable you to continue shopping in Turkey even after returning home.

# PART II

# Great
# Destinations

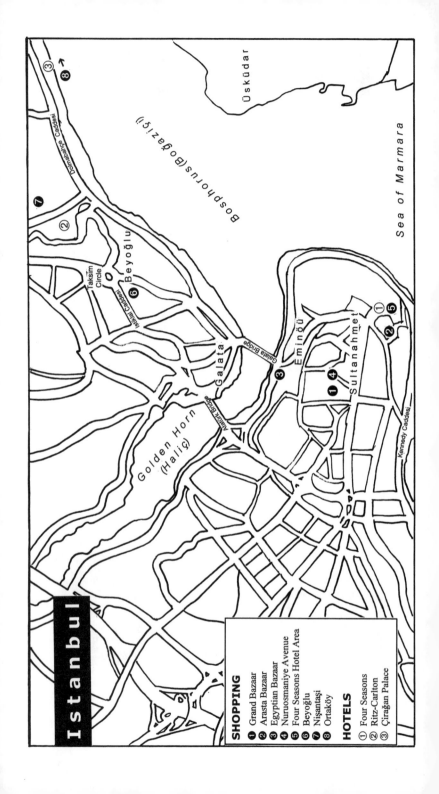

# Istanbul

**SHOPPING**
1. Grand Bazaar
2. Arasta Bazaar
3. Egyptian Bazaar
4. Nuruosmaniye Avenue
5. Four Seasons Hotel Area
6. Beyoğlu
7. Nişantaşı
8. Ortaköy

**HOTELS**
1. Four Seasons
2. Ritz-Carlton
3. Çırağan Palace

Üsküdar

Bosphorus (Boğaziçi)

Sea of Marmara

Dolmabahçe Caddesi

Beyoğlu

Taksim Circle

İstiklal Caddesi

Galata

Galata Bridge

Eminönü

Sultanahmet

Kennedy Caddesi

Atatürk Bridge

Golden Horn (Haliç)

# Istanbul

WELCOME TO AMAZING ISTANBUL, ONE OF the world's most exotic, romantic, and intoxicating cities – and a travel-shopper's paradise. Straddling both Europe and Asia at the fabled Bosphorus Straits, which link the Black Sea to the Sea of Marmara and eventually into the Mediterranean Sea, this beautiful, energetic, and throbbing city of over 12 million people hosts nearly 10 million visitors each year who often begin and end their Turkey adventure in this fascinating place. It's a city that begs to be discovered on foot or by boat, tram, subway, or car. Through many narrow winding streets, colorful bazaars, grand mosques, spiraling minarets, and well preserved palaces and museums to fine shops, restaurants, bars, and hotels, Istanbul has it all – a virtual gold mine of delights that can easily occupy a busy week of shopping, dining, sightseeing, cruising, and entertainment. The city constantly unfolds with a never-ending stream of surprises. Many visitors to this city have only one complaint – they didn't plan enough time to fully enjoy Istanbul's many treasures and pleasures. Well, you can always come back! And many soon do.

## A City of Contrasts

If you like big, attractive, diverse, colorful, and intriguing cities with lots of great character, you'll love legendary Istanbul with its many wonderful sights and sounds. Originally built on seven hills, like its model, Rome, today Istanbul is a large, sprawling, and energetic water-bound metropolis that is simultaneously traditional and modern. Next to ancient walls and monuments tracing Istanbul's Greek and Roman past stand impressive mosques, graceful minarets, bustling markets, busy docks, bobbing boats, modern high-rise buildings, glittering five-star hotels, and sophisticated shops, bars, restaurants, and discos. Formerly Constantinople, this is a city that spans several centuries in a single moment as you survey its delightful architecture and budding skyline of the old and new. Rich in history and challenging to the imagination, this was once the capital of three great empires – Roman, Byzantine, and Ottoman – which left in their aftermath evidence of combined Western and Oriental grandeur.

❑ Istanbul constantly unfolds with a never-ending stream of surprises.

❑ This is a large, sprawling, and energetic water-bound metropolis that is simultaneously traditional and modern.

❑ Istanbul was once the capital of three great empires – Roman, Byzantine, and Ottoman – which left in their aftermath evidence of combined Western and Oriental grandeur.

❑ This is the perfect place to both start and end any trip to Turkey.

Haggling in crowded and exotic bazaars is often accompanied by cups of tea and amidst ringing cell phones. This is a stimulating city of fascinating contrasts that is both a photographer's delight and a travel-shopper's delight.

Istanbul also is a city of pleasant contradictions. While most everyone complains about the obvious traffic congestion, which comes with such urban territory, many of the same people also marvel at the wonderful ferryboat cruises along the Bosphorus – a great escape from the city's concrete and asphalt. The streets, sidewalks, and bazaars may be crowded and noisy with people, but that's what gives Istanbul much of its compelling character. While cosmopolitan Istanbul may not represent the real Turkey, it does showcase the best of the best this country has to offer visitors. It's the perfect place to start and end any trip to Turkey.

# GETTING TO KNOW YOU

Much of the city's contrasts and contradictions seem to be purposeful design features exacerbated by a heady geography that has always emphasized Istanbul as being an international center for something important. Halfway between Europe, Asia, and the Middle East, Istanbul simply looks and feels grand.

## A CENTER OF SOMETHING IMPORTANT

The city is literally divided into two continents linked by bridges and ferryboats. It's the world's only city that functions as a bridge between east and west as well as north and south. Indeed, it's caught between and accommodates many economic, political, and cultural forces that pass its way and sometimes give it a bit of a shady character. During World War II and the Cold War, for example, it was an important meeting place for spies, exiles, fugitives, and journalists in search of truth and anonymity but who often fell in love with the city and each other. Today Istanbul also is a center for trade, commerce, finance, and tourism in search of new relationships, products, and money.

## EUROPEAN ISTANBUL

The European side of Istanbul is further divided into north-south sections – an old and new city which are separated by a body of water called the Golden Horn and linked to each other by vehicular bridges. The Old City to the south, also known as Old Stamboul and centered in the historic district of Sulta-nahmet, is the crowded, congested, and often confusing part of Istanbul. It exudes a great deal of Third World Asian and Middle Eastern character. It's where East meets West at the confluence of two continents. This is where Istanbul showcases its many major historic sites of interest to millions of visitors each year: the Topkapi Palace, Sultanahmet (Blue) Mosque, Basilica of Hagia Sophia, Hippodrome, and numerous muse-ums. It's also home of the famous Grand Bazaar and Egyptian (Spice) Bazaar as well as reputedly (and we agree) the world's number one hotel, the Four Seasons. The sights and sounds here are often chaotic and exotic but always fascinating and fun. It's a great place to explore on foot, whether in the Grand Bazaar with its labyrinth of more than 4,000 shops or along its many meandering cobblestone streets that take you to mosques, museums, and carpet and jewelry shops galore. This is where shopping takes on all the character of a Third World bazaar complete with aggressive touts and haggling merchants in colorful and festive settings. Cash-and-carry bargaining is both expected and accepted as the rule for determining prices. There's lots to see and do here. Indeed, you may decide to spend most of your time in Istanbul exploring this vibrant and colorful section of the city.

Immediately north of the Golden Horn is the newer European section of the city. Here the city has a distinctive European character with often narrow perpendicular and meandering streets, small shops, bars, restaurants, and a popular pedestrian mall which runs for nearly one kilometer along Istiklâl Caddesi immediately southwest of Taksim Circle and in the district of Beyoğlu. The restaurants, bars, nightclubs, and shops here tend to be trendy and especially appealing to the young and professional crowds. Farther north is the upscale suburb of Nişantaşi with its many fine boutiques and restaurants. This is also Istanbul's modern business and residential center with a few major attractions such as the Dolmabahçe Palace, Çirağan Palace (hotel), Ortaköy, and the Galata Tower which offers a panoramic view of the city. Many visitors prefer to stay in this area but do most of their daily sightseeing and shopping in the Sultanahmet area of the Old City.

*While Istanbul may not be the real Turkey, it showcases a very special side of Turkey you may quickly fall in love with.*

## ASIAN ISTANBUL

Istanbul also boasts an Asian side which is still very European but primarily residential. Known as Üsküder, it lies immediately to the east of the European side and along the east bank of the Bosphorus. This side of Istanbul tends to be relatively upscale with many restaurants and shops catering to locals who prefer the quiet of this area to the more crowded and noisy European side of Istanbul. The Asian side has very little to offer visitors in terms of sightseeing and shopping, although it does boast several good restaurants. Driving along its main streets and passing by numerous furniture and home decorative shops and high-end car dealerships will quickly convince you that Asian Istanbul is very self-contained and inward looking. The most appealing parts of Istanbul remain on the well-trafficked European continent.

## Where The Action Is

While Ankara is the country's political, governmental, administrative, and diplomatic capital, Istanbul is its economic, social, cultural, and historical center as well as the country's most important window to the rest of the world. Istanbul is where the action is. It has the best hotels, restaurants, shopping, sightseeing, and entertainment in the country. A sophisticated international city, it's simultaneously Turkish and European with many other international influences evident in its music, culture, and fashion. Here your choices for everything are both numerous and convenient. Top quality design, fashion, and style make this an extremely attractive city for most visitors and residents alike. Indeed, by comparison, much of the rest of Turkey has a decided "up country" look and feel. While Istanbul may not be the real Turkey, it showcases a very special side of Turkey you may quickly fall in love with.

## Quick and Easy Istanbul

Any large metropolis can be confusing for first-time visitors who need to quickly get a visual fix on where to best focus their limited time and attention. While Istanbul may initially appear confusing, it's really not all that difficult to get oriented to its various sections. Armed with a good map and some sense of direction, you should be able to quickly make sense of how to navigate the city.

### Istanbul on the Web

In preparation for your Istanbul adventure, you may want to visit a few websites that provide information on the city:

- **Istanbul City Guide**    www.instanbulcityguide.com
- **Explore Istanbul**    www.exploreistanbul.com
- **Istanbul**    www.istanbul.com
- **The Guide Istanbul**    www.theguideturkey.com
- **Istanbul Guide**    www.istanbulguide.net

- Istanbul Travel Guide www.istanbultravelguide.net
- Istanbul Convention
  and Visitors Bureau www.icvb.org
- Tourism Turkey www.tourismturkey.org
- The Turkey Guide www.turkeyguide.com
- Istanbul Life www.istanbullife.org
- Istanbul Hotels www.istanbulhotels.online.com
- Istanbul Hotels www.istanbulhotels.com
- Turkish Hotels www.turkishhotels.com

## LOCAL PUBLICATIONS

For online access to Turkey's only English language daily news-paper, *The Turkish Daily News*, visit www.turkishpress.com. But for more direct information on specific destinations, including Istanbul, go directly to this URL:

www.anatolia.com/anatolia/destinations/default.asp

Once you arrive in Istanbul, look for the following monthly English-language publications which may be available at your hotel or in various newsstands:

*City Plus Istanbul*
*Time Out Istanbul*
*The Guide Istanbul*

Each of these publications includes information on museums, hotels, restaurants, shopping, arts, culture, entertainment, and travel as well as informative articles about life in Istanbul.

## SIX BASIC ISTANBULS

For travel-shoppers, Istanbul can be conveniently divided into six major sections for shopping, sightseeing, and dining:

1. **Old City:** This is Istanbul's prime tourist destination, the historic district of Sultanahmet. It includes the Grand Bazaar, Egyptian (Spice) Bazaar, Arasta Bazaar, mosques, palaces, churches, museums and adjacent streets jam–packed with shops offering a dazzling array of carpets, jewelry, leather goods, copperware, and handicrafts. You can easily spend three days shopping and sightseeing in this richly rewarding area of fascinating sights, sounds, people, and products.

2. **New City:** This is the European section of Istanbul with its many trendy shops, restaurants, cafes, hotels, bars, discos, and nightclubs. Much of this area's shopping, dining, and entertainment activities are centered along Istiklâl Caddesi in Beyoğlu. Here you'll find numerous antique shops, bookstores, and music shops along with trendy boutiques, and the main Vakko department store. A charming tram runs up and down this main pedestrian walkway to make covering the area especially convenient and pleasant. Functioning as a central business district, this whole area is full of wonderful surprises as you explore its many meandering side streets. This section of the city is especially popular with young people.

3. **Nişantaşi:** Located just 10 minutes north of Taksim Circle, the tree-lined suburb of Nişantaşi is Istanbul's major upscale shopping and lifestyle area. It's Turkey's version of Rodeo Drive and Fifth Avenue in the U.S. Its main streets are lined with quality carpet, home decorative, art, antique, jewelry, clothing, leather, and accessory shops. Given its many restaurants, you can easily spend a couple of days engaged in lifestyle shopping.

❑ The Old City around Sultanalımet is Istanbul's prime tourist destination for sightseeing and shopping.

❑ The New City around Istiklâl Caddesi in Beyoğlu is a major center for shopping, dining, and entertainment.

❑ Nişantaşi is Istanbul's most upscale shopping and lifestyle area – the city's version of Rodeo Drive and Fifth Avenue.

❑ Ortaköy, a small arts and crafts community on the Bosphorus, is the city's most popular night spot.

4. **Ortaköy:** East of Nişantaşi, near the Bogazici Bridge and situated along the Bosphorus, is the small arts and crafts community of Ortaköy. This is a pleasant area to stop and browse through numerous quaint shops and vendor stalls and enjoy its many restaurants. The area is especially popular on weekends when it becomes an arts and crafts flea market. It's also the most popular night spot along the Bosphorus for seafood restaurants, jazz clubs, nightclubs, and bars.

5. **Akmerkez:** Farther north of Ortaköy in Etiler, near the Fatih Bridge, lies the huge Akmerkez Shopping Mall, one of the largest in Europe. Immensely popular with locals, this complex offers many surprises for individuals interested in good quality jewelry, clothes, and accessories.

It's also a great place to people watch, especially after having experienced the exotic sights and sounds of the crowded Grand Bazaar and Egyptian Bazaar in the Old City.

6. **Üsküder:** If you have time, you may want to visit the Asian side of Istanbul at Üsküder. Easily accessible by ferryboat from the European side, Üsküder is primarily an upper-class residential area with little of the chaos found elsewhere in Istanbul. Except for a few excellent restaurants and some interesting architecture, Üsküder has very little of interest to visitors, who are well advised to spend more time in the European side.

---

# THE BASICS

## GETTING THERE

Istanbul is serviced by several major international airlines. From the United States, both Turkish Airlines and Delta fly directly into Istanbul from New York City which takes about nine hours. Turkish Airlines also flies from Chicago and Miami. Since no direct flight connects Canada to Turkey, Canadians must find connecting flights in the United States or Europe. Most major European airlines have direct flights into Istanbul from their main hubs – Air France, Alitalia, Austrian Airlines, British Airways, Iberia, KLM, Lufthansa, and Swissair.

## ARRIVAL

Arriving by air into the new Atatürk International Airport (opened in February 2000) is relatively quick and easy. A rather sterile and utilitarian steel and aluminum structure, the airport is very functional, enabling ease of getting in and out of its premises. If you already have a visa, proceed immediately to immigration which should process you through within a few minutes. If you need a visa, go directly to the two visa windows which are located to your right, just before the immigration lines. Unlike many other countries, you need not complete disembarkation forms or other documentation prior to arriving at the immigration desks. Just present your passport and visa. After completing immigration, go directly to the large baggage retrieval area. Here you will find luggage carts (trolleys) which can be rented for US$1 (1.5 million TL) – pay the people who operate the machines that dispense the carts. It may take some time for your luggage to arrive since the delivery of bags to this area is much slower than the immigration process. While waiting, you may want to check out several duty-free shops adjacent to the luggage carousels. The same products, especially liquor, will cost much more once you leave the airport. After you get your bags, proceed to the customs section which may or may not be operating. During our recent arrival, no officials were staffing this section. Once you exit to the arrival hall, you'll find numerous services for handling money, transportation, and hotel reservations. The various service windows are found to your right. They include several money exchange windows and representatives of car rental firms, and two tourist information desks. The money exchange windows offer competitive rates, with most charging commissions. The Post Office window, which is next to the tourist information office, does not charge commissions. They only change cash.

Getting from the airport to the city is relatively convenient. If you are not being met by a tour group or hotel representative, the quickest way to get into the city is by taxi. They are metered and will cost from US$10 to US$20, depending on the traffic and your hotel location. Since the airport is located approximately 15 kilometers south of the city, the trip from the airport to your hotel will probably take 30 to 45 minutes. There's also a less expensive shuttle bus service (Havaş)that operates between the airport and the Taksim and Akaray areas. The cost is US$3 per person. From these drop-off points, you'll need to take a taxi to your hotel. If you're traveling with a companion or companions that can share the cost of transportation, it will be more convenient to just take a taxi into the city.

## GETTING AROUND

The most convenient way to navigate Istanbul is by taxi or with a car and driver. The ubiquitous yellow **taxis** seem to be everywhere. They are metered.

You can arrange for a **car and driver** through your hotel or a local travel agency.

While you may be tempted to **rent a car** and drive on your own, it's really not recommended since parking is relatively difficult and the costs of using taxis or hiring a car and driver are relatively inexpensive compared to the cost of renting a car and handling parking problems.

**Trams** and the **subway** operate through certain parts of the city. They are relatively inexpensive and convenient to use, if you know where they go – which is not always easy to detect.

**Buses**, both large and small (dolmuş or minibus), are ubiquitous throughout the city. While inexpensive, they also tend to be crowded, and it is often difficult to understand exactly where they go because of signage problems.

**Ferries and seabuses** are delightful ways to travel along the Bosphorus and to cross from Europe to Asia. Eminönü is the main disembarkation point. One of the highlights of visiting Istanbul is to spend six hours taking ferries up and down the Bosphorus to see major sights along the way.

You'll see very few **motorcycles or motorbikes** in the city. Istanbul is primarily a city of cars and buses.

## SHOPPING ISTANBUL

Istanbul is one of the world's great shopping destinations. From the crowded bazaars and fascinating carpet, jewelry, ceramic, and copper shops of Sultanahmet to the antique centers, upscale boutiques, arts and crafts shops, hotel shopping arcades, and shopping centers of the New City, Istanbul offers visitors a dazzling array of shopping choices for just about any budget and taste, from the cheap and tacky to the expensive and sophisticated, and everything in between. Just step into the famous Grand Bazaar and you'll immediately discover that Istanbul has a very long and well developed shopping culture dating from early Ottoman times. Or visit the many shops in the New City and you would think you were shopping in any modern city of the world.

### TWO SHOPPING CULTURES AND STYLES

Nowhere else in Turkey do you encounter two distinct shopping cultures so close to one another. The first shopping culture is that of the noisy and crowded bazaar – Istanbul's original shopping mall. Here goods tend to be crammed into small shops where they are often difficult to see without taking them outside the shop into better lighting. The ubiquitous type of shops fitting this description offer carpets, rugs, textiles, leather goods, copper, brass, antiques, jewelry, ceramics, meerschaum pipes, and assorted arts and crafts. This is also a highly personalized shopping experience where merchants invite you into their shops for tea, coffee, soft drinks, and conversation. Here you first establish a personal relationship with the merchant in the process of acquiring products. In fact, this highly personalized shopping process may result in major contacts with the local people. Visit many of these shops and indulge in this local ritual and you'll soon find your shopping day goes very slowly. But you will meet some very interesting people along the way, perhaps establish some long-term friendships, and find this to be a very rewarding shopping experience. You'll learn a great deal about products and the people behind them. This also is a culture of price indeterminacy and bargaining. While prices are seldom displayed on goods, once quoted, you are expected to bargain. However, the rules of bargaining are never quite clear. In some places you may end up with something at 50, 60, or 70 percent of the initial asking price. In other places you may only receive a 10 or 20 percent discount, and some places may give no discount. This also is frequently a "cash and carry" culture – many merchants do not accept credit cards, nor do they pack to international standards. Expect to pay cash and take the item with you in a plastic bag or wrapped in a newspaper.

❑ Istanbul has a very long and well developed shopping culture dating from early Ottoman times..

❑ The rules of bargaining are never quite clear – discounts can range from 10 to 70 percent, depending on the shop and your negotiation skills.

❑ Street touts, tour guides, and drivers expect to receive 10 to 30 percent commissions on everything their clients purchase.

❑ Shopping on your own in Istanbul is easy, fun, and rewarding.

The second shopping culture is that of the boutique, department store, hotel shopping arcade, and shopping mall. Here goods tend to be nicely showcased in windows and display counters. Salespeople tend to keep their distance, letting customers browse on their own. Prices tend to be both displayed and fixed. While you may be able to negotiate some discounts, especially in street shops and jewelry stores with high ticket items, for the most part prices are inflexible, except during advertised sales periods. Most of these shops accept major credit cards and will pack and ship. This shopping culture also is very lifestyle-oriented, with many restaurants, cafes, and food courts to make shopping a very convenient social event.

Many visitors to Istanbul feel more comfortable with the second shopping culture which is similar to shopping back home. They are often intimidated by the first shopping culture, especially when it comes time to "do a deal" – bargain over the price. Not knowing how to properly bargain, they often avoid these shops or pay the first asking price, which is usually too much. Savvy travel-shoppers in Istanbul learn how to handle both shopping cultures well.

## TOUTS, GUIDES, AND THE COMMISSION GAME

Hovering over both shopping cultures are street touts, tour guides, and drivers who expect to receive commissions for bringing you to specific shops. They often claim to have a brother, cousin, or a friend who can give the visitor a very special price. This usually means they have prearranged deals with shops that give them 10 to 30 percent on everything their clients purchase. Invariably these are often mediocre tourist shops that depend on traffic being brought into their shops through such sources who prey on tourists. Not surprisingly, if you buy in such shops, you end up indirectly paying the commissions through the shop's inflated prices. If you are being taken to a shop by a local, chances are you are indeed being taken! Many of the carpet and handicraft emporiums located just outside the Grand Bazaar (along Nuruosmaniye Caddesi) fit this tour group pattern. You'll see groups of tourists, especially cruise ship passengers on a sponsored shopping adventure, being led inside these shops where their tour group leaders make a great deal of money from their mediocre purchases.

## SHOPPING ON YOUR OWN

Shopping in Istanbul is both easy, fun, and rewarding. You don't need, nor want, a guide to take you around to his recommended shops. All you need is a good map, this book, and a sense of adventure. In most cases, you can easily get around by taxis. However, you may find it more convenient to hire a car and driver if you're planning to cover a large area in a single day. But taxis are relatively easy and inexpensive to get around in Istanbul. If you practice the basic shopping rules for Turkey, which we outlined in Chapter 3, and visit many of our recommended shops in this chapter, you'll come in contact with the best of the best Istanbul has to offer. You'll operate effectively in both shopping cultures, meet some wonderful people, and leave Istanbul with several memorable treasures. If you are like many other visitors, you'll want to soon come back to experience more treasures and pleasures of Istanbul.

# WHAT TO BUY

Since Istanbul is a major crossroads, everything seems to end up in this intriguing city. Whether trendy European fashion or unique Turkish carpets and ceramics, Istanbul is the center for shopping. Selections and quality here are hard to beat.

## ARTS AND ANTIQUES

Numerous galleries and antique shops offer a wide range of arts and antiques. Look for miniature paintings and antiques in the Grand Bazaar, especially at **Galeri Sufi**, prints and drawings in the bookshops in and around Istiklâl Caddesi in Beyoğlu, galleries in a few major hotel shopping centers, and antique shops along Çukurcuma Street in Beyoğlu. Shops such as **Sofa, Atrium, Erdüm Collection, Eskidji, Antikarnas, Şamdan Antique, Hikmet & Pinar,** and

**Koleksiyon Auction House** offer some of best arts and antiques in Turkey. If you're interested in old furniture and collectibles, the five-story **Horhor Bit Pazari** (flea market) is the place to visit. For high-end European-style antiques, be sure to visit the **Antique Palace**. You'll find contemporary art galleries in Istanbul but very few. **Sofa** combines contemporary art with antiques and collectibles.

## JEWELRY

Jewelry shops in Istanbul offer some of the best designs and selections that you will find anywhere in Turkey. Several shops, such as **Urart, Efendy,** and **Hilat Collection**, offer wonderful gold reproduction jewelry with Roman and Ottoman themes. Many of the top jewelry shops are found in the major hotels, such as the Ritz-Carlton, Swissôtel, Çirağan Palace Hotel Kempinski, as well as in and around the Grand Bazaar, and in Nişantaşi. Some of our favorite jewelers include **Urart, Gilan, Fibula, Sait Koç, Sponza, Hilat Collection,** and **Efendy**. The Grand Bazaar includes numerous gold and jewelry shops. Some of the best jewelers, such as **Gilan** and **Sait Koç** have shops in the Akmerkez Shopping Mall in Etiler.

## CARPETS AND RUGS

Like elsewhere in Turkey, carpet and rug shops are everywhere. Indeed, this is one of the most confusing and challenging purchases you may make in Turkey. Istanbul has hundreds of shops offering a full range of Turkish carpets as well as rugs from other countries. Whom can you trust? What should you

pay? How will you get your purchase home? These questions
frequently arise with visitors who face a daunting task of
selecting from so many carpet shops. The largest concentration
of carpet shops is found in and around the Grand Bazaar and
the nearby Arasta Bazaar. You'll also find carpet shops in and
around the major hotels, especially the Four Seasons Hotel, and
in the suburb of Nişantaşi. Whether you want to or not,
chances are you will leave Turkey with at least one carpet,
although two to five carpets are more likely. Be sure to buy only
what you need or fall in love with rather than make an impulsive buy or because it appeared to be a steal. You'll most likely

regret purchasing carpets based
solely on impulse and price. Follow our advice on buying carpets
in Chapter 3 in order to avoid
the pitfalls of buying carpets in
Turkey. Carpets can be great
buys in Istanbul, but only if you
know what you are doing. Some
of our favorite carpet shops,
which offer excellent quality,
good selections, and fair prices,
include **Güneş Carpet and Kilim House** in Nişantaşi, **Şengör**
and **Adnan & Hasan** in the
Grand Bazaar, and **Maison du
Tapis D'Orient** in the Arasta Bazaar. For quality over-sized
carpets, visit **Asia Minor** near the Four Seasons Hotel.

In preparation for any rug purchases in Istanbul or elsewhere in Turkey, you may want to review our tips in Chapter
3 as well as the information on Turkish carpets and rugs found
on the following websites:

> www.about-turkey.com/carpet
> www.tourarium.com/info/carpets
> www.awildorchid.com/carpets.htm
> www.turkishnews.com/DiscoverTurkey/culture/carpets
> www.kilim.com

## TEXTILES AND EMBROIDERY

From rich silks and elaborate Ottoman fabrics to beautiful
embroideries and antique textiles from Turkey and Central
Asia, Istanbul is an important center for fabrics in addition to
its famous carpets and rugs. For a fine collection of Ottoman
fabrics, be sure to visit the fourth floor of the main **Vakko**

department store in Beyoğlu. For an exquisite collection of antique textiles and embroideries from central Asia, be sure to visit **Maison du Tapis D'Orient** in the Arasta Bazaar. Many shops within the Grand Bazaar offer a wide range of textiles and embroidered goods.

## BOOKS, MAPS, ENGRAVINGS

If you enjoy browsing for books and discover old maps, prints, and engravings of the Ottoman period, Istanbul will not disappoint you. Indeed, you can easily get lost in shops that offer fascinating selections of such collectibles. Several bookshops specialize in old maps and engravings. Most of these shops are found in the Beyoğlu district of the New City, although you'll find a few such shops in the Grand Bazaar. Some of the best places to discover nice selections of books, maps, prints, and engravings are **Eren**, **Ottomania**, **Atrium**, and **Sufi**.

## CERAMICS

Turkey is rightly famous for its many multi-colored ceramics. An art form developed and refined in Turkey, ceramics come in many different forms: plates, bowls, vases, trays, tiles, and figures. Most ceramics repre-sent two different art forms – Iznik with its distinctive blue, white, and red patterns and Kütahya which are blue and white. Some of the best ceramics shops are found in the Grand Bazaar and Arasta Bazaar. Some of our favorite ceramic shops include **Iznik Tiles**, **Iznik Classics**, **Topkaji Çini**, **Orient Iznik-Nicaea**, and **Anatolia Dreams**. For antique ceramics, be sure to visit the two **Sofa** shops near the Grand Bazaar. For one of the best collections of Çanakkale ceramics and pots, be sure to visit **Haci Cevdet Olcay** on the third floor of the Horhor Pitpazari.

## LEATHER

Turkey produces a wide range of leather goods, from coats, jackets, clothes, handbags, and accessories to briefcases, cushions, backpacks, and footwear. While numerous shops and factories in Istanbul offer excellent quality leather products, don't expect to find top quality Italian, German, and French leather goods here. Most leather shops in and around the bazaars offer inexpensive leather products which are not particularly fashionable nor flattering. The best quality leather shops will be found in the New City, especially in Beyoğlu, Nişantaşi, and the Akmerkez Shopping Mall as well as in the factory outlet shops along the road to the airport in the Old City. Some of our favorite leather shops include **Derishow, Vakko, Beymen, Matras, Derimod, Kiriclar,** and **Vincere.** For made-to-order knock-off handbags (Gucci, Hermes, Longchamp, Chanel) try **Serpan.**

## CLOTHES AND FASHION

Istanbul is the country's major center for trendy clothes and fashion. European and local designers are well represented in the many boutiques and department stores found in the New City. The best quality boutiques are located in Nişantaşi and in the Akmerkez Shopping Mall. For a good sampling of Istanbul's best clothing and fashion offerings, visit **Vakko** (both men's and women's), **Derishow, Beymen, Yargici, Cotton Bar,** and **Silk and Cashmere.** However, don't expect to make many clothing purchases in Istanbul. With the exception of stylish Vakko and trendy Derishow, many locally produced clothes are not particularly appealing to visitors who can probably do much better back home with styles, colors, fabrics, designs, and prices. Turkey is not a noted center for international clothing designers who are more oriented to the European market than to local residents and international visitors.

## HOME FURNISHINGS AND ACCESSORIES

Home furnishings and accessories in Istanbul are influenced a great deal by French and Italian style as well as by the local Ottoman style. In fact, within the past decade, Ottoman style with its rich colors and velveteen fabrics has seen a rebirth in Istanbul. For a good overview of home furnishings and accessories, in a fabulous Ottoman collection, be sure to visit the main **Vakko** department store in Beyoğlu. **Mimarca,** a new and trendy home decorative offshoot of the famous local design house of Derishow, offers excellent quality home furnishings and accessories with many unique designs that will fit into any home.

## SILVER

Silver lovers have a great time shopping for all types of attractive silver items, from antique silver and jewelry to bowls, plates, cups, and serving pieces. For a wide selection of silver jewelry, be sure to visit the three **Sponza** jewelry shops in the Ritz-Carlton, Swissôtel, and Ciragan Palace Hotels and **Dargent** in Nişantaşi. Quality antique silver can be found at **Sofa**. For a nice selection of silver serving pieces at good prices, visit **Melda Silver** in the Grand Bazaar. Our favorite silver shop, **Urart**, which has several branches in Istanbul (try the main Nişantaşi shop), produces very attractive silver bowls, plates, cups, and accessory pieces.

## HANDICRAFTS, SOUVENIRS, AND GIFTS

You'll find no shortage of handicrafts and souvenirs in Istanbul's numerous bazaars and shops. Many of these items make wonderful gifts, add to special collections, or serve as home or office decorative pieces. For special gift items, such as unique rock candles, marble bowls, and silver accessories, be sure to visit the **Urart** shops. The government-operated **Dösin** shops offer a wide range of handicrafts produced in several regions throughout Turkey. **Mimarca** is a great source for excellent quality and designed gift items, especially table accessories. Many of the shops in and around the Grand Bazaar and Arasta Bazaar offer a wide range of handicrafts and souvenirs – brass and copper pots, meerschaum pipes, Russian and Turkish icons, wood boxes, ceramic balls, lanterns, miniature paintings, dolls, tribal lacquer boxes from Afghanistan, inlaid boxes, knives, and ceramic animal figures. Indeed, you can easily spend a whole day in these two bazaars shopping just for handicrafts and souvenirs. Several of the museum shops, such as the Museum of Turkish and Islamic Art and the Dolmabahçe Palace, have good selections. **Fiyonk** in Nişantaşi offers a very nice collection of quilted gift and craft items. Several shops in the Ortaköy area, such as **Kevser** and **Atelye Negül**, specialize in arts and crafts. **Atrium** in the Beyoğlu area remains one of our favorite all-purpose art, antique, and handicraft shops that yields lots of unique treasures. Many visitors to the Grand Bazaar, Arasta Bazaar, and Egyptian Bazaar find the Turkish delights (candies), apple tea (actually apple cider), and spices make nice gift items.

## WHERE TO SHOP

However chaotic, shopping areas within Istanbul are relatively well defined and easily accessible. Once you get your urban bearings, head for the following shopping areas where you'll discover most of Istanbul's best treasures.

### OLD CITY AND SULTANAHMET AREA

The Old City, especially in the Sultanahmet area, offers many exciting shopping opportunities. Most shopping in this area is centered in and around the major bazaars, with the Grand Bazaar being the ultimate shopping experience.

### GRAND BAZAAR

Also known as the Kapali Çarsi, or Covered (Bedesten) Bazaar (www.mygrandbazaar.net), this is one of the world's great markets, a shopping and cultural tour de force. Claiming to be the world's oldest and largest covered shopping arcade, the

Grand Bazaar accommodates between 250,000 and 400,000 visitors a day. Crowded, noisy, and often disorienting, it's an intoxicating place that may well become one of your highlight experiences in Turkey. Whatever you do, don't miss this place. While you may not buy much here, you'll at least experience Turkey's original shopping mall with all its colorful Asian and Middle Eastern character. But chances are you will end up buying something, be it a carpet, antique, ceramic, handicraft, leather jacket, or piece of jewelry. While this place may initially seem intimidating, because of its unusual layout, narrow passageways, dense shops, and aggressive merchants, it's really a very friendly and fun place to visit. Just walk into a shop and start asking questions and you'll quickly strike up some interesting conversations and learn a great deal about the market, the merchants, the products, and the buying process. You should have a great time visiting this bazaar. Plan to arrive early – before all the crowds – and initially spend two to three hours here. Then plan to come back again. You're going to meet some very interesting people in the process of passing through this delightful labyrinth that is the mother of all bazaars.

Originally constructed in the 15th century, over the years the Grand Bazaar became the victim of several fires and earthquakes and has been reconstructed several times. What you see today is the latest sprawling creation of a bazaar that keeps on living and giving. In its current form, the bazaar covers an area of 30 hectares, with 60 streets, and over 4,000 shops. At the center stands the Old Covered Bazaar – Iç Bedesten – which now specializes in antiques, carpets, jewelry, and copper. Surrounded by stone walls, the Grand Bazaar is one huge labyrinth of streets, passages, commercial sectors, and shops – literally a city within a city, unquestionably one of the great cultural tours of Istanbul. Much of the bazaar also extends beyond the walls, especially the north/south Çadircilar Caddesi along the western wall of the bazaar. Many of the streets tend to specialize in a single product, such as jewelry, carpets, leather and suede, copper, textiles, silver, and antiques. However, many streets are mixed with a large variety of goods. Spend a few hours here and you'll discover a fabulous collection of treasures, an exciting market atmosphere, and delightful architecture. Without a good map, compass, or sense of direction, you can easily get disoriented here, although signage is relatively good. Some hotel shops and newsstands sell *The Grand Bazaar* map which provides sufficient details for navigating the various sections of the bazaar. Also, look for *Istanbul: The Hali Rug Guide,* which includes a useful section on this bazaar.

The Grand Bazaar is more than just a collection of retail shops. It's an integrated community that also houses restaurants, cafes, banks, moneychangers, mosques, storehouses, and 40 hans. The hans, which are both inside and outside the bazaar's walls, are commercial buildings where many items in the bazaar are made, repaired, and sold.

While there are several entrances to the bazaar, most visitors enter through either the southeastern **Nuruosmaniye Gate**, just off of the main shopping street of Nuruosmaniye Caddesi, or the southwest **Beyazit Gate**, just off of Çadircilar Caddesi. At either entrance, you'll probably encounter very persistent touts who want to become your guide through the bazaar. They may make you think the bazaar will be intimidating without their help, and they invariably will tell you they know where to shop for cheap carpets – the brother's, cousin's, or friend's shop. Don't establish eye contact or speak to them – just keep moving into and through the entrance to the bazaar. Both entrances immediate put you on the famous street of gold shops, Kalpakçilar Caddesi. From this street, the rest of the bazaar is easily accessible. In fact, the main thoroughfares within the wall of the bazaar include the following:

- **Kalpakçilar:** The street of gold shops that connects the east/west gates and links the major north/south streets and lanes.

- **Terzi Başi Sokaği/Kuyumcular/Aci Çeşme Sokaği:** Runs north and south near the eastern side of the bazaar. Includes several jewelry, carpet, and antique shops. The exit at the northern end takes you to several hans just outside the bazaar wall.

- **Takkeciler:** Begins at the center of Kalpakçilar Caddesi, this major north/south street is lined with handicraft, ceramic, and carpet shops. Halfway up Takkeciler you can turn right onto Zenneciler and go into the famous old covered bazaar, lç Bedesten, with its many antique, jewelry, and copper shops. The major carpet area – the intersecting east/west street called "The Street of the Carpet Dealers" (Halicilar Çarşisi Caddesi) – has two rows of pillars running down the middle of the street. Welcome to the fascinating world of Turkish carpets!

- **Sipahi Caddesi Feraceciler/Yağlikçilar Sokaği:** Runs north and south near the western side of the bazaar. Includes a wide range of shops with primary emphasis on textiles.

Starting at the wide arched Kalpakçilar Street which is literally lined with gold, the shops here offer very similar gold jewelry, from traditional to modern designs. One of the oldest and most famous jewelry shops is **Sait Koç** (No. 94/96, Tel. 526-6847). They are especially noted for their excellent designs, good quality, and reasonable prices (their largest and most upscale shop is at the Akmerkez Shopping Mall in Etiler). At the center of this goldsmith street, turn north along Takkeciler Street which will take you into the center of the bazaar. Along the way, stop at a tiny ceramics shop called **Orient Iznik-Nicaea** (Takkeciler Sok, 17-18-19-31-33-34-36, Tel. 526-4798) for one of the nicest collections of fine quality ceramic plates and tiles. If you turn right onto Zenneciler, you will be at the center of the bazaar and in the famous **lç Bedesten**. Here you can spend a couple of hours browsing through numerous small antique, art, copper, ceramic, jewelry, bronze, silver, and collectible shops. Indeed, this section of the bazaar may become your favorite haunt. Some of our favorite places here include **Erdün Collection** (No. 34-39 Beyazit, Tel. 526-7628, website: www.erduncollection.com) for old copper pots, plates, lanterns, and acoustic ceramic balls; **Galeri Sufi** (1ç Bedestan Şerif Aga Sokak No. 42-43, Tel. 512-3404) for miniature paintings; and **Iznik Classics** (1ç Bedestan Şerif Aga Sokak No. 188, Tel. 520-2568) for some of the best ceramic plates, bowls, and tiles in Turkey. Just north and west of the Bedesten are the bazaar's two major carpet streets, Halicilar and Takkeciler. **Halicilar Çarşisi Caddesi** is known at "The Street of the Carpet Dealers." You can quickly become overwhelmed with the many carpet shops and dealers who beckon you into their shops for a drink and carpet demonstration. Our favorite carpet dealer here is **Şengör** (Takkeciler No. 65-83 ve 98, Tel. 527-2192, website: www.sengorhali.com), the oldest carpet dealer in the bazaar with its excellent collection of kilims and Anatolian carpets, excellent service, and reasonable prices. Other carpet shops worth exploring include the reputable **Adnan & Hasan** (Halicilar Caddesi 89-90-92, Tel. 527-9887, website: www.ad nanandhasan.com) for Anatolian carpets and kilims, and **Resat Gümüsgerdan** (Kavaflar Sokak No. 27, Tel. 513-7150), a tiny shop that functions as a wholesaler of silk carpets and kilims to other shops. A nearby shop called **Bay** (Kavaflar Sokak No. 40-41, Tel. 527-5014), offers an interesting collection of antique copper, brass, marble, and Russian and Istanbul icons.

The remainder of the Grand Bazaar includes thousands of shops selling all types of leather goods, fabrics, clothes, antiques, books, silver, copper, bronze, bedding, and souvenirs. Be sure to visit the various "hans" which specialize in producing, repairing, and selling different products: carpets, leather goods, clothes, scarves, shawls, furs, silver, and jewelry.

Just how good of a deal can you get in the Grand Bazaar compared to shops elsewhere in Istanbul? It's hard to say, especially since this is also a tourist mecca and merchants understand tourist pricing. If you come accompanied by a tour guide, expect 10 to 30 percent of your cost will go directly to the guide as his shopping commission. If you are serious about buying an item and you made the mistake of coming with a guide, tell him to take a 30-minute break and meet him at one of the main gates. Then go shopping on your own. Your ability to get a good deal in the bazaar largely depends on how well you bargain on your own. Since most merchants speak enough English to determine pricing, language should not be a problem. Indeed, you're dealing with very experienced and savvy merchants who know the art of the deal. Take your time, do comparative shopping, and don't pay an initial asking price. Like in most bazaars, with bargaining you may end up paying anywhere from 20 to 60 percent of the first quoted price.

The Grand Bazaar can be a very intense experience with its crowds, chaos, colors, and sounds. After three or four hours exploring this place, you may feel the need to escape from its narrow lanes and dense in-your-face shops. You may also want to get away to do some comparative shopping for similar items outside the bazaar. Our advice: Don't try to do the Grand Bazaar on one visit like the many one-day cruise ship visitors who only have time to stop here for their Istanbul shopping experience. There's simply too much to absorb in a single visit. Come back another day – perhaps in the evening – to further explore this place. A break will most likely give you a much needed perspective which often gets lost on the first trip through the Grand Bazaar. A second visit will most likely result in additional surprises as the bazaar continues to reveal its many shopping, architectural, and sightseeing secrets.

## ARASTA BAZAAR

Located behind the Blue Mosque, the pleasant street-front Arasta Bazaar is a favorite of many visitors. After experiencing the hustle and bustle of the Grand Bazaar, this bazaar offers a nice change of pace. Small, laid back, and easily accessible, the Arasta Bazaar is a delightful place to shop for quality carpets, textiles, ceramics, arts, and crafts. Less touristy than the nearby Grand Bazaar, few cruise ship passengers and organized tour groups have time to come here after their one-stop Grand Bazaar experience. However, many independent travelers and collectors have discovered the many treasures in this area. Many of them prefer the Arasta Bazaar over the Grand Bazaar for both quality and value. Serious collectors will come to the Arasta Bazaar first and then check out the Grand Bazaar.

Some visitors have difficulty finding the Arasta Bazaar because it's tucked between the Blue Mosque and a few side streets. If you leave the front door of the Four Seasons Hotel and walk directly up Utangac and Torum streets and turn right at Mimar Mehmet Ağa, you'll be at the southeast side of the bazaar. Alternatively, the southern entrance to the bazaar can be found at the intersection of Tuvukhane Sokak and Aya Sofia Caddasi, which are just around the corner from the southern end of Torum Sokagi. If you have difficulty finding the entrances to the bazaar, just ask anyone around the area and they will direct you to them. Not surprisingly, many of these "helpers" may also want to take you to their father's, brother's, or uncle's carpet shop, which may or may not be in the Arasta Bazaar! If you follow them, you should expect spending time going through the tea, coffee, and carpet demonstration rituals.

This is a relatively small bazaar with only 63 shops lining both sides of a pedestrian walkway, with both upper and lower sections. You can easily spend two to three hours in this bazaar – and longer if you end up in a few very interesting shops operated by serious collectors. A few of our favorite shops here include the following: **Maison du Tapis D'Orient** (Arasta Çarşisi No. 151, Tel. 517-6808) for an incredible collection of antique carpets and ikat textiles from Central Asia – don't miss this one; **Iznik Classics** and **Iznik Tiles** (Arasta Çarşisi No. 67 & 73, Tel. 517-1705) for excellent quality ceramic tiles, plates, vases, and bowls based upon classic Iznik designs; **Topkapi Çini** (Arasta Çarşisi No. 161, Tel. 517-1705) for an inexpensive line of handmade ceramics produced by Iznik Classics and Iznik Tiles; **Motif Nomad Art** (Arasta Çarşisi No. 77, Tel. 517-6798) for a nice collection of tribal rugs from Central Asia and lacquer boxes from Afghanistan, Turkmanistan, and Uzbekistan; **Seyitağaoğulari Carpet Kilim Hand-Craft Industry & Exp. Ltd. Co.** (Arasta  Çarşisi No. 159, Tel. 516-4173) for an unusual selection of rugs and carpeted slippers, handbags, notebooks, boxes, and collapsible lanterns; **Eymen Halicilik** (Arasta Çarşisi No. 107, Tel. 516-0733) for tribal textiles and rugs from all over Central Asia and lacquer boxes from Afghanistan; **Meerschaum Pipes** (Arasta Çarşisi No. 63, Tel. 516-4142) for an interesting collection of nicely carved meerschaum pipes; **Turkish Handicraft and Art** (Arasta Çarşisi No. 119, Tel. 517-7430) for miniature paintings, dolls, bone boxes, and ethnic clothes; and **Ares Handycraft and Art** (Arasta Çarşisi No. 121, Tel. 517-6800) for special watercolors and engravings produced by two Turkish artists.

## EGYPTIAN (SPICE) BAZAAR

Located next to the Yeni Valide Mosque and adjacent to the waterfront in Eminönü, the Misir Çarsisi or Spice Bazaar is also frequently referred to as the Egyptian Bazaar. Many visitors find the many outdoor commercial activities on the way to, as well as around, the Egyptian Bazaar to be one of the real highlights of visiting this place. Commerce spills into the streets and lanes of this very crowded commercial area that extends from the Grand Bazaar to the Yeni Valide Mosque. While bargains can be found everywhere, few of the cheap items in this area are particularly attractive to visitors; it's the colorful and chaotic street theater that impresses most people. If you're coming from the Grand Bazaar, the Egyptian Bazaar is about a 10-minute walk to the northeast. Along the narrow streets and lanes you will pass by hundreds of street shops and vendors selling a variety of inexpensive and very dated-looking local goods – footwear, clothes, toys, appliances, and jewelry. This area also abounds with knock-off name brand clothes, leather goods, and watches. The Egyptian Bazaar is housed in a rose brick $17^{th}$ century building. Inside you'll find a colorful and aromatic market offering a combination of produce and spices. Look for a large selection of exotic culinary and medicinal spices along with dried fruits, Turkish delights, apple tea, and caviar. The open area between the Egyptian Bazaar and the pigeon-infested Yeni Valide Mosque is a great place to people watch and enjoy the ambience of the Old City's waterfront.

NURUOSMANIYE AVENUE

The main street leading to the east gate of the Grand Bazaar is Nuruosmaniye Caddesi. Both sides of this pleasant tree-lined avenue have numerous upscale carpet, antique, and jewelry shops well worth visiting. Indeed, some of the largest dealers in Istanbul are found along this street. The best place to start is at the eastern end of the street, where it intersects with Bab-l ali Caddesi, and walk west toward the entrance to the Grand Bazaar. Several of the shops here operate as one-stop emporiums designed to handle tour groups, especially large groups from the cruise ships which dock nearby. Shops such as the very popular **Bazaar 54** (Nuruosmaniye Caddesi 54-65-67, Tel. 511-2150) offer a wide range of carpets, jewelry, ceramics, handicrafts, and souvenirs under one roof and over several levels. As might be expected, most of these shops make exaggerated claims about having the best quality and prices on everything in Istanbul. Don't believe them – it's part of the standard sales pitch. Many of the carpet shops also include a jewelry section – the ultimate one-stop shop for tourists. Seasoned in working with tour groups, these shops and emporiums are well staffed to take care of all your buying needs – obligatory carpet demonstrations, free drinks, credit cards, packing, and shipping.

Since so many of the shops here are organized for tour groups, you can expect the prices to be high and the quality to be less than what is advertised, despite claims to the contrary. This is definitely bargaining country since most shops are very eager to sell to what are essentially here-today-gone-tomorrow tourists. They also want you to buy with them now, before you wander around in the Grand Bazaar. This is also an area where you can waste a lot of precious shopping time on what are essentially tourist traps. Be prepared to say "No" in many of these shops, especially when offered another time-consuming carpet demonstration. Your goal should be to move on as quickly as possible to the shops that offer the "good stuff"!

We have a few favorite shops here that go beyond what we consider to be the typical tourist traps of Nuruosmaniye Caddesi. For some of the best antiques, arts, and collectibles in all of Turkey, be sure to visit the two **Sofa** shops on this street: Nuruosmaniye Caddesi Nos. 42 and 106-B, Tel. 527-4142 and 529-2850. These two high-end shops are for serious shoppers and collectors who appreciate good quality, whether old or new. For fabulous one-of-a-kind jewelry, as well as unique paintings, be sure to visit the exclusive **Efe Jewelry** (Nuruosmaniye Caddesi Nos. 41-47, Tel. 520-9505, website: www.efegold. com). One of Turkey's top jewelers has its head office on this street: **Gilan** (Nuruosmaniye Caddesi No. 58, Tel. 519-3010, website: www.gilan.com.tr; its largest and most impressive shop is at the Akmerkez Shopping Mall). Two of the largest and most reputable carpet dealers in Istanbul are **Hereke Hali** (Nuruosmaniye Caddesi No. 57, Tel. 513-6474, website: www. herekecarpet.com) and **Hali Sarayi** (Nuruosmaniye Caddesi No, 66-68, Tel. 514-1700, website: www.halisarayi.com).

If you're in a hurry to get this shopping exercise over within an hour, get in line with all the tour groups and explore the six floors of **Bazaar 54**. This is one-stop shopping heaven for many shoppers with limited time. You'll find lots of interesting merchandise in this impressive emporium. Be sure to strike up a good bargain for everything you buy here. Even if you don't plan to buy anything, at least browse through this impressive place. You also can get a free shoeshine here!

As you approach the entrance to the Grand Bazaar, turn right and go two blocks until you come to the **Serefhan Building**. This is one of the largest centers for jewelry shops in Istanbul with more than 60 jewelry shops showcasing their wares on three floors. One of the most popular shops here is **Hilat Collection** (Şerefefendi Sokok, No. 58, Şerefhan, First Floor, 95-98, Tel. 520-0171) with its distinctive gold reproduction designs.

## FOUR SEASONS HOTEL AREA

The Four Seasons Istanbul has a rightly deserved reputation as the top hotel in the world. If you splurge on only one hotel in Turkey, make sure it's the Four Seasons Istanbul. Occupying the grounds of a former prison for high-class political prisoners, it draws a very exclusive clientele that appreciates good quality travel and shopping. Nicely located in the shadows of Istanbul's major sights – the Blue Mosque and Hagia Sophia Mosque – the Four Seasons Istanbul also is centrally located for shopping. The concierges at this hotel dispense lots of good shopping advice, but the hotel itself does not have a shopping arcade. It does feature a few top-end shops in its showcases, such as Sofa and Hilat Collection. Many shops are along the street just outside the hotel. Indeed, the surrounding streets are lined with good quality carpet, textile, ceramic, and leather shops, as well as some very good restaurants, which are well worth exploring. The hotel is also within five minutes walking distance from the pleasant Arasta Bazaar and 10 minutes walking distance from the Grand Bazaar. Within this area, we found the following shops well worth visiting: **Asia Minor** (Kutlugün Sok, Tel. 516-5132, website: www.asiaminorcarpets.com) for top quality oversized carpets; **Jasmin Rug Store** (Tevkifhane Sokak No. 8/A, Tel. 638-3061) for a good collection of wool and silk carpets; **Aytek** (Cankurtaran Ha. Seyit Hasan Sokak No. 24, Tel. 516-6307, website: www.aytekcarpets.com) for a wide range of carpet designs ; and **Anatolia Dreams** (Kutlugün Sok, No. 16-A, Tel. 517-8433) for ceramic tiles and plates. Several attractive showcases in the lobby of the Four Seasons Istanbul feature the products of the city's top jewelry, art, and antique shops.

## ROAD TO AIRPORT

Kennedy Avenue, the scenic coastal route that connects Sultanahmet District with the international airport, offers a few interesting shopping opportunities. Midway to the airport, you'll see a group of factory outlet leather and fashion shops on your right: **Derimod, Kircilar, Vincere,** and **Gianni.** The first three shops are open to the public; Gianni is only open to the trade. While these are ostensibly factory outlet shops, in reality they are basically large showrooms that offer a better range of selections then their smaller retail shops. **Derimond** (Tel. 547-1604) offers excellent quality leather shoes, coats, jackets, and handbags – much better than their other shops in Istanbul which primarily offer shoes. **Kircilar** (Tel. 582-5555) offers very stylish leather coats, jackets, handbags, and belts; this is their only shop in Istanbul. **Vincere** (Tel. 546-2036) offers more colorful and trendy leather jackets and coats (and loud music) than the other shops. If you travel farther west toward the airport, you'll soon come to the **Galleria Shopping Mall** and the adjacent Crowne Plaza Hotel. The shopping mall primarily caters to local middle-class shoppers. However, it does have branches of two shops of interest to visitors: **Matras** (Tel. 559-4572) for nice leather accessories and **Silk and Cashmere** (Tel. 559-4516) for good quality scarves, sweaters, and silk blouses.

## NEW CITY AND BEYOĞLU AREA

The Beyoğlu area in the New City is one of Istanbul's trendiest and fun places for shopping, dining, and entertainment. While you may not buy much here, nonetheless, you'll find the area most interesting to explore. Chances are you will find a few treasures along the way. In many respects, this whole area is great street theater for people who enjoy exploring new areas and encountering the unexpected.

Stretching for nearly one kilometer southwest of Taksim Square, the Beyoğlu area is dominated by one main street which functions as a convenient pedestrian mall – Istiklâl Caddesi. A charming red tramway travels up and down this street. Very European, outdoors, and festive in character, this popular area is a great place to explore numerous shops along the main street as well as on several side streets. It's also a great place for people watching, from beggars, children, and street musicians to bread vendors and young lovers. Watch where you walk since the tram can quietly sneak up on you and delivery cars often compete with pedestrians for street space. It's the type of area that always seems to yield new surprises each time you visit.

The best way to explore this area is to start at **Taksim Circle**. This busy circle is usually crowded with buses, taxis, and cars. You can't miss **Istiklâl Caddesi** since it's a stone paved pedestrian walkway filled with people and highlighted by the red tram that terminates near the circle. If you walk southwest along this street, you'll see numerous small shops, restaurants, cafes, and bakeries. Several music shops blare loud music onto the street in hopes of attracting customers to their latest featured selections. **Beyoğlu ADA Kültür** (Istiklâl Caddesi, Orhan Adli Apaydin Sok. lst. Barusu Alti, No. 20, Zemin Kat, Tün, Tel. 251-3878) is one of the best music shops for a good selection of CDs and tapes of local and international music. Most shops here cater to local residents, especially boutiques, clothing, shoe, and jewelry stores for young people. Some of the better shops along this street include **Desa** (Istiklâl Caddesi No. 140, Tel. 243-3786) for leather shoes, handbags, coats, wallets, briefcases, and luggage; **Paşabahçe** (Istaklal Caddesi, No. 314, Tel. 244-0544) for quality glassware; and **Vakko** (Istiklâl Caddesi No. 123/125) department store. The real highlight here is Vakko. This is the main department store for the upscale Vakko chain, Turkey's version of Neiman Marcus and Saks Fifth Avenue. It includes five floors of top quality clothes, home furnishings, and textiles. If you visit only one shop in Istanbul, make sure it's this exquisite Vakko store. For basic custom-designed ladies shoes and handbags, visit **M. Nazaryan** (Siraselviler Caddesi No. 65, Tel. 293-7179) which is located just south of Taksim Circle.

The real treasures in this area found along several side streets which include shops selling arts, antiques, prints, and books. Many of the small streets leading directly from Istiklâl Caddesi include restaurants, cafes, discos, and nightclubs – streets that draw crowds in the late evening. Shoppers head for two major areas – **Tünel** for prints, books, and collectibles and **Çukurcuma** for antiques and home decorative items. In the Tünel area visit the small **Sufi Gallery** (Tünel Square No. 6, Tel. 251-1966) for a nice collection of miniature paintings, watercolors, prints, bookmarks, cards, and bone boxes; **Lavant Koleksiyon** (Tünel Meydani No. 8, Tel. 293-6333) for paintings, prints, and cards; **Eren** (Tünel, Istiklâl Caddesi, Sofyali Sokak No. 34, Tel. 251-2858) for arts books on Turkey; **Ottomania** (Tünel, Istiklâl Caddesi, Sofyali Sokak No. 30-32, Tel. 243-2157) for a large collection of old maps, prints, and calligraphy; and **Atrium** (Tünel Geçidi 7, Tel. 251-4302) for a wonderful collection of antiques, paintings, prints, ceramics, rugs, wood mortars, and collectibles – our favorite in the whole Tünel area.

The Çukurcuma area includes many small antique and home decorative shops which are particularly popular with collectors and designers. The whole area, with its narrow streets and small shops, has a very European feel to it. Along the way, look for **Serpan** (Yeni Çarşi Caddesi No. 33/A, Tel. 244-3146) for handmade knock-off handbags (Hermes, Longchamp, Chanel);

**Stoa** (Hayriye Caddesi No. 18/1, Tel. 251-4098) for hand-crafted modern wood furniture and accessories, especially creative lamps and lighting systems; **Hikmet and Pinar** (Faik Paşa Yokuşu 36/A, Tel. 293-0575) for old French-style furniture, Ottoman embroideries, and home decorative items; **Şamdan Antique** (Kuloğlu Mahallesi Altipatlar Sok. No. 20, Tel. 245-4445) for a very nice collection of unique antiques, from Anatolia wall panels and wood ceilings to Turkmanistan oil bowls and tin and copper pots and bowls; **Asli Günşiray** (Çukurcuma Caddesi 72A Firuzağa, Tel. 231-3605) for home furnishings and fabrics, including some nice Ottoman and Chinese accent pieces; and dusty, disorganized, but always reliable **Antikarnas** (Kuloğlu Mahallesi Falkpaşa Yokuşu No. 15 Çukurcuma, Tel. 251-5928) for a designer's hard-to-find collection of Turkish, Ottoman, and European antiques, paintings, pictures, clocks, stone animals, and architectural pieces.

## NIŞANTAŞI AREA

The Nişantaşi area, located approximately one kilometer north of Taksim Circle, is Istanbul's most upscale shopping area. Often crowded and confusing with one-way streets, this pleasant shopping neighborhood is lined with elegant boutiques and jewelry, carpet, antique, home decorative, and gift shops. Several nice restaurants and cafes make this a great place for lifestyle shopping.

Nişantaşi is a relatively small, compact, and at times very congested suburban community with one main street – Valikonaği – and several connecting one-way streets. Since parking is a real problem here and most of the shops are close together, it's most convenient to walk the main shopping streets. Start at Valikonaği Caddesi and branch out to Abdi Ipekçi Caddesi, Rumeli Caddesi, Halâskârgazi Caddesi, Mim Kemal Öke Caddesi, and Akkayak Sokak. Along the way you'll discover lots of interesting shops. While many of them are upscale boutiques offering international name brand items (Tommy Hilfiger, Esprit, Benetton, Mango/MNG), other shops are less exclusive and offer good value. Some of our favorite places in this area include **Güneş Carpet and Kilim House** (Mim Kemal Öke Caddesi No. 5, Tel. 225-1954, website: www.ishoparoundthe world.com/gunes) for one of the nicest collections of old and new carpets in Turkey; **Urart** (Abdi Ipekçi Caddesi No. 18/1, Tel. 246-7194) for a unique collection of beautifully designed silver and gold jewelry, reproduction (antiquity) gold and black pearl jewelry, silver serving pieces, and marble and silver plates; **Yargici** (Valikonaği Caddesi No. 30, Tel. 225-2952) for fashionable men's and women's clothes as well as its own line of toiletries and skin products; **Derishow** (Valikonaği Caddesi No. 85, Tel. 231-1510) for very fashionable and trendy leather coats, handbags, shoes, accessories, and clothes: **Salabi** (Mim Kemal Öke Caddesi) for an exclusive collection of beautiful Ottoman, Chinese, and European antiques and collectibles; **Orient House** (Valikonaği Caddesi Saroğlu Atp. No. 83D, Tel. 224-7620) for quality Asian furniture and accessories: **Fiyonk** (Valikonaği Caddesi No. 12/1, Tel. 225-1921) for a cute collection of quilted gift and craft items; **d'Argent** (Valikonaği Caddesi Akkavak Sokak Orkide Apt. No. 4/1, Tel. 224-1734) for uniquely designed silver jewelry, pewterware, and handpainted trays (also has a nice cafe next door); and **Ev+** (Valikonaği Caddesi Akkavak Sokak Albayrak Apt. 9/3, Tel. 323-1758) for colorful contemporary tableware. While in this area, check out a few of Nişantaşi's fine restaurants for lunch and dinner, such as **Hünkar** (Mim Kemal Öke Caddesi No. 21, Tel. 225-4665) and **Borsa** (Istanbul Convention and Exhibition Centre, Tel. 232-4201).

## ORTAKÖY AREA

Located just south of the Boğaziçi Bridge along the Bosphorus and near the Akmerkez Shopping Mall, Ortaköy, "The Middle Village," is a delightful riverfront arts and crafts community with several restaurants, cafes, shops, and vendor stalls arrayed along its cobblestone streets and lanes. If you've traveled to Kas or Kalkan in southwest Turkey along the Mediterranean, you'll notice many "village" similarities to Ortaköy. This is an especially popular place during the weekends when many visitors disembark from the ferries to enjoy a few hours of ambient shopping and dining. Parking can be a real problem along the main street, Muallim Naci Caddesi, which fronts the Ortaköy area. On Sundays the place becomes a very popular arts and crafts market offering lots of inexpensive jewelry, crafts, and ceramics. In the evenings, Ortaköy becomes one of the most popular areas for entertainment given its many jazz clubs, nightclubs, and bars.

Some of our favorite shops here include **Kevser** (Muallim Naci Caddesi No. 72, Tel. 327-0586) for a nice selection of painted ceramic plates, bowls, and serving pieces; **Hazal Kilim** (Mecidiye Köprüsü Sokak No. 27, Tel. 227-4071, website: www.hazalkilim.com) for an excellent collection of carpets and kilims in a pleasant old two-story commercial building with several small rooms for demonstrating their unique line of textiles; and **Atelye Negül** (Ortaköy Sahili Değirmenci Sokak

No. 10, Tel. 261-8599) for interesting decorative colored glass items, especially glasses, pots, and bowls.

## HOTEL SHOPPING ARCADES

A few of Istanbul's top hotels in the New City have small shopping arcades which primarily cater to their upscale clientele. The largest arcades are found at the Çirağan Palace, Ritz-Carlton, Swissôtel, and Hilton. Many of these shops are branches of shops found elsewhere in Istanbul. Offering jewelry, carpets, arts, crafts, and decorative items, they cater to business travelers and cruise ship passengers who stay in these hotels.

One of the best hotel shopping arcades is found in the **Çirağan Palace Kempinski Hotel** (Çirağan Caddesi 84, Beşiktaş, Tel. 258-3377). Here you'll find a very exclusive collection of shops: **Koleksiyon Auction House** (Tel. 236-6890) for a large collection of quality carpets, antiques, ceramic pots, glass, and paintings from Turkey and Iran; **Chantique** for a small but good collection of antiques, jewelry, paintings, rugs, glass, and porcelain; **Abdullah Export** (Tel. 266-0811) for reproduction brass pots and antiques; and **Efendy** (Tel. 236-2183) for a small but top quality collection of reproduction gold and one-of-a-kind jewelry using diamonds, rubies, emeralds, sapphires, turquoise, and old coins.

The relatively new **Ritz-Carlton Hotel** (Elmadağ Askerocaği Caddesi No. 15, Tel. 344-4444) has a nice shopping arcade which is beginning to take shape in the aftermath of a major downturn in tourism which took place when the property opened in the immediate aftermath of the September 11. Look for the **Hilat Collection** for fine jewelry; **Sponza** for silver, diamond, gold, and pearl jewelry; and **Kutahya Porselen** for a nice collection of ceramics and porcelain.

The **Swissôtel** has a few quality shops well worth visiting: **Antik Palace** for porcelain, clocks, and silver; **Sponza** for jewelry; **Bvlgari** (owned by Sponza) for jewelry and watches; and **Urart** for unique jewelry and silver pieces.

Both the Hilton and Conrad Hilton Hotels have small shopping arcades with very familiar shops found in other hotel shopping arcades: **Koleksiyon Auction House** and **Urart**.

## SHOPPING MALLS

Shopping malls have become very popular with local residents. However, most of these places are of little interest to visitors in search of unique local items. After all, most shops in the malls cater to local needs with a disproportionate number of clothing and accessory shops for young people. One exception to this general rule is the big, noisy, and crowded **Akmerkez** Shopping Mall in Etiler. This is Turkey's largest and most up-market shopping mall. If you visit only one shopping mall, make sure it's Akmerkez. It has everything for young and trendy shoppers, including major jewelry, clothing, and leather stores. Its middle to upper middle class clientele pack this place on Saturdays. It also attracts many European visitors.

As soon as you arrive at Akmerkez, be sure to visit the Information Desk where you may be eligible to receive a one day "Courtesy Card" that entitles you to five to 15 percent discounts in selected shops. The shopping mall has many name brand stores, such as **Lacosta, Benetton, Polo Ralph Lauren, Ferre, Façonnable, Pierre Cardin,** and **Esprit.** It represents some Turkey's best leather and accessory shops, such as **Derishow, Derimod,** and **Teodem.** But the real stand-out store here is fashionable **Derishow** (No. 314/315, Tel. 282-0408) with its extensive leather, clothing, furniture, and home furnishings sections. This is one of the best shops in Istanbul for local designer goods fashioned with Italian leather and fabrics, and it's the most extensive of the Derishow shops. Service and selections here are simply outstanding. Also look for trendy and up-market fashions at **Beymen, Vakko, Vakkorama,** and **Silk and Cashere.**

The Akmerkez Shopping Mall also is home to several of Istanbul's top jewelers. Be sure to visit both **Gilan** (No. 123, Tel. 282-0576, website: www.gilan.com.tr) and **Sait Koç** (No. 267, Tel. 282-2547) for top quality jewelry. **Bijoux Noemi** (No. 240, Tel. 282-2710), just around the corner from Sait Koç, offers an nice collection of quality costume jewelry made in Israel and France.

Other popular shopping malls with locals include the **Galleria** in Ataköy (near the airport), **Carousel Mall** in Bakirköy, and **Atlas Passage** in Beyoğlu. The best of these shopping malls is Galleria. More middle class and less up-market than Akmerkez, Galleria is located on the road to the airport and adjacent to the Crowne Plaza Hotel. However, there's not much of interest to visitors except for branches of **Matras** (Tel. 559-4572) for fine leather goods and **Silk & Cashmere** (Tel. 559-4516, website: www.silkcashmere.com.tr) for fashionable men's and women's clothing and accessories with special emphasis on cashmere sweaters. It does have a large food court (McDonald's, Burger King, Dominos Pizza, Pizza Hut, KFC) with an ice skating rink in the food court/atrium area.

## ANTIQUE EMPORIUMS AND FLEA MARKETS

Istanbul has several antique emporiums and flea markets that are open during the week or on weekends. One of the largest and best organized is the **Horhor Bit Pazari** at Aksaray (Horhor Caddesi, Kirma Tulumba) in the New City. If you love antiques, collectibles, and unusual treasures, Horhor may be just what you're looking for. This large, rambling, and dusty complex includes 215 shops which are found on six different levels. Most of the stops offer old furniture and accessories – tables, chairs, chests, beds, and pianos. Some include unique collections of collectibles, art, lamps, and pottery. While there is not much English spoken here and service is not readily apparent, you should be able to navigate this place with little difficulty. Someone who speaks

English will eventually help you. The best shops are found on levels, 1, 2, and 3. Look for **Haci Cevdet Olcay** (Kat 3 No. 141 Aksaray, Tel. 524-4156) for one of the best collections of the famous Çanakkale pottery; **Olcay ve Olcay** (Kat 1 No. 79-82 Aksaray, Tel. 532-7780) for a nice selection of unique leather chairs, furniture, glass, and silver; **Topaz** (Kirma Tulumba Sk. No. 13 Giriş Kati No. 59-60, Tel. 531-9226) for furniture, pots, statues, lamps, chandeliers, and mirrors; Kandil Çeşitleri (Kirma Tulumba Sk. No. 13/176, Tel. 532-9203) for a large collection of lamps and lanterns; **Sultan Antik** (Kiriktumba Sk. No. 13/150 Kat 4, Tel. 533-9255) for a good collection of lamps, tables, and jewelry; **Horlton Antik and Sanat** (#130) for many small and large paintings, both old and new; **Antik Avize** (Kat 2 No. 93, Tel. 534-2456) for a very large selection of colorful lamps in all forms and sizes; **Art Antik/ Gallery AAD** (Kirma Tulumba Sk. 13/149, Tel. 631-5231) for a unique collection of paintings and antiques, from furniture to bird baths; **Sedef Is** (Kirma Tulumba Sk. No. 13-75-76, Tel. 521-2813) for Ottoman and Turkish furniture, especially inlaid tables, chairs, and chests; and **Osmanli** (Kirik Tulumba Sk. No. 13/84 (Tel. 521-6832) for a fascinating collection of weapons, candle holders, victrolas, chests, silver, clocks, locks, hanging brass lamps, knives, guns, jewelry, and Ottoman boxes.

**Eskidji** (at the end of Dolapdere Mobilya Çarşisi and Yenişehir Dereotu Sokak in Beyoğlu) is another popular antiques emporium which also includes an auction house. It has four floors of art and antique shops. Most of the art shops are found on the fourth floor. Several furniture and home accessory shops, such as **Yilmazlar Mobilya** and **Ofisev**, are found along the main street leading to this emporium.

The rather hard to find **Antik Palace** (Spor Caddesi, Talim-yeri Sok, Maçka, Tel. 236-2460, website: www.antikpalace.com /tr), next to the Nişantaşi area, is Istanbul's premier antique auction house and emporium. It's also Europe's fourth largest auction house. Indeed, they are known as the "Sotheby's of Turkey." This nicely appointed old historic five-story yellow building includes high-end antiques, many of which are French in origin – furniture, clocks, statuary, lamps, and mirrors. This is the place for serious antique collectors. The Antik Palace also publishes the magazine *Antik & Dekor*.

**Raffi Portakal** (Mim Kemal Öke Caddesi 19, Tel. 225-4637) in Nişantaşi is a small but exclusive auction house offering high-end antiques, such as furniture, oil paintings, and chandeliers. You also can buy direct here.

Flea markets can be found throughout Istanbul. In the Beyazit district, look for the daily Sahaflar Çarşisi and Çomara. On Sundays you'll find a flea market between the Grand Bazaar and Sahaflar as well as between Büyükdere and Sariyer. Daily flea markets are open in Topkapi district, on Çukurcuma Sokak in Cihangir, on Büyük Hamam Sokak in Üsküdar, in the Kad-köy Çarşi Duraği area, and between Eminönü and Tahtakale.

## MUSEUM SHOPS

Most museums have small gift shops selling books, postcards, and souvenirs. A few of the shops are operated by the government Some of the largest and most interesting museum shops are found at the **Topkapi Palace** which is actually a **Dösin** arts and crafts shop operated by the Ministry of Culture. You'll also find a **Urart** jewelry and silver shop on the grounds of the Topkapi Palace (on the way to the Konyali Restaurant). The **Museum of Turkish and Islamic Art** has two shops near the entrance that offer a good collection of ceramics, carpets, copper pots, bone boxes, jewelry, shadow puppets, books, prints, paintings, cards, and bookmarks. The **Dolmabahçe Palace** has a nice gift shop near the exit that offers beautiful reproduction porcelain pieces, books, coins, textiles, carpets, and paintings.

# BEST OF THE BEST

If you have limited shopping time in Istanbul, you may want to focus your shopping attention on the top shops. We found the following shops to offer some of the best quality products for discerning travel-shoppers. While some of these shops may initially appear to be expensive, they generally offer good value for their quality selections.

## ARTS AND ANTIQUES

❑ **Sofa:** *Nuruosmaniye Cad. 42, Cağaloğlu, Tel. 527-4142 and Fax 527-9134; and Nuruosmaniye Cad. 106-B, Cağaloğlu, Tel. 527-5051. Website: www.kashifsofa.com. E-mail: kasif@kashif sofa.com.* These two shops, operated by the engaging Mr. Kâşif Gündoğdu, are filled with one of the best eclectic collections of quality arts, crafts, antiques, and collectibles found in Turkey. The first shop (Nuruosmaniye Caddesi 42) is the larger with three floors of ceramics, pots, needlework, jewelry, carpets, calligraphy, engravings, silkscreens, contemporary paintings, silver, weapons, and collectibles. The smaller second shop (106-B), near the entrance  to the Grand Bazaar, includes two floors with jewelry, Russian religious icons, and ceramics. Expensive but excellent quality and selections. Also has nice display windows at the Four Seasons Hotel and the Çirağan Palace Hotel. Visit Sofa's website for information about various product lines as well as examples of its inventory.

❑ **Atrium:** *Tünel Geçidi 7, Beyoğlu. Tel. 251-4302 or Fax 249-8983.* Located in a charming old building (circa 1885), fronting on a courtyard of cafes and restaurants, this three-room shop with tall ceilings includes a treasure-trove of antiques, paintings, prints, and small collectibles. Look for an extensive collection of old prints and paintings – both framed and unframed – along with stone candle stands, old ceramics, rugs, Konya mortars, cloth stamps, and copper items. Jam-packed with treasures, you'll need to do some serious browsing here to survey the complete inventory, which is often tucked away in cabinets or on the floor. Be sure to pick up one of their beautiful Ottoman bookmarks which also functions as their business card.

❑ **Antikarnas:** *Kuloğlu Mahallesi Faik Paşa Yokuşu 36/A, Çukurcuma, Beyoğlu, Tel. 251-5928 or Fax 251-4135.* A favorite for local designers, this dusty and chaotic shop includes a unique collection of antiques – huge ceilings, furniture, picture frames, lanterns, stone animals, pictures, paintings, clocks, candle holders – and collectibles.

❑ **Şamdan Antique:** *Kuloğlu Mahallesi Altipatlar Sokak No. 20, Çukurcuma, Beyoğlu, Tel. 245-4445. E-mail: SamdanAntique@ hotmail.com.* Located just around corner from Hikmet & Pinar, this delightful antique shop is filled with many unusual ethnic pieces from Anatolia and Turkmenistan. The Ottoman wall panels and ceiling pieces are wonderful, but they cannot be exported from Turkey. Look for tin and copper pots, Turkmenistan wood oil bowls, and ceramic pots from eastern Turkey. The emphasis here tends to be on country folk antiques.

❑ **Hikmet & Pinar:** *Faik Paşa Yokuşu 36/A, Çukurcuma, Beyoğlu, Tel. 293-0575.* This small but exclusive home decorative shop offers antique French and Ottoman style furniture and accessory pieces. Includes some nice antique ceramic and embroidery pieces. Primarily works with local designers.

❑ **Erdün Collection:** *Grand Bazaar, İç Bedesten, Şerif Ağa Sokak, No. 34-39 Beyazit, Tel. 526-7628 or Fax 250-9554. Website: www.erduncollection.com.* This relatively small, crammed, and cluttered shop in the middle of the old bazaar section of the Grand Bazaar offers a good collection of copper and brass pots, plates, vases, lanterns, bread boxes, and other items, both old and new. Popular with both tourists and collectors, this shop has something for everyone, regardless of taste or budget, with items ranging from US$5 to US$10,000.

❑ **Hakan Fikri:** *Grand Bazaar, İç Bedesten, Şerif Ağa Sokak.* Located next door to the Erdün Collection, this small shop offers similar items minus all the lamps. Specializes in old coffee grinders.

❑ **Galeri Sufi:** *Grand Bazaar, İç Bedesten, Şerif Ağa Sokak, No. 42-43, Tel. 512-3404.* This very small shop, located just two shops from the Erdün Collection, includes a nice collection of miniature paintings. Most are new paintings on old paper. Also look for watercolors and oils. The whirling dervishes are especially attractive. Expect to pay about US$50 to US$80 for a nice framed painting.

❑ **Horhor Bit Pazari** (Flea Market): *Kirma Tulumba, Aksaray, Fatih.* This rambling and dusty six-story building is an antique lover's paradise. It houses 215 shops offering a wide range of antiques and collectibles but with a heavy emphasis on furniture, lamps, chandeliers, paintings, and small collectibles. Some unique shops here include **Haci Cevdet Olcay** (3ʳᵈ floor, No. 141, Tel. 524-4156) with its fine collection of Canakkale pots, ceramics, and locks – the owner is Turkey's expert on Çanakkale ceramics; **Olcay ve Olcay** (1ˢᵗ floor, No. 79-82, Tel. 532-7780) for quality furniture, glass, and silver; and **Osmanli** (1ˢᵗ floor, No. 13/84, Tel. 521-6832) with its wonderful range of fascinating collectibles, including weapons, locks, combs, and Ottoman boxes. You can easily spend a couple of hours browsing through the shops in this complex. Many of the most interesting shops are found on the second, third, and fourth floors.

❑ **Eskidji:** *Dolapdere Mobilya Çarşisi and Yenişehir Dereotu Sokak in Beyoğlu.* Auction house with several antique, furniture, and art shops selling direct. See description above under "Antique Emporiums and Flea Markets."

❑ **Antik Palace:** *Spor Caddesi, Talimyeri Sok, Maçka, Tel. 236-2460 or Fax 236-2473. Website: www.antikpalace.com/tr. E-mail: antik@antikpalace.co.tr.* Known as the "Sotheby's of Turkey," this is the country's largest auction house which specializes in high-end French and Ottoman antiques. See description above under "Antique Emporiums and Flea Markets."

❑ **Koleksiyon Auction House:** *Çirağan Sarayi Beşiktas, Tel. 236-6890 or Fax 236-2145.* Located at the lower level of the palace section of the Çirağan Palace Hotel, this expansive shop offers a fine collection of Turkish and Iranian antiques, from ceramics and glass to boxes and furniture. Includes a large selection of paintings and carpets. Also has a shop at the Hilton Hotel in Ankara.

JEWELRY

❏ **Urart:** *Abdi İpekçi Caddesi No. 18/1, Nişantaşi, Tel. 246-7194 and Swissotel No. 13, Tel. 259-0221. Also has shops on the grounds of the Topkapi Palace in Istanbul and in Ankara and Izmir.* If you are looking for uniquely designed jewelry, this is the place to shop. Offers excellent quality jewelry using black pearls and precious stones as well as many beautifully designed silver serving pieces and marble bowls. Includes reproduction jewelry based on many pieces on display at the Istanbul Archeological Museum which date from the 3$^{rd}$ millennium BC and include works in the Anatolian-Persian style, and from the Hellenistic, Egyptian, Roman, Byzantine, Islamic, and Ottoman periods. Urart also has shops in Ankara (Hilton) and Izmir.

❏ **Gilan:** *Akmerkez Shopping Mall, Nispetiye Caddesi, No. 123, Etiler, Tel. 282-0576 or Fax 282-0579. Website: www.gilan.com. tr. E-mail: info@gilan.com.tr.* Produces a gorgeous line of luxury jewelry using its own designers. Especially noted for its unique designs using Tahitian black pearls and diamonds as well as its special Ottoman-style collection of gold jewelry. Produces some of the best quality black and white diamond jewelry we've seen in Turkey. Also has shops on the Asian side of Istanbul (Üsküdar), near the Grand Bazaar (Nuruosmaniye Caddesi No. 58), and in Ankara. However, this is their largest shop with the best selections.

❏ **Fibula/Efe Corporation:** *Nuruosmaniye Caddesi No. 41, Cağaloğlu, Tel. 520-9505 or Fax 528-0496. Website: www.efe gold.com. E-mail: info@efegold.com.* This very exclusive jeweler produces fabulous custom and limited editions of jewelry. Limited editions are restricted to just 24 pieces worldwide. Designed by artist and jeweler Hasan Kale, these creations are some of the most unique pieces of jewelry you will find anywhere in the world. Many are based on Anatolia designs. If you're looking for something very special in jewelry, be sure to visit this shop. Includes a small art gallery featuring Hasan's paintings.

❏ **Sait Koç:** *Akmerkez Shopping Mall, Nispetiye Caddesi, No. 267, Etiler, Tel. 282-2547 or Fax 282-2549; and Grand Bazaar, Kalpakçarşi, Tel. 526-6847 or Fax 512-3704. Website: www. saitkocjewellery.com.* This is one of Istanbul's most famous and respected jewelers, which always seems to be crowded with loyal customers. A real quality operation that offers an excellent range of nicely designed jewelry at reasonable prices. The diamond bracelets and necklaces are especially attractive. Sait Koç's largest shop with the best selections is at the Akmerkez Shopping Mall.

❏ **Sponza:** *Swissôtel, Tel. 259-0223; Ritz-Carlton Hotel, Tel. 251-6874; and Çirağan Palace Hotel shopping arcade.* Offers an excellent range of high-end jewelry in diamonds, gold, and silver. Many pieces are copies or reproductions of jewelry pieces found in the catalogs of major jewelers, such as Cartier and Tiffany's. They also do original designs. Be careful with the mirrored walls – it's easy to walk into them thinking they lead into another section of the shops. Also operates all Bvlgari jewelry and watch shops in Turkey. Also has shops in Izmir and Çeşme.

❏ **Hilat Collection:** *Şerefefendi Sokuk No. 58, Şerefefendi-First Floor, 95-98, Nuruosmaniye, Tel. 520-0171. Also has a shop at the Ritz-Carlton Hotel shopping arcade, Tel. 244-3171.* Includes great display cases in the Four Seasons Hotel and Çirağan Palace Hotel where it showcases its many gorgeous gold necklaces, bracelets, and rings. Behind these display cases is actually a small main shop housed in a jewelry center (Serethan Building) near the Grand Bazaar. Call ahead for an appointment to ensure you will be communicating with someone who speaks English. Specializes in reproduction gold pieces and its own uniquely designed 22-karat gold pieces. While in the jewelry center, check out the 59 other jewelry shops that occupy the five floors of the Serethan Building.

❏ **Efendy:** *Çirağan Palace Hotel, Shopping Arcade No. 10, Tel. 236-2183 or Fax 236-2185.* This small and exclusive shop offers one-of-a-kind top-quality jewelry pieces designed with 22-karat gold, precious stones (diamonds, rubies, emeralds, sapphires, turquoise), and old coins.

## CARPETS, RUGS, AND TEXTILES

❏ **Güneş Carpet and Kilim House:** *Mim Kemal Öke Caddesi No. 5, Nişantaşi, Tel. 225-1954, 225-1968 or Fax 225-1940. Website: www.ishoparoundtheworld.com/gunes. Email: enozta@ turk.net.* May be difficult to find since the sign on the awning outside only says "Carpet and Kilim." This is not your typical bazaar-style rug dealer catering to walk-by tourists whose needs have yet to be identified for carpets with strange colors and designs and questionable quality. This is a very comfortable and trusted class operation that delivers good quality and value – a shop and gallery you wish you had closer to home. You need to spend some time finding this place on a pleasant one-way side street in the upscale residential and shopping neighborhood of Nişantaşi in Istanbul – a 10- to 20-minute taxi drive from most major hotels. But your search will be justly rewarded with a very special trusted and talented dealer – Günes Öztarakçi. Turkey's leading female rug dealer for more than 25 years, Günes has the knowledge of a seasoned expert, the eye of an artist, and the tastes of a fine interior designer for selecting some of the best quality carpets and kilims for her international clientele. Loving what she does, her enthusiasm for

these woven works of art, as well as for her interested clients, is infectious. Offering Turkish weaves, rare antique rugs, colorful Anatolian kilims, exquisite Hereke silk rugs, and fine vegetable dyed carpets in all sizes and price ranges, her friendly and inviting shop in one of Istanbul's most exciting yet crowded neighborhoods is a virtual art gallery jam-packed with two floors with three rooms of old and new rugs.

Spend an hour or more here and you will surely find the perfect carpets or kilims to grace your home or office. Go elsewhere and you are likely to return again to this very reputable and trusted shop. Best of all, you'll learn a great deal about these works of art, many of which are commissioned by Günes, a very engaging and personable expert who has an good eye for selecting appropriate colors and designs. Working with villages in the south and southeast Turkey, she is especially well known for producing quality reproductions of old carpets, for using colors that especially appeal to interior designers and their fashion-conscious clients, and for exhibiting her "collector pieces" at major shows. You don't need to bargain here since her prices are both fixed and fair. Nor does she play the tour guide commission game – come here on your own or tell your guide you'll need some time alone in this shop. Does excellent packing and will arrange international shipping.

❑ **Şengör:** *Grand Bazaar, Kapalıçarşı, Takkeciler, No. 65-83 ve 98, Tel. 527-2192 or Fax 522-4115. Website: www.sengorhali. com. E-mail: info@sengorhali.com.tr.* In the heart of the Grand Bazaar, adjacent to many other appealing and aggressive rug shops, this long-established (since 1918) and reputable four-generation family carpet and kilim shop offers good selections and quality at reasonable prices. The very personable family runs two small shops next to each other. Their shops have been well recommended for quality and reliability, but we would have been persuaded to enter even if they had not been recommended because of the manner in which they welcomed the "visitor" to their inviting and comfortable shop. The first shop on the left is where most business and socializing gets done along a comfortable pillowed sitting area reminiscent of a carpeted tent. The two shops are piled high with a wide selection of attractive rugs. But it's the warm, personal, enthusiastic, and infectious service that is the real highlight of this shopping experience. The emphases here are on selections, quality, price, and service. They include many old carpets as well as reproduction carpets and kilims from Turkey, Turkmenistan, Afghanistan, and Georgia. Rug prices appear reasonable, starting as low as US$20; many nice pieces can be acquired for under US$500. A delightful place to learn about carpets and kilims and make friends with a very delightful family of rug experts.

❑ **Adnan & Hasan:** *Grand Bazaar, Kapalıçarşı, Takkeciler, Nos. 89-90-92, Beyasit 34440, Tel. 527-9887, 513-9359, Tel./Fax 528-0885. Website: www.adnanandhasan.com. E-mail: info@and anandhasan.com.* Located in the heart of Istanbul's Grand Bazaar, these three shops are situated across from each other. Long established and reputable, Adnan & Hasan offer a wide selection of quality carpets and kilims to their many international clients.

❑ **Reşat Gümüşgerdan:** *Grand Bazaar, Kapalıçarşı, Kavaflar Sokak No. 27, Tel. 513-7150 or 520-6954.* You wouldn't know its value by first impressions. Indeed, you would probably pass by this shop because it looks very undistinguished. But this could be your lucky stop. This crammed rug shop is literally a hole-in-the-wall that wholesales silk carpets to other shops in the Grand Bazaar. If, for example, you're looking for a particular silk carpet in a shop that may not have it in their current inventory, they may ask you to wait a moment as they run over to Reşat Gümüşgerdan to get more inventory. You can cut out the middleman by shopping at this source. Reşat Gümüşgerdan also wholesales wool carpets and kilims. He's also a supplier to other rug shops in Turkey as well as abroad. Good English spoken when the owner's son is minding the shop.

❑ **Asia Minor:** *Basdogan Carpets, at the intersection of Tevkijhane and Kutlugün Sok., near the Four Seasons Hotel, Sultanahmet, Tel. 516-5132 or Fax 516-5133. Website: www.asiaminorcar pets.com.* Specializing in gorgeous oversized carpets, which you'll immediately see on display in their store windows, this is one of Istanbul's high-end rug shops. Many of the rugs are made to look old by producing them with short piles. Includes five shops in the United States (New York City, Atlanta, and High Point, North Carolina) and often advertises in *Architectural Digest*. Top quality with excellent designs and colors. Very expensive compared to most rug shops in Turkey.

❑ **Jasmine:** *Tevkifhane Sokak No. 8/A, 34400 Sultanahmet, Tel. 638-3061 or Fax 571-1085. E-mail: adem@galleryugur.com.* Located across the street from the Four Seasons Hotel, this large carpet and kilim shop includes a demonstration area near the front door where a woman sits working on a loom weaving a double knot silk rug. The engaging and enthusiastic owner, Adem Ayten, will give you a personal tour of his shop and building. The shop also operates a new boutique hotel and restaurant next door – Seven Hills Hotel (Tel. 90-212-516-9498, Fax 90-212-517-1085, website: www.hotel sevenhills.com). Take the elevator to the restaurant on the top floor where you can get wonderful views of the Blue Mosque, Hagia Sophia, and the Old Prison, which is now the Four Seasons Hotel.

❑ **Hazal:** *Mecidiye Köprüsü Sokak No. 27, Ortaköy, Tel. 227-4071. Website: www.hazalkilim.com.* E-mail: edemirkol@hazal kilim.com. Offers an excellent collection of kilims, carpets, and pillows made from grain bags. Housed in a lovely old two-story building in the delightful Ortaköy area. Several small rooms serve as demonstration areas.

TEXTILES AND EMBROIDERY

❑ **Maison du Tapis D'Orient:** *Arasta Bazaar (Arasta Çarşisi), No. 151, Sultanahmet 34400, Tel. 517-6808 or Fax 638-1553. E-mail: mcetinkaya2002@yahoo.com.* This small but richly adorned shop is a real find for serious textile collectors in

Istanbul. It includes a fabulous collection of textiles, embroidery work, and rugs from Uzbekistan and Turkmenistan.
Offers an especially gorgeous collection of rare velvet silk
ikat coats (1860-1910 circa). The very knowledgeable owner, tall bearded Mehmet Çetinkaya, regularly travels to
neighboring Uzbekistan and Turkmenistan to add to his
growing collection. He also has a large depot/gallery at
another location where he takes serious buyers interested in
his much larger textile collection. The shop also includes a
few small wooden spice boxes, collectibles, and books (one
of the few places you can buy the informative *Istanbul: The
Hali Rug Guide* book for only US$10, while supplies last). A
great shop for serious collectors and buyers rather than
tourists, although many tourists will appreciate learning
about collector-quality textiles from Mehmet.

❑ **Vakko:** *Istiklâl Caddesi No. 123/125, 80600 Beyoğlu, Tel.
251-4092 or Fax 245-4099. Website: www.vakko.com.tr.* Vakko
in Turkey is synonymous with quality clothing, accessories,
and home furnishings – Turkey's equivalent to Saks Fifth
Avenue and Neiman Marcus in the U.S., very high-end,
classy, fashionable, and expensive. Vakko's main shop in the
Beyoğlu district of Istanbul includes three floors of wonderful textiles, from its special Ottoman collection of fabrics to
bed linens and towels. Start at the very top – the fourth
floor of the second building (the first building has nine
levels), which functions as Vakko's showroom ("Home
Collection") for showcasing its fabulous collection of handmade silk velvet, burnt velvet, silk, and embroidered fabrics,
garments, table runners, furniture, and accessories designed
around old Ottoman designs. This is a gorgeous high-end
decorator's center. They also have their own coffee table
book of Vakko's Ottoman designs, which will give you a
good idea of what exactly Vakko is up to these days with
such textiles. The second floor includes two sections of
fabrics and fabric samples – upholstery and garment – which
can be purchased by the meter. The third floor includes less
interesting bed linens. If you want to see what's happening
with retro-Ottoman textiles, and the role Vakko is playing
in promoting these rich fabrics, colors, and designs – it's
often a fashion and home decor pace setter in Turkey – be
sure to visit the fourth and second floors of this Vakko
department store. You can view their Ottoman art collection
by clicking on to the "Vakko Decor" section of their website. The other floors of this shop include Vakko's trade-
mark men's and women's clothing, accessories, and fra-

grances, which are readily available in several other Vakko shops in Istanbul (Akmerkez, Nişantaşi, Suadiye) and other cities in Turkey (Adana, Ankara, Bursa, and Izmir).

## BOOKS, MAPS, ENGRAVINGS

❑ **Eren:** *Tünel, Istiklâl Caddesi, Sofyali Sokak No. 34, Beyoğlu, Tel. 251-2858 or Fax 243-3016. E-mail: eren@erenbooks.com.* This well established publisher and bookstore, who also owns the nearby Ottomania, offers one of the best collections of art books on Turkey. Most titles are in Turkish.

❑ **Ottomania:** *Tünel, Istiklâl Caddesi, Sofyali Sokak No. 30-32, Beyoğlu, Tel. 251-2157 or Fax 243-3016. E-mail: eren@turk. net.* Offers a wonderful collection of old maps, prints, and calligraphy. Can purchase these items either framed or just matted. A fun place just to view such interesting collectibles that remind one of Turkey's compelling history.

❑ **Atrium:** *Tünel Geçidi 7, Beyoğlu, Tel. 251-4302 or Fax 249-8983.* While primarily an antiques and collectible shop (see entry under "Arts and Antiques"), this shop includes many nice prints among its many other attractive choices.

❑ **Sufi:** *Tünel Square No. 6, Beyoğlu, Tel. 251-1966. E-mail: galerisufi@yahoo.com.* This small shop includes a very nice collection of miniature paintings, watercolors, and prints.

## CERAMICS

❑ **Iznik Classics:** *Two shops in the Grand Bazaar: Kapaliçarşi Iç Bedesten, Serifaga Sok No. 188 and Nos. 18-21 (Old Bazaar). Tel. 520-2568. Also at Arasta Bazaar (Arasta Çarşisi) No. 67-73, Sultanahmet, Tel. 517-1705 or Fax 517-1121. E-mail: iznik classics@hotmail.com.* This is one of Istanbul's best shops for acquiring top quality reproductions of ceramic plates, bowls, vases, and tiles. Its three artists produce replicas of famous designs appearing in the Ottoman palaces from the 15$^{th}$ to 17$^{th}$ centuries. The best selections are found in the Grand Bazaar shops.

❑ **Iznik Tiles:** *Arasta Bazaar (Arasta Çarşisi) No. 73. Tel. 517-1705 or Fax 517-1121. E-mail: iznikclassics@hotmail.com.* Owned and operated by Iznik Classics, this shop specializes in reproductions of classic Iznik ceramic tiles. Includes beautiful tiles made from quartz.

❑ **Topkapi Çini:** *Arasta Bazaar (Arasta Çarşisi) No. 161. Tel. 517-1705 or Fax 458-0664. E-mail: iznikclassics@hotmail.com.* Also owned and operated by Iznik Classics, this is the general souvenir ceramic shop of the company and the Iznik Foundation. It includes good quality but inexpensive ceramic plates, bowls, and figures for those not interested in collecting the more expensive reproduction ceramics and tiles offered by the company's other ceramic shops.

❑ **Orient Iznik (Nicaea):** *Grand Bazaar (Kapaliçarşi İç Bedesten), Divrik Sok, 19-21-25; Takkeciler Sok. 17-18-19-31-33-34-36. Tel. 526-4798 or Fax 528-5693.* This tiny shop in Istanbul's Grand Bazaar offers a small but very fine collection of ceramic plates and tiles which are all nicely displayed in wood cabinets and niches. The more expensive quartz tiles are beautiful works of art.

❑ **Haci Cevdet Olcay:** *Horhor Antikacilar Çarşisi, Kat 3, No. 141 Aksaray, Tel. 524-4156.* This small and dusty shop yields what is perhaps the largest collection of Çanakkale ceramics and pots in all of Turkey. The owner is a famous collector of these unique ceramics, especially the attractive decanters or "Testi." The owner does not speak English. If need a translator, see his son who operates one of the best antique shops in the Horhor antique complex – **Olcay ve Olcay** (Kat 1, Not. 79-82, Tel. 532-7780) – who will come and translate as well as help with the transaction.

## LEATHER

❑ **Derishow:** *Akmerkez Shopping Mall, No. 314/315, Tel. 282-0408) and Valikonaği Caddesi. No. 85, Nişantaşi, Tel. 231-1510.* This is one of Turkey's most fashionable leather and clothing boutiques for women's jackets, coats, purses, and accessories designed by some of Turkey's leading fashion designers. The Akmerkez shop is the largest and most comprehensive store which also includes the owner's home furnishings line under the label Mimarca. Look for beautifully designed and trendy leather clothes and accessories using Italian leather designed and fabricated in Turkey. The leather quality and designs here are exceptional compared to most leather you find in Turkey. The clothing lines include classic and trendy sweaters, blouses, skirts, pants, and "boucle" wool coats with fox fur. Branch shops are found in Nişantaşi, Suadlye, Ankara, and Izmir. Derishow also is well noted for its excellent displays and customer service.

❑ **Vakko:** *Istiklâl Caddesi No. 123/125, 80600 Beyoğlu, Tel. 251-4092 or Fax 245-4099. Website: www.vakko.com.tr.* Also has shops in Suadiye, Akmerkez, and Nişantaşi. Like so much else offered by the upscale Vakko department shorts, leather goods here are top quality. For more information on Vakko, see above entry under "Textiles and Embroidery."

❑ **Beymen:** *Akmerkez Shopping Mall, Etiler, Tel. 282-0380; Suadiye, Tel. 467-1845; and Nişantaşi, Tel. 241-1273. Website: www.beymen.com.tr.* This is one of Turkey's most upscale and fashionable stores for men's and women's clothing, accessories, cosmetics, and homewares. Offers a good selection of quality leather coats, especially the extensive leather collection on the upper level of the Akmerkez shop. Look for many international fashion name brands, such as DKNY, Sonia Rykiel, Etro, Armani, Christian Dior, Zegna, and Donna Karan.

❑ **Matras:** *Akmerkez Shopping Mall, Etiler, Tel. 282-0215; Galleria Shopping Mall, Ataköy, Tel. 559-4572; and three other locations in Istanbul and seven other locations in Turkey.* Offers excellent quality leather goods, especially nicely designed handbags, belts, and wallets. A good place to acquire small leather gift items.

❑ **Derimod:** *Demirhane Caddesi H. Reşit Bey Geçidi No. 18, Zeytinburnu, Tel. 547-1604 or Fax 547-1669. E-mail: derimod @superonline.com.* Located next to a few other leather showrooms on the road to the airport, this is the factory outlet or depot shop for one of Turkey's most popular leather companies. While most Derimod shops specialize in shoes, this large showroom has a very nice selection of leather coats, jackets, and handbags which are not available in most of their other shops. Offers discounts on cash payments.

❑ **Teodem:** *Akmerkez Shopping Mall, No. 258, Etiler, Tel. 282-0188.* Offers a good selection of leather coats, handbags, shoes, and boots with fur.

❑ **Desa:** *Istiklâl Caddesi No. 140, Beyoğlu, Tel. 243-3786. Also includes stores in 10 other Istanbul locations and eight other locations in Turkey.* Offers a large selection of leather shoes, handbags, coats, wallets, briefcases, and suitcases. Desa brand shoes are basically Italian-designed but Turkish-made.

❑ **Kircilar:** *5 Kardeşler 4, Sokak. No. 18, Tel. 582-5555 or Fax 546-8881.* Located next to a few other major leather outlet showrooms on the road to the airport, this company offers very fashionable coats, jackets, handbags, and accessories on two levels. Everything is produced at their factory in Bursa. This is the only Kircilar shop in Istanbul.

❑ **M. Nazaryan:** *Siraselviler Caddesi No. 65, Taksim, Tel. 293-7179.* Located just off Taksim Circle, this shop designs and makes shoes and handbags – from scratch – for women only. One of the few shops in Istanbul that still does this type of custom work. Allow yourself some time to use this shop since it takes about 15 days to produce custom-made shoes and seven days to make a handbag. The owner/designer, Muhtar Nazaryan, does all his own designs rather than make copies from photos or produce knock-offs, which has both advantages (unique designs) and disadvantages (not the most stylish). You'll see numerous racks of his shoes on display as well as several handbags behind the counter. His shoes are customized to each foot rather than made in reference to set patterns or lasts. Most handbags cost from US$40 to US$70. Most shoes run about US$60. Be sure to communicate well your design preferences since not much English is spoken here.

## CLOTHES AND FASHION

❑ **Derishow:** *Akmerkez Shopping Mall, No. 314/315, Tel. 282-0408) and Valikonağı Caddesi No. 85, Nişantaşi, Tel. 231-1510. Website: www.derishow.com.* Offers very fashionable and trendy clothes. See above entry under "Leather."

❑ **Vakko:** *Istiklâl Caddesi No. 123/125, 80600 Beyoğlu, Tel. 251-4092 or Fax 245-4099. Website: www.vakko.com.tr.* Offers top quality men's and women's clothing under its own Vakko label. Produces excellent quality men's shirts and ties. See above entry under "Textiles and Embroidery."

❑ **Beymen:** *Akmerkez Shopping Mall, Etiler, Tel. 282-0380; Suadiye, Tel. 467-1845; and Nişantaşi, 241-1273.* See above entry under "Leather."

❑ **Yargici:** *Vali Konağı Caddasi No. 30, Nişantaşi, Tel. 225-2952. Website: www.yargici.com.tr. E-mail: yargici@yargici.com.tr.* Offers very fashionable men's and women's apparel as well as their own line of toiletries and skin products.

❏ **Silk and Cashmere:** *Galleria Shopping Mall, Ataköy, Tel. 559-4516. Website: www.silkcashmere.com. E-mail: fab@silkcash mere.com.tr.* Especially popular with expats and visitors, this shop specializes in men's and women's cashmere sweaters, mink scarves, Pashmina shawls, and silk blouses. While not as fashionable and upscale as Vakko and Derishow, it does have a loyal clientele who appreciate its products.

❏ **Cotton Bar:** *Akmerkez Shopping Mall, Tel. 282-0142.* Especially noted for offering good quality men's shirts and ties.

HOME FURNISHINGS AND ACCESSORIES

❏ **Mimarca:** *Yeşil Çimen Sokak No. 91, Beşiktaş, Tel. 259-7255. Website: www.derishow.com.* This newly opened home center includes the "Home Collection" designed and produced by the husband/ wife owners of Derishow (see entry above under "Leather") who are architects by training. The three floors of tastefully designed furniture, accessories, and home products (serving trays, ceramics, cutting boards, glass) include many wonderful items.

❏ **Vakko:** *Istiklâl Caddesi No. 123/125, Beyoğlu, Tel. 251-4092 or Fax 245-4099. Website: www.vakko.com.tr.* See above entry under "Textiles and Embroidery."

❏ **Antique and home decorative shops:** Check out the many antique and home decorative shop found in two major areas of Istanbul: Çukurcuma area in Beyoğlu, the Horhor Bit Pazari (Flea Market) at Kirma Tulumba in Aksaray, and the Antique Palace in Maçka. See entries under the above "Arts and Antiques" section.

HANDICRAFTS, GIFTS, AND SOUVENIRS

❏ **Dösim:** *Topkapi Kültür Ürünleri Satiş Mağazasi, Topkapi Sarayi Giriş Avlusu, Sultanahmet, Tel. 513-3134; Haseki Hamani Hali ve Kilim Satiş Mağazasi, Ayasofya Karşisi, Sultanahmet, Tel. 638-0035; and Istanbul Prestij Mağazasi, Istanbul Ayasofya Girişi, Tel. 512-6689. Website: www.kultur. gov.tr.* If you're looking for a one-stop shop for a wide range of Turkish handicrafts, be sure to visit the Dösim shops which are operated by the government's Ministry of Culture. They are found in several other areas throughout Turkey. Established to both showcase and promote Turkish handcrafted items, the shops usually include a good selection of quality items: ceramics, textiles, embroidery, carpets, silk, glassware, leather goods, wood carvings, reproductions, jewelry, earthenware, copper dishes, and silver.

❑ **Urart:** *Abdi İpekçi Caddesi No. 18/1, Nişantaşi, Tel. 246-7194 and Swissôtel No. 13, Tel. 259-0221.* See above entry under "Jewelry." Offers several beautifully crafted silver and marble pieces that make lovely gift items.

❑ **Fiyonk:** *Nişantaşi Vali Konaği Caddesi No. 12/1, Tel. 225-1921.* This small corner shop in the heart of Istanbul's most upscale neighborhood offers an interesting collection of gift and craft items – pajama holders, attractive boxes, jewelry, baskets, "evil eyes," and children's items.

---

## ACCOMMODATIONS

Istanbul offers an excellent range of accommodations for just about every budget. It boasts several five-star hotels that rank among the best in the world, including the Four Seasons Hotel which has been ranked the number one hotel in the world by major travel publications.

Before deciding on where to stay, be sure to consider the advantages and disadvantages of staying either in the Old City or the New City. The Old City has a more Third World feel to it – often crowded, chaotic, and noisy. The New City feels more modern and European. In fact, you may want to stay in both areas since the experiences are very different. If you're planning on six days in Istanbul, we recommend staying three days in each area. Some of Istanbul's best properties include the following:

❑ **Four Seasons Hotel Istanbul:** *Tevkifhane Sokak No. 1, 34490 Sultanahmet-Eminönü, Istanbul, Turkey, Tel. (90-212) 638-8200, Toll-free from U.S. 800-332-3442 or Canada 800-268-6282 or Fax (90-212) 638-8210. Website: www.fourseasons .com/istanbul.* Welcome to one of the world's very best hotels. Sparkling like a rare jewel in Istanbul's most historic and interesting quarter, the Four Seasons Istanbul artfully combines graceful, award-winning service with an exquisite, residential style ambience. Meticulous attention to details and a staff dedicated to making every guest feel truly at home contributed to the Four Seasons' distinction as the #3 hotel in the entire world and the only hotel to receive a perfect score of "100" on its guestrooms on *Condé Nast's*

"2001 Top 100 Best in the World." The attention to detail began when the old Sultanahmet Prison, with its Turkish neoclassic architecture, was renovated to be converted into a boutique hotel. The prison exterior was maintained while the interior was gutted and reconfigured to, like a phoenix, rise again – only this time more spectacular than at its beginning.

Situated in the heart of the Old City, the guest has views of both the Hagia Sophia and the Blue Mosque and is within easy walking distance of the Grand Bazaar, Arasta Bazaar, and the treasures of the Topkapi Palace. Each time the guest returns to the hotel, he is greeted with a sincere "welcome back" or "welcome home" from the staff. The 65 guestrooms, which include 11 suites on four floors, are spacious and beautifully appointed. Each one differs somewhat

in layout – necessitated in part by the original structure and taken advantage of by the Four Seasons to further the "boutique" nature and "exclusive private home" feel of the hotel. The famous Four Seasons' bed with crisp white cotton sheets, pillowcases, and duvet cover over a fluffy lightweight comforters is inviting. The attention to detail is in evidence when you notice that the headboard subtly reflects the architecture of the mosques. The slight curve of the wooden headboard is suggestive of the dome of the mosque and the posts flanking either side reflect the spiral of the minarets.

Artwork of the region – prints or delicate embroideries worked with silver or gold threads – grace the walls of the guestrooms while art of significant painters and beautiful antiques culled from the local area have been tastefully arranged in the public spaces. The marble bathrooms, which are as large as the guestrooms in some hotels, feature a comfortable soaking tub and a separate glass shower enclosure – which is thoroughly cleaned and dried each day! There is also a separate enclosed area for the toilet and many bathrooms feature double vanity sinks. Lighting in both the guestroom and the bath is excellent, allowing choices from soft ambient lighting to plenty of light for reading or working in the room.

In fact, the hotel is filled with natural light as well. The windows in the guestrooms are tall, most rooms have several windows which allow light to filter in during the day, and the public areas have many glass-covered atriums. The glass atriums are used to cover the areas that were added to the original structure and to connect areas of the original prison building that needed cover to protect guests from inclement weather as they walk from one section of the hotel to another on the top (fourth) level.

*Seasons Restaurant* offers international cuisine and local specialties. During warm weather months, guests enjoy the absolutely spectacular views of both Hagia Sophia and the Blue Mosque from the rooftop terrace. With the lighting on the domes and spires set against a night sky, you feel a sense of history, beauty, and romanticism which is truly magnificent. 24 hour Business Services; Health/Fitness Facilities (no pool); Meeting/Banquet Facilities.

What could possibly be any better than this? Only the combination of the present Four Seasons in Sultanahmet, and the yet-to-be-opened Four Seasons on the Bosphorus projected for late 2003 or early 2004. The new hotel situated on the shore of the Bosphorus will be a 160-180 room property and guests may travel by private boat between the two hotels. In fact, guests may experience the luxury of both properties with only one check-in and check-out!

❑ **Ritz-Carlton:** *Suzer Plaza, Asher Ocagi Caddesi No. 15, 80280 - Elmadag, Istanbul, Turkey, Tel. (90-212) 334-4444, Fax (90-212) 334-4455, or Toll-free from U.S. & Canada, 800-241-3333. Website: www.ritzcarlton.com.* Opened in October of 2001, the Ritz-Carlton Istanbul has already been awarded (in March 2002) the "Five Star Diamond Award" by the American Academy of Hospitality Services. Located in the heart of Istanbul in the Dolmabahçe district overlooking the Bosphorus Straits, the Ritz-Carlton offers the luxurious accommodations and impeccable service their hotels are renowned for around the world. Though the hotel is newly constructed, blending the old world with the new is evident throughout the hotel's public spaces where glass mosaic tiles, teak wood columns, beige, green and earth-toned marble floors and hand-woven Turkish carpets in muted pastel colors combine to give a sense of place while maintaining a sense of serenity. Beautifully carved antique wood doors are decoratively mounted on one wall within the lobby. These are flanked by two antique wood columns and form the backdrop for registered antique furniture found in

Turkish homes and purchased for the hotel. Decorative elements from the Ottoman Empire are carried through to the 244 deluxe guestrooms which include 39 rooms on the Club Level, 21 executive suites, and one Ritz-Carlton suite. Guestrooms are decorated in soft hues, and handcrafted furniture and carpets grace the rooms and complement the views of the Bosphorus and Golden Horn. Bathrooms are clad with marble brought from Turkey's Afyon region and cobalt blue and red İznik tiles are used for accent. All amenities are at hand – even goose down and non-allergenic pillows. In-room fax machines are provided on request. The Technology Butler is on call 24 hours a day to fix the guests' computer and technology troubles. Club floors offer additional services and facilities including five complimentary food and beverage presentations throughout the day.

Çintemani offers traditional Mediterranean cuisine blended with Turkish specialties. A nice touch at breakfast is the juice selection placed on the table offering three fresh fruit and vegetable juices for the guest to sample. Turkish bread, fresh from the wood-burning oven, is offered at lunch and dinner. The terrace restaurant, *Güney Park*, overlooking the Bosphorus Straits is open May to September. The *Lobby Lounge* offers afternoon tea or an evening cocktail. The *RC Bar* offers an exclusive collection of single malt whiskies and an extensive collection of cigars.

The indoor swimming pool features a wall aquarium of colorful fish, and twinkling "stars" illuminate the ceiling. The mosaic pool and columns surrounding it convey a feeling of the Byzantine period of Istanbul. Health/Fitness Center (with Turkish Hamam, sauna, steam bath, massage therapy rooms, training and exercise room); Business Center, Meeting/Banquet Facilities; Shopping Arcade.

❑ **Çırağan Palace Hotel Kempinski:** *84, Beşiktaş, 80700 Istanbul, Turkey, Tel. (90-212) 258-3377 or Fax (90-212) 259-6687. Toll-free from U.S. or Canada, (800) 426-3135. Website: www.ciragan-palace.com. E-mail: reserve@ciraganpalace.com.tr.* A member of *The Leading Hotels of the World*, the Çırağan Palace was truly a Sultan's Palace, first built in wood at the end of the 16th century and rebuilt in marble in 1857. Badly damaged by fire in 1910, it lay derelict and abandoned until 1986, when the Kempinski Hotel Group lovingly restored the palace with amenities and luxury expected by today's discriminating travelers. Situated on the European shores of the Bosphorus, the Çırağan Palace is actually two hotels: the restored Sultan's Palace itself and a modern five-star luxury hotel built for the hotel's opening in 1991, and decorated in the spirit of its traditional neighbor. The Palace offers 12 VIP spacious suites and the Hotel offers 204 guestrooms and 20 suites which provide all the expected amenities. *Tuğra Restaurant* specializes in traditional Ottoman cuisine with many of the recipes having been translated from historical documents as well as nouvelle Turkish cuisine. With its view overlooking the Bosphorus, Ottoman atmosphere including classical Turkish music, authentic menu including award-winning dishes, and quality service, Tuğra is a treat. The *Caviar Bar* offers authentic Russian cuisine. *Laledan Restaurant* is the hotel's fine dining restaurant offering "new world cuisine"– a fusion of the latest cuisine from USA with Mediterranean influences – in an elegant setting overlooking the Bosphorus. The *Gazebo Lobby Lounge* serves an a la carte menu throughout the day and high tea in the afternoon. Every night except Sunday, *Sultan's Night* which includes dinner and a show is presented in the Palace Blue Room. Health/Fitness Center (swimming pool right beside the Bosphorus); Business Services; extensive Conference/Banquet Facilities.

❑ **Ceylan Inter-Continental Istanbul:** *Asker Ocaği Caddesi, No. 1 Taksim 80200, Istanbul, Turkey, Tel. (90-212) 231-2121 or Fax (90-212) 231-2180. E-mail: istanbul@interconti. com.* Located next to Taksim Park with fashionable shops and the business district just a short stroll away, the Ceylan Inter-Continental is one of the recipients of *Condé Nast Traveler's* readers' awards. 355 guestrooms and 55 luxuriously appointed suites with views of the Bosphorus offer spacious accommodations with expected amenities. Three floors of Club Rooms offer VIP accommodation for the discerning traveler. With the Bosphorus as a backdrop, the *City Lights Bar, Safran Turkish Restaurant,* and *Citronelle* French/Thai restaurant offer specialty cuisines in dramatic settings. The club atmosphere of the *English Bar,* afternoon tea at the *Tea Lounge,* a business rendezvous at the *Palm Terrace,* or open buffet and light specialties at the *California Brasserie* offer additional options. Health Club; Business Center; Conference/Banquet Facilities.

❑ **Hyatt Regency:** *Taskisla Caddesi, 80090 Taksim, Istanbul, Turkey, Tel. (90-212) 225-7000 or Fax (90-212) 225-7007. E-mail: concierge@hyatt.com.* Located at the center of the city's business district on Taksim Park, the Hyatt's atrium lobby with landscaped gardens and fountains welcomes visitors.

360 guestrooms and suites offer the expected Hyatt amenities and 71 Regency Club rooms offer additional services
and amenities. The *Café* restaurant serves Turkish and international cuisines. Try *Takarabune Japanese Restaurant* for
Japanese cuisine or the Italian restaurant. There is also a
Tea Lounge, Businessmen's Lounge, Fun Pub, Pool-side Bar
and Grill as well as a deli and pastry shop. Health/Fitness
Facilities; Business Center; Conference/Banquet Facilities.

❑ **Swissôtel Istanbul - The Bosphorus:** *Bayildim Cadessi 2,
Maçka, Beşiktaş, 80680 Istanbul, Turkey, Tel. (90-212) 326-
1100 or Fax (90-212) 326-1122. Website: www.swissotel.com.
E-mail: bosphorus@swissotel.com.* Located in a park setting in
the city center with views of the Bosphorus and Dolmabahçe Palace, Swissôtel is a member of *The Leading Hotels of
the World.* Its 500 guestrooms and 100 suites are spacious
with plenty of workspace for the business traveler. Among
the 14 dining and beverage venues are *Tas, lik Turkish
Restaurant* for Turkish cuisine, and *La Corne d'Or* for French
fine dining, as well as Continental, Japanese, Chinese, and
Swiss restaurants. The *Lobby Lounge* and *Les Ambassadeurs
Bar* feature live music. A private boat offers daily cruises on
the Bosphorus. 14 elegant boutiques on premises. Spa and
Fitness Center; Business Center; Conference/Banquet Facilities.

❑ **Istanbul Hilton:** *Cumhuriyet Caddesi, Harbiye 80200, Istan-
bul, Turkey, Tel. (90-212) 231-4650, Fax (90-212) 240-4165,
or Toll-free from U.S. 800-321-3232. Website: www.hilton.com.*
Situated within 13 acres of gardens and overlooking the
Bosphorus Straits, the Hilton is within walking distance of
business, shopping and entertainment areas near Taksim
Square. The 498 guestrooms, including 15 suites and 51
Executive Rooms, have private balconies – most with a
Bosphorus view. Executive Floor guests experience additional personal service and the privacy of the Executive
Clubroom. The *Bosphorus Terrace* is for casual breakfast,
lunch, or dinner. The *Roof Restaurant* offers traditional Turkish and Mediterranean dining with elegance and a spectacular Bosphorus view. *Dragon* offers Chinese cuisine. In the
summertime, the *Pool Café* and the *Veranda Bar & Grill* serve
light summer cuisine. Fitness Center; Business Center;
Conference/Banquet Facilities.

❑ **Conrad International Istanbul:** *Yildiz Caddesi, Beşiktaş
80700 Istanbul, Turkey, Tel. (90-212) 227-3000 or Fax (90-*

*212) 259-6667. Website: www.conradhotels.com. E-mail: informa tion@conradistanbul.com.* Overlooking the Bosphorus, the closest hotel to the bridge linking European Istanbul to Asian Istanbul, the Conrad offers stunning views of the city. 600 guestrooms including a variety of suites, long-term apartments, and more than 100 Executive Rooms. Executive floor guests enjoy a private reception and concierge desk, butler service, complimentary local phone calls, and Internet connection. *Monet Restaurant & Terrace* offers French cuisine, *Prego* serves Italian selections. *Manzara*, serving Turkish-international cuisine, recently received a five-star diamond award. Health Club; Business Center; Conference/Banquet Facilities.

❑ **The Armada Hotel:** *Ahirkapi, 34400, Istanbul, Turkey, Tel. (90-212) 638-1370 or Fax (90-212) 518-5060. Website: www. armadahotel.com tr*. Located at the heart of Istanbul's histori-cal peninsula, surrounded by the ancient city walls affording views of Hagia Sophia and the Blue Mosque, Hotel Armada opened its doors to guests in 1994. The building was constructed on the site of a series of row houses, which were built for marine soldiers in the 16th century. The houses were demolished by fire and Armada was designed to faithfully replicate the facade of the original buildings. Elements of modern comfort and convenience have been carefully blended into the historical atmosphere. The 110 guestrooms are decorated in the Ottoman style and offer all expected modern amenities. Sixteen guestrooms are inter-connected, and two are fully equipped for wheelchair access. There is a view of the Old City from the *Armada Terrace Restaurant*. Two other restaurants, *Ahrkap Restaurant* and *Armada Sera*, offer a variety of cuisines. Business Center; Conference/Banquet Facilities.

❑ **Seven Hills Hotel:** *Tevkifhane Sok. No. 8/A, 34400 Sul-tanahmet, Istanbul, Turkey, Tel. (90-212) 516-9497 or Fax (90-212) 517-1085. Website: www.hotelsevenhills.com. E-mail: info@ hotelsevenhills.com.* Offering the wonderful Sultanahmet loca-tion, the Seven Hills Hotel is like 'the little engine that could.' Across the street from the Four Seasons Hotel, this small family owned and operated hotel obviously attempts to emulate its luxurious neighbor. And although no one would mistake it for the Four Seasons, the Seven Hills offers a similar impressive view and a warm welcome to its guests – for less money, of course. As their brochure states, "The hotel is like the house of an old friend but with fewer social obligations and considerably better room service." 14 spacious guestrooms include one deluxe room and three suites. Suites have a jacuzzi. Guestrooms are lovingly furnished and have hardwood floors and king-sized beds. The *Terrace Bar and Restaurant* commands an impressive view of the Blue Mosque and Hagia Sophia. It is a small hotel with homespun luxury in a great location.

## RESTAURANTS

Great cities tend to be renowned for their great restaurants. Istanbul is no exception to this general rule. As befits its waterfront location on the Bosphorus, Istanbul is noted for its many fine seafood restaurants. Indeed, you can order fish everywhere you dine and not tire of the many selections. At the same time, Istanbul is well noted for its many traditional Turkish and Ottoman restaurants serving excellent appetizers, kebabs, grilled meats, and desserts. It also offers many good international restaurants, from French and Italian to Chinese, Japanese, and Thai cuisine. One of the added bonuses of dining in Istanbul are restaurants with gorgeous views of the Bosphorus and city skyline.

*Istanbul is noted for its many fine seafood restaurants as well as wonderful Turkish and international cuisines.*

Since some of today's best restaurants will change chefs, management, ownership, and locations in the future, you are well advised to check with your hotel concierge on the latest favorite restaurants for their guests as well as among fellow concierges. Also check out these English-language publications for recommended restaurants: *Time Out Istanbul*, *The Guide Istanbul*, *City Plus Istanbul*, and *The Turkish Daily News*. Also check out the Restaurant or Dining sections of these websites for the latest information on restaurants:

- Istanbul City Guide    www.instanbulcityguide.com
- Explore Istanbul       www.exploreistanbul.com
- Istanbul               www.istanbul.com
- The Guide Istanbul     www.theguideturkey.com

Keep in mind that such recommendations may be less than objective since many are based upon advertising rather than surveys of actual diners.

On our recent visit, we found the following among Istanbul's best restaurants:

❑ **Iskele:** *Yahya Kemal Caddesi No. 1, Reumelihisari, Sariyer, Tel. 263-2997 or Fax 263-4064.* Especially popular with locals, this seafood restaurant is located along the Bosphorus. Offers an excellent range of fresh seafood and salads. Often crowded and noisy. Be sure to make reservations for an inside window table or a terrace table when weather permits.

❑ **Rami:** *Utangac Sokak No. 6, Cankurtaran, Tel. 516-6593 or Fax 517-6593.* Located near the Four Seasons Hotel and Arasta Bazaar, this intimate restaurant serves excellent Ottoman cuisine. The best tables in this charming three-story old white house are on the third floor with a gorgeous view of the Blue Mosque. Be sure to make reservations for a window table on the third floor. Try the wonderful kebabs as well as the baklava and rice pudding for dessert. Gives a five percent discount for cash.

❑ **Boğaziçi Borsa:** *Lütfi Kirdar Convention and Exhibition Centre, Harbiye, Tel. 232-4201 or Fax 232-5856.* This popular restaurant offers excellent service along with fine Turkish cuisine. Everything here is good, especially the appetizers, roasted lamb shank "Konya Style" and grilled minced meat with Kaşar cheese. Located near Nişantaşi, this is an excellent choice for either lunch or dinner. Offers both indoor and outdoor dining options with excellent views of the Bosphorus.

❑ **Develi Kebab:** *Kalamuş Yatch Marina Kalamiş, Fenerbahçe Tel. 418-9400, Balik Pazari (Fish Market) Gümüşyüzlük str, 7 Samatya, Tel. 529-0833. Tepecik Yolu, No. 22, Etiler, Tel. 263-2571.* Serves traditional Turkish kebabs and grilled dishes as well as an excellent selection of appetizers. Offers very large portions at reasonable prices.

❑ **Vogue:** *Spor Caddesi BJK Plaza, A Blok Kat No. 13 Akaretler, Beşiktas, Tel. 227-4404 or Fax 258-8872.* This very trendy restaurant draws lots of beautiful people with its romantic setting overlooking the Bosphorus and Golden Horn on the 14th floor of an office building. When not real busy (before 9pm), it offers excellent service. The place becomes very crowded, noisy, and smoky after 9pm. Given its trendy fashion theme, the restaurant runs fashion videos on its TV monitors. Serves excellent Continental dishes and offers a separate sushi menu. Try the local fish – bonita. After midnight Vogue becomes a bar.

❏ **Hünkar:** *Mim Kermal Öke Caddesi No. 21, Nişantaşi, Tel. 225-4665 or Fax 296-3611.* Located just a few doors from our favorite carpet shop in Nişantaşi, this friendly restaurant is operated by one of Istanbul's top chefs – Feridun Ügümü – and serves excellent Ottoman cuisine. Unlike most restaurants that have menus, here you go through a line and select your dishes, which are then served at your table.

❏ **Hamdi:** *Tahmis Caddesi. Kalçin Sokak No. 17 Eminönü, Tel. 528-0390. Website: www.hamdietlokantasi.com.* Located near the Egyptian Bazaar with a nice view of the water and New City. Serves excellent kebabs. The cracked wheat and meat balls (içli köfte) are very good. The best seats for a view of the city are on the second floor.

❏ **Hacibaba:** *Istaklâl Caddesi No. 49, Beyoğlu, Tel. 244-1886.* Located just off Taksim Circle, this pleasant well established restaurant, overlooking a garden, offers a good selection of mesas (buffet style) and meat dishes, especially kebabs. A good stop for lunch.

❏ **Le Select:** *Vakko, Istiklâl Caddesi No. 123/125, Beyoğlu, Tel. 251-6565. Website: www.le-select@vakko.com.tr. Open 10am to 10pm.* Here's the ultimate café and restaurant to indulge oneself in lifestyle shopping. Located on the second floor of the Vakko department store and adjacent to the store's art gallery, this richly appointed café draped in velvet red, serves Italian and French dishes along with sandwiches and salads. The paintings in the gallery next door are part of the owner's private collection and thus not for sale. The sculptures in the café/restaurant can be purchased.

❏ **Körfez:** *Körfez Caddesi No. 78, Kanlica, Tel. 413-4314.* Located on the Asian side, this restaurant can be reached by taking a private boat across the Bosphorus from Rumeli Fortress. One of Istanbul's most chic and romantic seafood restaurants. Reservations essential. Try the sea bass.

❏ **Circus:** *Abdi İpekçi Caddesa Arzu Apt. No. 5/3, Nişantaşi, Tel. 219-9675.* Noted chef Carlo Bernadini serves excellent Italian and Asian cuisine in a sophisticated setting. Offers a good selection of desserts and wines.

❑ **Sarabi:** *Istihlâl Caddesi No. 174, Beyoğlu, Tel. 244-4609.* This cosy restaurant set in a large wine cellar at the lower level serves excellent Mediterranean cuisine. Try the carmelized beef steak and ravioli.

❑ **Paper Moon:** *Akmerkez Shopping Mall, Tel. 282-1616.* Serves excellent traditional Italian cuisine in an elegant setting. Includes a very popular bar and lounge. Reservations recommended.

❑ **Sabaşi Lokantasi:** *Çarşikap, Nuruosmaniye Caddesi No. 48 Nuruosmaniye, Tel. 522-4762.* Small but well Turkish established restaurant just inside the made entrance to the Grand Bazaar.

## SEEING THE SITES

Istanbul offers a wealth of interesting sightseeing opportunities to occupy two to three full days of city touring. The most popular sites are mosques, churches, palaces, and museums which are primarily found in the Old City within a one-half kilometer radius of the major bazaars – Grand, Egyptian, and Arasta. Your best use of time in this area will be to combine shopping with sightseeing. Indeed, most of the bazaars, shops, mosques, churches, palaces, and museums are within easy walking distance (five to 15 minutes) of each other within the adjacent Old City areas of Sultanahmet, Cağaloğlu, Beyazit, Eminönü, and Küçükprazar. Combining shopping with sightseeing and dining in this relatively compact area makes for an exciting lifestyle shopping experience!

Sightseeing in the New City is very limited – four to eight hours here should be sufficient. With the exception of the Dolmabahçe Palace, Galata Tower, Çirağan Palace Hotel, and a few other sites, the New City is primarily an area for shopping, dining, and entertainment.

### MOSQUES AND CHURCHES

❑ **Ayasofya:** *Ayasofya Square, Sultanahmet, Tel. 522-1750. Admission US$6. Open Tuesday to Sunday from 9:30am to 4:30pm.* Also known as the Hagia Sophia, St. Sophia, and Church of the Holy Wisdom, this ancient basilica was originally constructed in the 4th century by Constantine the Great. For nearly 1,000 years, until the construction of St. Peter's Basilica in Rome, this was the largest Christian church in the world. However, with the demise of Christianity and the rise of Islam in Constantinople, in the 15th century St. Sophia was converted into a mosque and in subsequent years four minarets were added. A victim of earthquakes, conquests, and neglect, Ayasofya has been reconstructed several times. In 1936 it was converted into a museum. So is it a church, a mosque, or a museum? It's all three, depending on your perspective. Constantly under restoration, today it primarily functions as a museum and important historic site for both Christians and Muslims. It's a fascinating building, one of Turkey's most memorable sites. A masterpiece of dome construction (the center dome is 55 meters high and 31 meters in width), this massive building is most noted for its fascinating architecture and beautiful old Byzantine mosaics and frescos. At the same time, it's a very worn building, especially dark and dreary, which has seen better days. It includes an interesting museum shop selling books, postcards, and souvenirs.

❑ **The Blue Mosque:** *Sultanahmet Square, Sultanahmet, Tel. 518-1330. Admission US$1.50. Open daily from 9am to 5pm.* Also known as the Sultan Ahmet Cami or the Mosque of Sultan Ahmet, this picture-postcard structure is a major symbol of both Istanbul and Turkey and a masterpiece of the famous architect Sinan. Located opposite St. Sophia, this massive structure with its multiple domes and six minarets draws thousands of worshipers and sightseers each day. While the interior with its 20,000 blue Iznik ceramic tiles and 260 stained-glass windows is interesting, it's less impressive than the overall exterior architecture. Visitors must remove their shoes before entering the mosque. Women are supposed to wear skirts and cover their heads, although this rule is relaxed, and slacks were permitted when we visited. Just don't arrive wearing shorts and looking too immodest or you may be stopped and asked to do a quick make-over using their supplied skirts and scarves.

❑ **Süleymaniye Camii:** *Süleymaniye Caddesi. Located near the northern gate to Istanbul University. Open daily.* Also known as the Mosque of Sultan Süleyman the Magnificant, this is considered by many visitors to be the largest and grandest mosque in Istanbul. Constructed between 1550 and 1557 by Süleyman I, it is probably the most beautiful and spiritual imperial mosque in Turkey. Located on a hill with four minarets and soaring architecture, it houses the tomb of Süleyman the Magnificant.

❑ **Rüstem Paşa Mosque:** *Hasircilar Caddesi. Open daily.*
Located just north of the Egyptian Bazaar, this small
mosque was designed by the famous architect Sinan and
built in 1561. It is especially noted for its beautiful interior
which is decorated with lovely Iznik tiles.

❑ **Yeni Mosque:** Located at Eminönü, this is one of the city's
landmark sights. Built between 1597 and 1663, it's especially noted for its beautiful fountain and Iznik tiles.

### PALACES

❑ **Topkapi Palace:** *Gülhane Park, near Sultanahmet Square. Tel.
512-0480. Admission US$4 and US$2 for the harem tour. Open
Wednesday to Monday, 9:30am to 4:30pm.* This is Istanbul's
most popular tourist site. This maze of buildings and
courtyards served as the royal residence for the Ottoman
sultans from the 15$^{th}$ to the 19$^{th}$ centuries. It housed nearly
5,000 people who lived and "served" here in various capaci-
ties as relatives, bureaucrats, guards, concubines, eunuchs,
and slaves. In 1868 Sultan Abdül Mecit I moved from here
to the newly constructed Dolmabahçe Palace in the New
City along the Bosphorus. Since this place can become very
crowded with tourists, it's best to arrive here early, before
the tour groups start coming in around 10am. Plan to spend
two to three hours here and include the extra harem tour.
The highlights of this place include the Imperial Treasury
with its jewels and thrones and the harem. A visit here will
give you a good idea of the power, splendor, and lifestyle of
the Ottoman sultans. If time permits, plan to have lunch at
the Konyali Restaurant on the palace grounds (go down a
flight of stairs behind the Treasury) which serves excellent
kebabs and offers a wonderful view of the Bosphorus. Along
the way you will pass a Urart jewelry shop.

❑ **Dolmabahçe Palace:** *Dolmabahçe Caddesi, Tel. 258-5544.
Admission US$10. Open Tuesday, Wednesday, Friday, and
Sunday, from 9am to 4pm.* This is a very impressive palace
complex and a monument to court excesses. Constructed
between 1843 and 1856, this massive structure with its
beautiful fountain and nicely manicured grounds became
the official residence of Turkey's last sultans. The government literally went bankrupt financing this extravaganza
modeled along exaggerated European lines – eclectic French
Baroque and Rococo styles which at times verge on being
tacky. You'll find very little Ottoman architectural style

here, although an occasional Ottoman element appears unexpectedly. The palace grounds offer nice views of the Bosphorus. You can only visit the grounds by joining official
guided tours which depart at specific times (the last tour for
the day departs at 3pm). Be sure to check on the times for
different language tours. You have two tour options – main
and harem tours. Both tours can be completed within two
hours. The first or main tour is the more interesting, especially when seeing the impressive huge rooms, parquet wood
floors, large chandeliers (1-4 tons), crystal staircase (actually, just the banisters are crystal), large Turkish carpets,
and ornate ceilings and walls. The impressive Grand Throne
Room (2,000 square meters and 36-meter high ceiling) is
still used for major state receptions. It's worth paying extra
to take the harem tour which takes you into the personal
residence of the sultans. Here you'll get to see the apartments of the official and unofficial wives, grand rooms, and
the bedroom and bed in which President Kemal Atatürk,
Turkey's founding father, died in 1938. As you exit this
complex, you'll find an excellent shop near the exit which
offers many reproduction porcelain pieces (some sell for
US$2,600), books, coins, carpets, paintings, and other
souvenir items.

## MUSEUMS

❑ **Museum of Turkish and Islamic Arts (Türk Ve Islâm
Eserleri Müzesi):** *Atmeydani 46, Sutanahmet, Tel. 518-1385.
Admission US$1.50. Open Tuesday to Sunday from 9:30am to
5:30pm.* This is one of the best and most interesting museums in Turkey, especially if you are interested in Turkish
textiles, carpets, kilims, and culture. Indeed, if you are
planning to buy carpets and kilims in Turkey, this is a "must
see" museum for better understanding the origins, history,
and quality of such items. Even if you're not planning to
make such a purchase, you should still come here since you
will probably become an "accidental carpet buyer" sometime
during your stay in Turkey! Housed in an old palace
(Ibrahim Paşa Sarayi, circa 1524), room after room unfolds
with a partial collection of over 40,000 objects. Some
carpets date from the 13th century. Everything here is nicely
displayed. The downstairs area includes an ethnographic
section with displays of the various peoples and cultures of
Turkey, including tents, houses, and shop life in Istanbul
during the 19th and 20th centuries. You'll also find two
museum shops near the entrance – one for ceramics, carpets,

jewelry, and souvenirs and another for books, prints, paintings, and cards.

❑ **Istanbul Archaeology Museums:** *Gülhane Park, on the perimeter of the first court of the Topkapi Palace. Open Tuesday to Sunday, 9:30am to 4:30pm.* Two museums here include an interesting collection of antiquities. The **Archaeological Museum (Arkeoloji Müzesi)** includes such noted classical antiquities as the Alexander Sarcophagus and the Athena Temple from Assos, as well as many white marble statues from Roman times. The collection of elaborately carved sarcophagi is especially intriguing. The newly opened (September 2000) **Museum of the Ancient Orient (Eski Şark Eserleri Müzesi)** is one of the most interesting museums in Turkey. It includes a rare collection of antiquities from the Sumerian, Babylonian, Assyrian, Hatti, Hittite, Egyptian, Mesopotamian, and pre-Islamic civilizations.

❑ **Tiled Pavilion (Çinili Köşkü):** *Gülhane Park, on the perimeter of the first court of the Topkapi Palace. Open Tuesday to Monday, 9:30am to 4:30pm.* Located on the same grounds with the Istanbul Archaeology Museums, the museum includes an interesting collection of Turkish tiles and ceramics. Several rooms display ceramic plates, lamps, bowls, and vases from the Seljuk (10th to 13th centuries), Iznik (14th to 17th centuries), and Kütahya (18th century) periods.

### OTHER

❑ **Galata Tower (Galata Kulesi):** *Büyük Hendek Caddesi, Tel. 245-1160. Admission US$3. Open daily 9am to 8pm.* Located in the Jewish section of the New City, this imposing 68-meter stone tower, which was built by the Genoese in 1348, is a great place to get a panoramic view of the city, including the Golden Horn, Bosphorus, bridges, ships, mosques, residential and commercial areas, traffic, the Asia side, and Istanbul's seven hills. Take the elevator to the seventh floor and climb two additional floors where you finally reach a narrow observation ledge that circles the complete tower. The top floors house a restaurant (eighth) and a nightclub and bar (ninth).

❑ **Sultanahmet Square and the Hippodrome:** *Atmeydani, Sultanahmet. Open all the time.* Located in front of the Blue Mosque, the Hippodrome once served as a center for Byzantine civic life. With a stadium that held up to 100,000 spectators, it was the site of numerous chariot races and circuses. You can still see the outlines of this arena which you can fill in with your imagination. Only three monuments now remain on this site: Obeliks of Theodosius, the bronze Serpentine Column, and the Column of Constantine. Numerous tourists congregate in this rich sightseeing area along with street vendors and peddlers offering postcards and souvenirs.

❑ **Çirağan Palace Hotel:** *Çirağan Caddesi No. 84, Beşiktaş, Tel. 258-3377.* Constructed by Sultan Abdül Aziz in 1863, this palace along the Bosphorus was later restored and converted to a luxury hotel. If you are not staying here, you may want to visit the impressive hotel and grounds. See "Accommodations" above for information on this unique property.

---

## ENJOYING YOUR STAY

Other highlights of any visit to Istanbul might include the following:

❑ **Bosphorus cruise:** One of the most delightful things to do in Istanbul is to take a cruise along the Bosphorus. You can easily and inexpensively do this by just taking one of the regular passenger boats that starts at Eminönü and goes back and forth to the Asian and European sides of the city. A complete trip will take about six hours. Along the way you will see mosques, minarets, hotels, yali (old wooden villas), palaces, fortresses, bridges, and small fishing villages. If you are interested in a more organized and focused excursion, private companies such as Plan Tours (Tel. 230-2272, 230-8118, 234-1056; website: www.plantours.com) offer half day and evening dinner cruises along the Bosphorus for US$30 to US$90 per person, depending on the type of cruise.

❑ **Turkish bath:** Many visitors to Istanbul make a point of trying a Turkish bath or hamam. The city has several historical hamams that are open to both men and women (separate sections). Most are beautiful old marble hamams with lots of history and character. Three in particular are worth considering: **Cağaloğlu Hamami** (Prof. Kazi Gürkan Caddesi 34, Cağaloğlu, Tel. 522-2424); **Çemberlitaş Hamami** (Vezirhan Caddesi 8, Tel. 522-7974); and **Galatasaray Hamami** (Sütterazi Sokak 24, Beyoğlu, Tel. 249-

4342). Most of these places are open daily from 5am to midnight for men and from 8am to 8pm for women. Self-service baths usually cost about US$10 and another US$5-10 for a vigorous bathing massage.

❑ **The Princes' Islands (Istanbul Adalari):** Located in the Marmara Sea about 20 kilometers from Sultanahmet, the Princes' Islands consists of nine islands which were once used as retreats by Byzantine princes. The major island, Büyükada, which once served as the home for exiled Russian leader Leon Trotsky, is a pine forested island with sandy beaches, horse-drawn carriages, hotels, restaurants, and cafes. The second largest island, Heybeli, also boasts popular beaches, cafes, and teahouses. Most cruises go to either or both of these resort islands. Companies such as Plan Tours (Tel. 230-2272, 230-8118, 234-1056; website: www.plan tours.com) offer a full-day tour of the Princes' Islands for US$60 per person.

❑ **Entertainment:** Istanbul comes alive at night, especially in the New City. Numerous popular discos, nightclubs, jazz clubs, and bars are found in the major hotels as well as in the area south of Taksim Circle, especially on the side streets that run off of Istiklâl Caddesi in Beyoğlu. The community of Ortaköy is considered to be the best place for nightlife along the Bosphorus with its many seafood restaurants, jazz clubs, nightclubs, and bars. For updated information on the latest in entertainment – from concerts and exhibitions to discos and bars – be sure to survey the listings in these local English-language publications: *Time Out Istanbul*, *The Guide Istanbul*, *City Plus Istanbul*, and *The Turkish Daily News*. Also check out the Art, Culture, Entertainment, or Nightlife sections of these websites for the latest in local entertainment:

- **Istanbul City Guide**      www.istanbulcityguide.com
- **Explore Istanbul**         www.exploreistanbul.com
- **Istanbul**                 www.istanbul.com
- **The Guide Istanbul**       www.theguideturkey.com

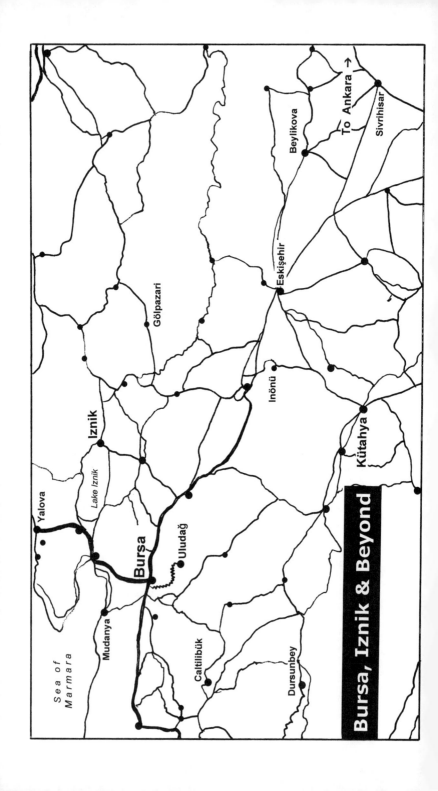

Bursa, Iznik & Beyond

# 5

# Bursa, Iznik, & Beyond

I
F YOU PLAN TO DRIVE SOUTHEAST OF ISTANBUL
to Ankara and Cappadocia, you should seriously consider
including two places along the way via the southern
Mamara region – Bursa and Iznik. These famous old cities
have a great deal to offer travel-shoppers, history buffs,
and thermal bath enthusiasts. They are often pleasant surprises
for travelers who know little about this region or who primarily
go there for sightseeing. For lovers of antiques, ceramics, and
silk, Bursa and Iznik are very interesting places to visit.

---

## WELCOME TO OLD BURSA

The old city of Bursa is a delight for many visitors who only
plan a day trip here from Istanbul. Drawn to Bursa primarily

133

for its historical, architectural, and thermal attractions, many visitors quickly discover this pleasant city also is a great place for shopping and dining. If you really want to enjoy the treasures and pleasures of Bursa, plan to stay over one or two nights to enjoy this city and its surrounding area, including a visit to the charming old ceramics town of Iznik.

A famous city in the history of Turkey, dating from 200 BC, Bursa played many important historical roles which culminated in becoming the first capital of the Ottoman Empire in the 1300s. Its early history is well represented in Bursa's architecture and historical sites, from museums to mosques and tombs. These are the major attractions that draw most tourists to Bursa for a day trip.

During the 20$^{th}$ century, Bursa grew into a major agricultural, industrial, and handicraft center. Today, with a population of over 1 million, it's a bustling city especially noted for fruit processing plants, automotive assembly factories, and textile and handicraft production facilities. Much of the textile and handicraft production, as well as antiques and collectibles, can be found in and around the many shops and stalls that line the walkways that lead to Bursa's major historical sites and in its Covered Bazaar and factories. Here you'll discover many of Bursa's treasures that often surprise visitors who did not come here with the expectation of shopping. However, since Bursa is famous for its textiles and handcrafted traditions, shopping is one of its major attractions for local visitors who come here to stock up on inexpensive cotton towels and silk textiles produced in Bursa's many factories.

- ❑ Drawn to Bursa primarily for its historical, architectural, and thermal attractions, many visitors quickly discover this pleasant city also is a great place for shopping and dining.

- ❑ Bursa played many historical roles, including being the first capital of the Ottoman Empire in the 1300s.

- ❑ A city of over 1 million, Bursa is especially noted for fruit processing plants, automotive assembly factories, and textile and handicraft production facilities.

- ❑ Local visitors come here to buy inexpensive cotton towels and silk textiles produced in Bursa's factories.

Bursa is one of Turkey's most pleasant and attractive cities. This sprawling metropolis lies at the foothills of Mt. Uludağ which also includes ski resort facilities within an hour's drive of the city. Many of the narrow streets of the old city meander through the hills, offering wonderful views of the valley below. Lunch at a restaurant overlooking the city, especially adjacent to the Green Mosque, is one of the highlights of a brief visit to Bursa.

# BURSA BASICS

## GETTING THERE

Bursa is located 250 miles south of Istanbul via the Mamara Sea. While you can drive or take a bus east of Istanbul around the coast of the Mamara Sea to reach Bursa, this is a long trip that can take up to five hours. The fastest and most pleasant way to get to Bursa is via the ferry east of Istanbul (Yenikapi docks, Tel. 517-7137) that goes directly to Yalova on the eastern shore of the Mamara Sea. From here it takes about 50 minutes to cross the Mamara Sea. The ride costs US$10 per car regardless of the number of passengers, and the ferries usually depart every half hour. Once you arrive at the docks in Yalova, the trip by road to Bursa takes about one hour. Several buses also await travelers at the Yalova docks.

## GETTING AROUND

Bursa has plenty of metered taxis for getting around the city. Since most major attractions are found within easy walking distance of **Heykel**, once you reach this square, plan to walk to most of Bursa's major attractions. Most places, from the Green Mosque to the Covered Bazaar, can be reached on foot within 15 minutes. If you stay at one of the major hotels west of the city center, take a taxi to the square (a 15-minute ride in average traffic) and spend the rest of your day exploring the center of the center.

# GETTING TO KNOW BURSA

Bursa sprawls from east to west along the valley and slope of Mt. Uladağ. From the hills of the city, this is a very picturesque community. Its quaint narrow vehicle-clogged streets, which frequently change names, can be a challenge to navigate for first-time visitors who arrive without the aid of a good map, compass, or guide. Consequently, be prepared to get lost several times and frequently ask for directions.

## AT THE CENTER

The center of the city, which is located in the old city, is usually designated as **Heykel** or Republic Square (Cumbhuriyet Alani), which has a huge equestrian statue of Atatürk at its center. This square is found at the intersection of Atatürk Caddesi and Inönü Caddesi. If you walk directly west along Atatürk Caddesi, within four blocks you'll come to a large pedestrian area which includes the Tourist Information Office, a park, Municipal Building (Belediye Sarayi), mosques (Ulu Camii and Orhan Camii), Covered Bazaar (Kapali Carşi), silk bazaar (Koza Han), and numerous shops, which are all located on the north side of Atatürk Caddesi. This area is rich with sites, shops, and restaurants. It's also a pleasant pedestrian area for strolling, window shopping, and people watching. Indeed, you can spend a good part of a day exploring the many streets and lanes in this rich shopping and sightseeing area.

### Getting Started Right

We recommend first stopping at the **Tourist Information Office** (Tel. 517-7137) which is located in a small shopping center beneath the main street (Atatürk Caddesi) and between the Municipal Building and Orhan Camii and near both the Covered Bazaar and Silk Bazaar. Here you can pick up an excellent detailed map of the city (one of the best in Turkey) as well as a useful 96-page book on Bursa and brochures on various attractions in and around the city. The guide includes all of the city's major sightseeing attractions and travel agencies as well as a directory to hotels in both Bursa and Uludağ and restaurants, cafes, and bars in Bursa. This office also can answer any questions and help with tours, guides, and transportation.

If you walk east of Heykel for a few blocks and then turn left onto Yeşil Caddesi, you'll soon come to the famous **Green Mosque** (Yeşil Camii) and **Green Tomb** (Yeşil Turbe), two of Bursa's major architectural highlights and popular tourist attractions. Along the way to these two sites are several noteworthy antique, handicraft, and clothing shops. In fact, some of Bursa's most interesting shopping can be found along the walkways that lead to these two monuments.

## Shopping Bursa

Bursa yields several unplanned treasures and pleasures for visitors who primarily go there to view the city's architecture and historical monuments. Indeed, we did some of our best shopping in all of Turkey during our visit to Bursa. A relatively well developed city with a thriving economy, Bursa offers a great deal of shopping opportunities for both local and international visitors. While not quite a shopper's paradise and not the most fashionable shopping center, the city holds its own in comparison to most cities and products in Turkey.

## WHAT TO BUY

Bursa is famous for a variety of products which are quickly apparent in and around its markets and tourist sites. It is especially noted as one of Turkey's major centers for hand-crafted products. These include:

- **Silk:** Bursa is Turkey's premier silk center. Numerous villages in the surrounding area produce silk as well as finished silk garments and accessories. Bolts of solid color and printed silk are available in the markets and cloth shops and can be purchased in meter lengths. But for many visitors, the really exciting shopping experience for silk is found in the Silk Bazaar which is located in a separate building (**Koza Han**) directly across from the Tourist Information Office just north of Atatürk Caddesi. Here you will discover 53 small silk boutiques offering a wide range of surprisingly fashionable silk garments and accessory pieces, from jackets and neckties to shirts, blouses, scarves, and handbags, at very reasonable prices. Also look for an excellent selection of silk fabric, garments, and accessory pieces at the **Yaşil Çarşi Shopping Center** (Yaşil Caddesi, Tel. 327-7283) next to the Green Tomb. This shop includes a nice selection of silk ties produced by the famous Turkish clothier Vakko.

> ❑ Bursa is Turkey's premier silk center. The Silk Bazaar (Kosa Han) is the key shopping center for silk.
>
> ❑ Bursa's famous cotton towels and terrycloth robes are primarily designed for local consumption.
>
> ❑ Most of Bursa's ceramics follow the traditional blue and red floral Ottoman patterns of the famous Iznik ceramics.
>
> ❑ Many of Bura's antiques shops are found near the Green Mosque and Green Tomb.

- **Towels and bathrobes:** Bursa is rightfully famous for its numerous textile factories that produce towels and bathrobes. These products are found in abundance in the **Covered Bazaar** as well as the famous factory shop **Özdilek** (Yalova Yolu 4. Km., Tel. 211-5240, website: www.ozdilek.com.tr). While cheap, interesting, and in abundance, don't expect to buy much in this product category. The towels and terrycloth robes are primarily designed for local consumption. The towels tend to be thin and produced in colors and designs that would look out of place back home. They are not something you will need to find much room for in your suitcase. The terrycloth bath robes are marginal – may or may not appeal to your tastes. Some of the best colors and designs are found at the Özdilek factory shop. Their beach towels also are relatively appealing with many attractive bold colors and designs.

- **Bedspreads and bed linens**: Bursa's textile factories produce an abundance of bedspreads and bed linens which are famous throughout Turkey. However, like Bursa's towels and bathrobes, most of these products are produced in colors, styles, and sizes which are more appropriate for local tastes and consumption. Numerous shops in the Covered Bazaar offer a wide range of such products – often next door to glittering wedding shops.

- **Ceramics**: Similar to other places in Turkey, shops in Bursa offer a wide range of handcrafted ceramic items, from  decorative tiles, plates, and bowls to coasters, lamps, and figurines. Most of the ceramics follow the traditional blue and red floral Ottoman patterns of the famous Iznik ceramics. Many other attractive ceramics, as found in the handicraft complex next to the Green Tomb (Yeşil Carsa), are from the noted ceramics town of Kütahya, which is located two hours east of Bursa.

- **Knives**: Bursa artisans are famous for producing decorative Ottoman-style knives with wood sheaves inlaid with mother-of-pearl. Most handicraft shops will offer these souvenir items.

- **Shadow puppet figures**: Several antique and handicraft shops offer small colorful flat leather puppets which are used in Turkish shadow puppet plays. These unique plays have been in existence in Turkey for more than 600 years. They purportedly began in Bursa from origins in India and Indonesia or perhaps even the Mediterranean region. These translucent camel leather marionette figures, colored with natural dyes, make nice collectibles for individuals interested in decorative handcrafted items. If you are interested in seeing a local shadow puppet performance, contact the Bursa Karagöz Theatre (Tel. 221-8727), which offers performances at 11am on Wednesdays and 11:30am on Saturdays at the Çekirge, Karagöz Art House. You also can meet the puppeteer, R. Şinasi Çelikkol, at his antique and handicraft shop, **Karagöz**, near the entrance of the Covered Bazaar where he often puts on a short shadow puppet demonstration using a makeshift screen. This shop, of course, offers several shadow puppet figures for sale. His brother, Şenol Çelikkol, who also is a puppeteer, operates another nearby antique shop, **Karagöz 2**.

- **Gold and silver jewelry**: Numerous shops offering gold and silver jewelry can be found in and around the Covered Bazaar. Primarily produced for local consumption, most of the jewelry tends to be basic functional designs rather than fashionable for international visitors. Most of the gold jewelry shops are found within the Covered Bazaar. Many silver jewelry shops are housed together in a separate building adjacent to the Covered Bazaar.

- **Antiques and collectibles**: Several of Bursa's antique shops offer a wide range of old furniture, collectibles, and junk.
Many of these shops are located near the famous Green Mosque and Green Tomb. Dusty and crammed to the rafters with an odd assortment of old and aging items, these shops can be real adventures in shopping. Many of these places look like junk shops that need a major house cleaning or at least someone with a basic talent in classification and display. Wander through a few of these places and you  may discover an old copper pot, bronze French statuary and clocks, German canteens, and Turkish knives and instruments. From old rugs, textiles, brass mortars, candle stands, ceramics, glass, and radios to telephones, phonographs, mirrors, guns, lanterns, icons, camera, saddles, and jewelry, the list of both desirable and undesirable collectibles seems

to go on and on. Near the Green Tomb, look for such shops as **Ekinci Ticaret Antik** (Yeşil Emir Caddesi No. 3, Tel. 328-4785), **Selçuk** (Yeşil Emir Caddesi No. 9/A, Tel. 328-0495), and **Güler** (Yeşil Emir Caddesi No. 18/B, Tel. 328-0569). In the Covered Bazaar, be sure to visit the Karagöz family of shops – **Karagöz** (Kapali Çarşi Eski Aynalı Çarşi No. 12, Tel. 224-221-8727, website: www.karagoz.8m.com) and **Karagöz 2** (Kapali Çarşi Eski Aynalı Çarşi No. 17, Tel. 222-6151).

■ **Canned and bottled fruits:** As a major agricultural region producing an abundance of fruits and vegetables, Bursa is known for its food processing plants. It's especially famous for offering packaged fruits such as roasted chestnuts. You'll find these in small markets and in a few handicraft shops such as the **Yaşil Çarşi Shopping Center** (Yaşil, Tel. 327-7283) next to the Green Tomb.

## WHERE TO SHOP

While Bursa offers numerous shopping opportunities throughout the city, most major shops of interest to international visitors are concentrated in two areas:

1. Around major mosques and sites, especially the Green Tomb and Green Mosque.

2. Covered Bazaar, especially the silk market.

### GREEN MOSQUE/GREEN TOMB AREA

The two streets that surround the Green Mosque and Green Tomb – Yaşil Caddesi and Yaşil Emir Caddesi – are lined with many souvenir, antique, and ceramic shops. While primarily catering to tourists, many of the antique shops especially appeal to serious collectors who are interested in old furniture, copper pots, and a wide range of collectibles. Many of these shops especially appeal to local visitors rather than international tourists. Some of the best shops in this area include:

❑ **Yaşil Çarşi Shopping Center:** *Yaşil Caddesi, Tel. 327-7283 or Fax 328-7676.* Located immediately to the right of the Green Tomb, this two-story shopping center consists of several adjoining rooms which offer a wide selection of jewelry, glass, ceramics, clothing, and foodstuff. This is actually a big handicraft shop that uses the term "shopping center" loosely. Most clothing is found upstairs in several rooms, including a good selection of Vakko neckties and shirts. The backroom, which goes into a courtyard, has a nice collection of Kütahya ceramics. If you want to sample Bursa's famous roasted chestnuts, check out the packed foodstuff area near the entrance to this shop. Most items here are souvenirs for tourists who visit the Green Tomb next door.

❑ **Ekinci Ticaret Antik:** *Yaşil Emir Caddesi No. 3, Tel. 328-4785.* Located just to the east of the Green Mosque and Green Tomb in Bursa, this combination antique and souvenir shop includes two adjacent shops. The first place is a crammed and dusty antique shop that primarily offers old furniture but also has a display of old copper pots, candle holders, and collectibles on tables in front of the shop. The second shop to the left is primarily an arts and crafts shop selling ceramics and related tourist items. If no one is minding the antique shop, go next door to the souvenir shop where they are probably transacting business, including packing items.

❑ **Selcuk:** *Yeşil Emir Caddesi No. 9/A, Tel. 328-0495.* This small dusty and somewhat disorganized antique shop is filled with copper pots and plates, glass, brass mortars, instruments, knives, carpets, bells, and other collectibles.

❑ **Güler:** *Yeşil Emir Caddesi No. 18/B, Tel. 328-0569.* This is literally chaos on the corner – two adjacent Ali Baba shops! These are real antique and junk shops packed to the rafters with just about every conceivable collectible you could imagine. You can hardly walk through the first shop, which has one of the most eclectic collections of small antiques and junk you'll find anywhere in Turkey – porcelain, glass, lamps, rugs, radios, telephones, bronze statues, German cuckoo clocks, phonographs, mirrors, pictures, and World War II canteens. The second shop is filled with jewelry, guns, vases, lamps, lanterns, cameras, icons, saddles, knives, and candle holders. In front of both shops you'll find an unusual display of door knockers, cameras, wagon wheels, boxes, and paintings. This is truly an international antique and junk shop with many items from Germany, France, and England. The aging owner, Abdullah Güler, also is as interesting a character as is his collection.

CENTRAL OLD CITY

Most of the best shopping in the central old city is found in and around the Covered Bazaar and nearby Silk Bazaar. Prices here are generally better than in Istanbul's Grand Bazaar, and the traffic tends to be a combination of local residents and local tourists. The bazaars are especially well noted for their inexpensive cotton towels, terrycloth robes, and bedspreads and linens as well as silk textiles and apparel. However, selections have a decidedly local look which is not particularly stylish for many international visitors.

COVERED BAZAAR (KAPAL CARŞI)

Bursa's Covered Bazaar feels more like a shopping mall than a bazaar. It includes separate sections for antiques, gold and silver jewelry, wedding gowns, bedspreads and linens, towels, terrycloth bathrobes, and household goods. Some of the best shops are found in the antiques and silver jewelry sections:

❑ **Karagöz and Karagöz 2:** *The Covered Bazaar, Kapali Çarşi Eski Aynali Çarşi No. 12, Tel./Fax 221-8727; and Kapali Çarşi Eski Aynali Çarşi No. 17, Tel. 222-6151. Website: www.kara goz.8m.com.* Operated by the Karagöz family, who are noted

antique dealers, shadow puppeteers, and travel agents in Bursa, these two small shops near the entrance to the bazaar offer a good range of antiques as well as arts and crafts. **Karagöz** is piled high with copper pots, textiles, clothing, brass plates, shadow puppets, pipes, lanterns, cooking utensils, jewelry, and knives. It also includes a small demonstration shadow puppet screen, which the owner activates to generate interest for attending his regularly scheduled (Wednesdays at 11am and Saturdays at 11:30am) shadow puppet shows at the Karagöz Art House (Çekirge Caddesi), where he also has a large textile collection. His brother's nearby antique and craft shop – just four shops closer to the entrance to the Covered Bazaar – **Karagöz 2**, includes copper and bronze pots, ceramics, inlaid picture frames and knives, candle sticks, and meerschaum pipes. The family also owns a couple of other shops, including a travel agency, across the walkway near the entrance to the Covered Bazaar.

❑ **Silver Section:** Housed in a separate building, the silver jewelry section includes more than 15 small shops offering relatively inexpensive silver jewelry.

### SILK BAZAAR (KOZA HAN)

*Koza Han, north of Atatürk Caddesi and near the old Municipal Building.* For many visitors to Bursa, the Silk Bazaar offers some of the best shopping, much better than the city's Covered Bazaar. Located adjacent to the Covered Bazaar, the Silk Bazaar has a sign at its entrance stating the historical significance of Bursa and the silk trade: "Bursa was the last stop on the great silk road to China."

Indeed, Bursa has a long history of being an important silk center in Turkey. Since the 15th century Bursa has been famous for its fabrics, especially its silk weaving. Today this tradition is focused on the Silk Bazaar, which is housed in a separate building (Koza Han) directly across from the Tourist Information Office, just north of Atatürk Caddesi and northwest of the old Municipal Building. Here you'll discover 53 small silk boutiques offering a wide range of silk garments and accessory pieces, from jackets and ties to shirts, blouses, scarves, pashminas, ties, and handbags, at very reasonable prices (scarves and ties cost US$3 to US$6 each). You also can purchase silk pillows and fabric by the meter. The Silk Bazaar is literally a one-stop shopping center for a wide range of colorful and surprisingly fashionable – especially after seeing Bursa's not-too-fashionable cotton towels, bathrobes, and bed linens – silk garments and accessories.

### OTHER PLACES

❑ **Özdilek:** *Yalova Yolu 4. Km., Tel. 211-5200 or Fax 211-5249. Website: www.ozdilek.com.tr.* This combination towel factory and department store offers some of the best towels in

Turkey. Just behind this retail store is the huge towel factory which also has a demonstration area. The towels, terry cloth bathrobes, and bedding here are more colorful, fashionable, and better packaged than similar items found in the covered market. However, they still may not meet your standards for quality and selections. The large colorful beach towels are a good buy at US$4 to US$5 each.

❑ **Çekirge Caddesi:** Running from the hotel section in the western part of city to the downtown area, this street includes several upscale clothing and accessory shops, such as Vakko, DKNY, Versace, and Benetton.

## ACCOMMODATIONS

While many tourists based in Istanbul only come to Bursa for the day, others stay overnight in order to explore Bursa and the surrounding area in more depth. You'll find plenty of accommodations in Bursa for all budgets, but the two top hotels which also include popular thermal baths are:

❑ **Kervansaray Termal:** *Çekirge Meydani, 16080 Bursa, Turkey, Tel. (90-224) 233-9300, Fax (90-224) 233-9324. Website: www.kervansaray.com.tr. E-mail: termal@kervansarayhotels.com.* Located on a hill in an upscale section of the city, yet away from the bustle of the city center, the Kervansaray Termal bills itself as a resort hotel – no doubt because of the thermal baths. Solarium-style glass on the top (5$^{th}$) level floods much of the interior public space with light. The 211 guestrooms are similar to what you might expect in a mid-range chain hotel. Though billed as five-star, most four- or five-star hotels outside the major cities are not the same as a five-star in Istanbul. Five-star is more likely to be earned by things such as the number of telephones in the guestrooms, whether there are exercise facilities, and the number of restaurants than by the luxuriousness of the carpet, bedding, and furniture. Guestrooms have balconies which provide a nice space to sit outside. Most (187) guestrooms have twin beds; 11 have French beds; and there are seven corner suites and six demi suites. Four restaurants: *Topaz, Bahçe, Safir Saloon a la carte Mercan,* and *Sedef.* The stone vaulted ceiling of the building housing the Turkish Bath, as well as some of the other health facilities, is a gem. With its constant supply of mineral water, the "Eski Kaplica" physical treatment center draws many of the guests to

Kervansaray Termal. Fitness/Health Facilities (outdoor pool and thermal open and enclosed pools); Conference/Banquet Facilities; Amatis Night Club and Han Disco Bar.

❑ **Hotel Çelik Palas:** *Çekirge Caddesi 79, 16070 Çekirge/Bursa, Turkey, Tel. (90-224) 233-3800 or Fax (90-224) 236-1910. Website: www.hotels.wec-net.com.tr/ernek/palas.html.* The property owners are presently building a new Çelik Palas behind the present one. Once completed, it will be the grandest in town. Scheduled for completion in 2002, it will probably open later, in part because of the worldwide economic and tourism slow-down. The present Çelik Palas, billed as five-star (see note above on Kervansaray Termal) is situated within the city but out of the noisy city center. The 173 rooms fit expectations of a mid-range chain hotel. There are 13 suites. Two restaurants, *Terrace* and *Marmara*, offer diners a choice of cuisine. Fitness Center features Turkish Bath with constant supply of natural mineral water; Conference/Banquet Facilities.

# FAVORITE BURSA RESTAURANTS

You'll find plenty of good restaurants in Bursa. The shopping area in the center of the old city has several relatively inexpensive restaurants and cafes. Two of our favorite restaurants are found here and near the Green Tomb:

❑ **Hümker:** *Yeşil Camii Yani No. 17-19. Tel. 327-8910.* Popular with many tour groups, this restaurant has a nice view of the city and valley as well as serves pizzas and pastas. But its famous specialty is the döner kebab (Bursa Iskender Kebab) which is served with tomato sauce, butter, and yogurt. Indeed, we tried lots of dönor kebabs in Turkey, but none came close to the outstanding one served here. Several other restaurants in Bursa also serve this local specialty dish.

❑ **Çiçek Izgara:** *Belediye Caddesi No. 15, Tel. 221-6526.* Located near the Covered Bazaar, this popular second floor restaurant is especially famous for meatballs.

# SEEING BURSA'S SITES

Bursa is famous for its many mosques, tombs, and museums. Some of the most popular places to visit include:

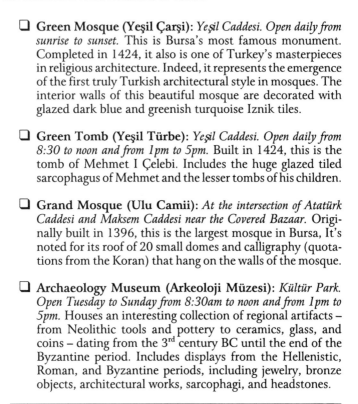

❏ **Green Mosque (Yeşil Çarşi):** *Yeşil Caddesi. Open daily from sunrise to sunset.* This is Bursa's most famous monument. Completed in 1424, it also is one of Turkey's masterpieces in religious architecture. Indeed, it represents the emergence of the first truly Turkish architectural style in mosques. The interior walls of this beautiful mosque are decorated with glazed dark blue and greenish turquoise Iznik tiles.

❏ **Green Tomb (Yeşil Türbe):** *Yeşil Caddesi. Open daily from 8:30 to noon and from 1pm to 5pm.* Built in 1424, this is the tomb of Mehmet I Çelebi. Includes the huge glazed tiled sarcophagus of Mehmet and the lesser tombs of his children.

❏ **Grand Mosque (Ulu Camii):** *At the intersection of Atatürk Caddesi and Maksem Caddesi near the Covered Bazaar.* Originally built in 1396, this is the largest mosque in Bursa, It's noted for its roof of 20 small domes and calligraphy (quotations from the Koran) that hang on the walls of the mosque.

❏ **Archaeology Museum (Arkeoloji Müzesi):** *Kültür Park. Open Tuesday to Sunday from 8:30am to noon and from 1pm to 5pm.* Houses an interesting collection of regional artifacts – from Neolithic tools and pottery to ceramics, glass, and coins – dating from the 3rd century BC until the end of the Byzantine period. Includes displays from the Hellenistic, Roman, and Byzantine periods, including jewelry, bronze objects, architectural works, sarcophagi, and headstones.

---

## Enjoying Your Stay in Bursa

Many people come to Bursa to enjoy its famous warm **mineral baths** which are reputed to have special curative powers for many ailments. The major hotels have their own public baths that are open to guests and the public. One of the largest and most popular bath houses is located next to the Kervansaray Termal Hotel – **Eski Kaplica** (Tel. 233-9300). Most thermal baths have separate sections for both men and women and charge less than US$10.

During the winter months, Bursa becomes a popular center for winter sports on the slopes of **Uludağ**, the tallest mountain in Western Anatolia that reaches a height of 2,543 meters. This also is Turkey's most important ski and winter sports center. You can take a chair lift from Bursa to the ski resort of Uludağ. See the end of this chapter for more information on the unique pleasures of Uludağ.

One of the highlights of visiting Bursa is to explore the historic ceramic and religious town of **Iznik**.

## DISCOVERING IZNIK

The small historic village of Iznik, located 83 kilometers northeast of Bursa and 60 kilometers southeast of Yalova, is well worth a day trip for surprising sightseeing and shopping. Famous as a political, cultural, religious, and learning center, as well as the production center for unique ceramic tiles, Iznik is a charming and friendly village on the shore of Lake Iznik. You can easily spend a half day strolling its narrow streets, visiting its numerous historic sites, and shopping its many art, antique, and ceramic shops. It's the perfect day trip for both history buffs and travel-shoppers who enjoy small-town ambience.

❑ Iznik is a virtual outdoor museum of monuments and historic sites.

❑ The most important historic sites can be covered within a few hours.

❑ Iznik is especially well known for the art of tile making and its distinctive Iznik designs which were widely used in Ottoman architecture.

❑ The art of tile making disappeared in Iznik during the 18th century. In the early 1990s Iznik's ceramic art tradition was revived.

❑ The town has several ceramic and decorative art shops offering everything from traditional Iznik designs to modern ceramic art designs.

As soon as you arrive in Iznik, be sure to stop at the **tourism office**, which is located directly behind the Church of Hagia Sophia (Museum of St. Sophia) at the very center of town where the two main streets intersect. There you can pick up a very informative map of the town, which includes all the major sites, as well as a detailed booklet on the historic sites of Iznik.

### A RICH HISTORIC TRADITION

With a history dating back to 2500 BC, Iznik is a virtual outdoor museum of monuments and historic sites. Its numerous ruins, buildings, and brick and stone structures represent the remains of flourishing Roman, Byzantine, Seljuk, and Ottoman periods in Iznik's history. It's an especially important town for Christians. Iznik was the site for convening the First and Seventh Eucumenical Councils. The First Council took place in the Senate Palace in 325 AD and resolved for Christians the question once and for all whether Christ was just a normal human being or the son of God. The Seventh Council in 787

AD, which was held in the Nicaea Hagia Sophia, established the dates of Christian holidays, issued the Nicaea Edicts, and ended the previous ban on producing and displaying church icons.

Using the historic map or booklet acquired through the tourist office, you can easily conduct your own self-guided tour of the town. However, given the numerous sites found in and around the town, it may take more than a day to see everything. Consequently, you may want to eliminate some of the many baths and tombs in the area – they all begin looking the same after a while. What you will see are several archeological sites, crumbling buildings, interesting mosaics and murals, a few well preserved churches and mosques, and a museum – all evidence that this was once, indeed several times, an important city in the history of Turkey. Except for the most recent structures of the Ottoman period, most structures you'll see are best classified as "ruins." Iznik's historic sites are organized by these major periods. We included an asterisk (*) next to the most important sites, which can easily be covered within a few hours:

- **Roman Period**
  The Walls*
  Palace of the Senate*
  Monument of Beştaş (Obelisk)
  Antique Theater
  Berber Rock
  Stone Bridge (Taş Köprü)

- **Byzantine Era**
  Church of Hagia Sophia*
  Hypoge (underground tomb)
  Aqueducts*
  Sacred Insect Spring (Ayazma)
  Church of Koimesis
  Church of Hygios Tryphonos
  Church of Hygios Tryphon

- **Ottoman Period**
  Green Mosque*
  Nilufer Hatun Soup Kitchen/
    Iznik Museum*
  Haci Ozbek Mosque
  Seyh Kutbettin Mosque and
    Tomb
  Esref-i Rumi Mosque and Tomb*
  Mahmut Çelebi Mosque*
  Yakup Çelebi Mosque and Tomb
  Mosque and Bath of Orphan Gazi

Suleyman Pasha School of
    Theology\* (converted in 2001
    into an attractive upscale
    ceramic arts shopping center
    with café)
Bath of Ismail Bey
Bath of Murat II
Bath of Murat I
Bath of Konak
Tomb of the Kyrgyz
Tomb of Sari Saltuk
Tomb of Alaaddin-i Musri
Tomb of Abdülvahap Sancaktarî
Tomb of Çandarli Halil Hayrettin
    Pasha
Tomb of Çandarli Ibrahim Pasha
Tomb of Çandarli Kara Halil
    Pasha
Tomb of Eşref Baba
Tomb of Ahiveyn Sultan
Tomb of the Moodies
Arab Mosque (Namazgah)
Excavation Zone of the Iznik Tile
    Ovens\*

## CERAMIC ART AND SHOPPING

While the history of ceramics in Iznik dates to 7000 BC, Iznik is especially well known for the art of tile making and its distinctive Iznik designs which were widely used in Ottoman architecture. Traditional designs included motifs of humans, birds, fish, rabbits, dogs, boats, tulips, carnations, hyacinths, and pomegranates glazed in blue, turquoise, and Edirne red colors. During the 15th to 17th centuries the town became famous for supplying decorative tiles to mosques, palaces, baths, libraries, and pavilions. By the 17th century Iznik had over 300 tile furnaces producing this art form. However, by the end of the 17th century, the art of tile making in Iznik declined dramatically, disappearing altogether in the 18th century. By then, tile production had shifted to the town of Kütahya.

It wasn't until recently (early 1990s) that Iznik's ceramic art tradition was revived. Initially started by a few artisans who came to Iznik and then promoted by the Iznik Teaching and Education Foundation that established the Research Center for Iznik Tile and Ceramics in 1993, Iznik once again is producing traditional tiles and ceramics. Indeed, Iznik might be best characterized as an important old ceramic tile production center which has just come of age as it once again discovers its illustrious past. For visitors, the result is the beginnings of a growing tile and ceramics trade that takes on both traditional and modern forms. In addition to producing decorative tiles, Iznik's new artisans are noted for their production of decorative plates, bowls, cups, mugs, coasters, and oil lamps. While many of the designs and colors are very traditional, representing famous classical patterns which are copied directly from museum publications, several artisans also produce modern creative designs representative of a more contemporary art tradition.

While history buffs can find plenty to do in Iznik, shopping is the real treat for many visitors to Iznik. The town includes several ceramic and decorative art shops that offer everything from traditional Iznik designs to modern ceramic art designs. Many shops will even copy famous designs represented in the Iznik ceramics of museums throughout the world. Since this is a small town, all of the shops can be easily reached on foot within 10 minutes of each other.

As you shop, keep in mind that you will be seeing two different levels of ceramic production. Many glazed titles and bowls are produced as stone quartz. These are much heavier, thicker, and more expensive than the glazed ceramics. They also are more attractive. But the difference in cost can be 10 to 1 – a quartz title that sells for $50 may only cost $5 if produced as a thin ceramic.

You should begin your shopping adventure on the street just behind the tourist office – **S. Demircan Sokak**. Here you will find a few attractive ceramic, gemstone, and antique shops:

❏ **Ebru Seramik:** *S. Demircan Sokak No. 12.* Includes a nice selection of ceramic plates, bowls, vases, and tiles in traditional designs. A few items are nicely framed as wall hangings.

❏ **Gemstones:** *S. Demircan Sokak No. 18/B. Tel. 757-2407. E-mail: verenakaya@yahoo.de.* This newly opened shop offers an attractive collection of geodes, fossilized wood, fossils, silver, jewelry, and old copper cooking pots and vessels.

❏ **Emin Altinölçek:** *S. Demircan Sokak No. 18/B. Tel. 757-1391.* This tiny, and sometimes smoky, antique shop includes an interesting collection of old ceramic tiles, plates, vases, pots, and plates as well as copper pots, small rugs, and collectibles.

Just around the corner (turn left) and up the street is perhaps Iznik's most interesting shopping complex for ceramic art. Opened in September 2001, the **Seramik Çarşisi** (Ceramics Bazaar) is housed in the newly renovated Süleyman Paş Medresesi (Suleyman Pasha School of Theology), one of Iznik's major historic buildings. Once serving as an Ottoman religious school (founded in 1332) with an open courtyard and 11 domed porticoes, today these porticoes have been converted into attractive small ceramic art

shops and a café – the perfect place for lifestyle shopping in Iznik. Browse through each of the shops and discover a different mix of ceramic art, from traditional to modern glazed tiles, plates, bowls, vases, mugs, and figures. The following shops offer some very nice selections of ceramics, each with their own unique designs and colors. Many of the shop owners are artists in residence:

❑ **Gülgün Acarol:** *Tel. 566-5901.* Offers ceramic bowls and plates.

❑ **Senanur Gündoğdu Doku-dur:** *Tel. 757-61-63.* Produces beautifully designed modern decorative ceramic plates and coasters.

❑ **Eşref Eroğlu Workshop:** *Tel. 757-1312.* Offers one of the most attractive selections of signed ceramic tiles – true works of traditional and contemporary art.

❑ **Adil Can:** *Tel. 757-6529.* This is our favorite shop for attractive ceramic bowls, tiles, pots, candle stands, and sculpture. Specializes in producing Byzantium, Seljuckian, and Ottoman style ceramics. Includes interesting stories behind many of the motifs.

❑ **Rasih Kocaman:** *Tel. 757-0679.* Produces small ceramic bowls, trays, and tiles.

This small but intimate complex is a good place to take a coffee or tea break at the restaurant in the center courtyard.

Most of Iznik's remaining ceramics shops are within 10

minutes walking distance of each other. Check out these places in particular:

❑ **Fettah:** *Kiliçaslan Caddesi No. 183/C, Tel. 757-6951.* Located along the main street, this ceramics shop offers a good selection of plates, tiles, coasters, and animal figures. The small duck figures are very appealing.

❑ **Kobalt Çini:** *Kiliçaslan Caddesi No. 201, Tel. 757-0927.* One of the largest ceramics shops in Iznik. Specializes in producing copies of classic handmade Iznik ceramics of the 1480 to 1560 period. Just flip through the beautifully illustrated *Isnit* art book and order any design by number. Since the book is available abroad, you also can order by page or plate number once you return home – just fax the shop your order. Custom orders take about eight weeks to complete and will be shipped by UPS. Offers a nice selection of both glazed ceramic and quartz tiles, bowls, and plates.

❑ **Bardakçi (Old Bazaar):** *Kiliçaslan Caddesi No. 205, Tel. 757-0529.* This small ceramics shop is jam-packed with ceramic plates, coasters, and tiles. Includes a few antique copper pots.

❑ **Ayasofya:** *Atatürk Caddesi, Tel. 757-7690.* Located on the main street adjacent to the Hagia Sophia Museum, this tiny but sprawling indoor and outdoor shop includes ceramic plates, bowls, tiles, and coasters as well as jewelry and antique copper pots. Sign on front of shop reads "St. Sophia Antique Shop Nicaea (Iznik)."

❑ **Kaşi Seramik:** *Ad Lis Karşisi Ziraat Odasi Yani, Tel. 685-5024.* Somewhat difficult to find (one block directly west of Atatürk Caddessi and the Mahmut Çelebi Mosque), this tiny hole-in-the wall ceramic factory is the workshop/studio of ceramic artist Kadir Yilmaz Atölyesi who can be found at his traditional foot-operated wheel producing copies of classic Iznik ceramics. Has a few items on display in this chaotic workshop/studio.

Iznik has a few local nondescript restaurants and small markets located along its two main intersecting streets – Kiliçaslan and Atatürk. For starters, try **Kenan Soup and Grill Saloon** (Atatürk Caddesi, Tel. 757-0235) or **Kar-pi Fast Food** (opposite Saint Sophia on Kiliçaslan, Tel. 757-4224).

# ULUDAĞ

Bursa also is noted as a center for winter sports and winter tourism. If you arrive in Bursa during the winter months (the season runs from December to April) and if snow in the mountains is sufficient for skiing, you may want to visit the nearby winter sports center of Uludağ, which is one of Turkey's premier ski resorts. Located 36 kilometers south of Bursa, Uludağ is a 40-minute drive or a convenient 20-minute cable lift ride from the center of the city. Representing the highest mountain peak in West Anatolia at 2,543 meters, Uludağ is also a National Park because of its rich flora and fauna.

Uludağ is a full service ski resort with seven cable ski lifts and eight cable seat lifts operating in the hotel area. Over 15 hotels in Uludağ accommodate skiers in this alpine village only during the ski season. During other times of the year visitors primarily use this area for trekking, camping, and picnicking. If you enjoy trekking, you may want to pick up a well illustrated book produced by the Bursa Provincial Directorate of Tourism on the flowers of Uludağ: *Alpine Flowers of Uludağ*. It's available through the tourist office in Bursa. The growing season for Uludağ's attractive flowers is during the months of March through August, with the summer months being the most spectacular.

# CUMALIKIZIK

If you're interested in traditional community architecture and spontaneous community development, you'll enjoy a short side trip to the nearby village of Cumalikizik. Located 12 kilometers east of Bursa (three kilometers south of the road that branches off of the Ankara Highway) at the foot of Uludağ Mountain, this village is perhaps the best example of an Ottoman village. The community consists of 350 crumbling three-story houses made of stone, brick, timber, adobe, and red roof tiles, which look like they are about to collapse due to their age and makeshift construction materials. Only 230 of these buildings are occupied by families. Its maze of narrow lanes, many of which lead to dead ends, give you a good idea of community life in a traditional Ottoman village. A very interesting community which also offers numerous photo opportunities.

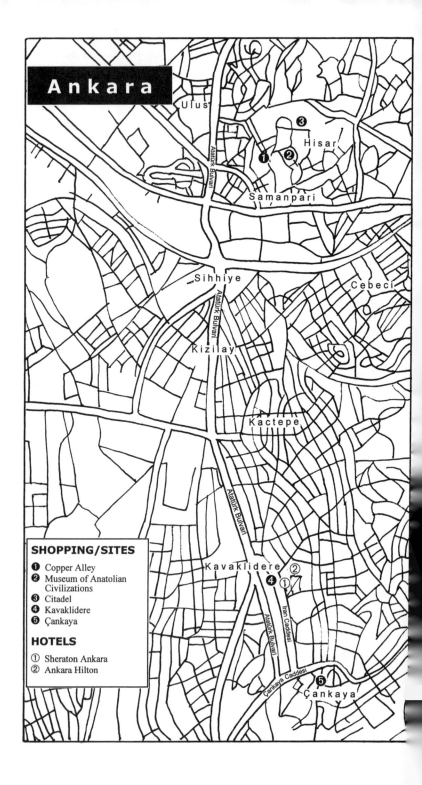

# Ankara

Ulus

Atatürk Bulvarı

**3** Hisar

**1** **2**

Samanpari

Sihhiye

Atatürk Bulvarı

Cebeci

Kizilay

Kactepe

Atatürk Bulvarı

Kavaklidere ②

**4** ①

## SHOPPING/SITES

**1** Copper Alley
**2** Museum of Anatolian
   Civilizations
**3** Citadel
**4** Kavaklidere
**5** Çankaya

## HOTELS

① Sheraton Ankara
② Ankara Hilton

Iran Caddesi

Atatürk Bulvarı

Çankaya Caddesi

**5** Çankaya

# 6

# Ankara

A BUSTLING GOVERNMENT AND BUSINESS CEN-
ter of over 4 million people, Ankara is a thoroughly
modern Western city that comes as a surprise to many
visitors who may be expecting something more Turkish and exotic, especially after visiting Istanbul and
areas east and south of Ankara. A relatively comfortable and
convenient city of wide boulevards, high-rise buildings, five-star
hotels, embassies, Mercedes, trendy restaurants, noisy discos
and nightclubs, crowded shopping centers, and an active artistic
and cultural scene, Ankara is the type of city some travelers like
to develop a negative attitude toward and disparage as being
too modern. Indeed, many visitors bypass Ankara altogether or
at best stop here overnight on their way to or from Cappadocia.
Few visitors spend more than a day in Ankara, which we find
unfortunate, especially after discovering many of Ankara's

hidden treasures and pleasures overlooked by other visitors who should know better.

---

## NOT TO BE MISSED

If you are a history and culture buff in search of more museums and monuments to explore and prefer small quaint towns and villages to large energetic metropolitan areas of fast food restaurants and shopping centers, Ankara may well disappoint you. That would be an unfortunate misreading of Turkish history and this city. For Ankara is very important to the contemporary history of Turkey, a city literally forged out of a backwater town to become the symbol of a newly independent and democratic Turkish republic that made a clean cut with many negative aspects of its past. Indeed, unlike Istanbul, which tends to symbolize a checkered past, Ankara represents the future – what Turkey wants to become, which is modern, Western, and secular, despite its long history of factional conflict, authoritarian rule, and potential religious (Islamic) extremism.

❑ Ankara is a thoroughly modern city that comes as a surprise to many visitors who expected a more Turkish and exotic place.

❑ Ankara is very important to the contemporary history of Turkey.

❑ Ankara deserves more than a perfunctory one-day stop on the way to somewhere else in Turkey.

❑ Ankara has a population of 4 million – up from less than 30,000 in 1923, the year Turkey became a republic.

But if you enjoy shopping, dining, people watching, and fine museums, Ankara deserves more than a perfunctory one-day stop on the way to somewhere else in Turkey. Full of interesting surprises for travel-shoppers, Ankara deserves at least a two- to three-day visit.

Like Washington, DC is the city of George Washington, Ankara is the city of Turkey's most illustrious founding father and national hero, Mustafa Kemal Atatürk. Forged with blood, sweat, and tears, Ankara is the symbol of the modern Turkish state – everything that democratic and secular Turkey would like to be if only it could realize its national dreams of economic growth and prosperity.

---

## CENTRAL ANATOLIA

Ankara lies on a plain in the heart of the culturally rich Central Anatolia region, an area that traces its ancient origins to the Bronze Age and the Hatti civilization. A center for numerous civilizations and various conquerors, this area was subsequently dominated by the Hittites, Phrygians, Lydians, Persians, Gallatians, Romans, Byzantines, Seljuk Turks, and Ottomans. These groups are well represented in Ankara's wonderful Anatolian Civilizations Museum, a "must visit" museum for all visitors to Turkey. On October 13, 1923, Mustafa Kemal Atatürk declared Ankara, a backwater town of fewer than 30,000 people, to be the capital of the newly established Republic of Turkey. Clearly a break with its Ottoman past and liberated from the decadence and corruption of Istanbul, Ankara soon symbolized a new democratic and secular Turkey. The city has grown remarkably over the past 80 years as a political, governmental, and business center. It's a great place from which to explore the many treasures and pleasures of the Anatolia region.

## GETTING TO KNOW YOU

Ankara is located 450 kilometers southeast of Istanbul. You can easily drive from Istanbul or Bursa to Ankara in three to four hours on good surfaced roads. The drive is somewhat boring given the relatively flat terrain, although the heavy and often challenging truck traffic will keep you alert. Ankara also is connected to Istanbul by several daily flights. A few international flights from New York City and European cities service Ankara. The train also connects Ankara with Istanbul, which takes from seven to nine hours. Driving to Ankara is especially convenient given the good roads and the relatively spread out Cappadocia area that will most likely be next on your travel agenda.

Once you arrive in Ankara, try to pick up copies of these two English language publications which are available at major hotels (ask at the front desk):

> *Ankara The Guide*
> *Ankara: The Professional's Business Reference*

You also can access information about Ankara on these two websites:

- **Tourism Turkey**     www.tourismturkey.org
- **The Turkey Guide**   www.turkeyguide.com

Ankara is a large and sprawling city with lots of parks, monuments, and uninspired government buildings. However, it often feels like a small and compact city compared to Istanbul. It has the feel of a youthful city with its many students, young professionals, chic boutiques, trendy restaurants, entertainment establishments, and vibrant cultural and artistic life.

The city includes both new and old sections, and has a basic north-south orientation. The northern section, or old city, is located on a hill which is accented by the old Citadel or fortress overlooking the city. The southern section, or new city, lies at the foot of the hill. This area includes wide boulevards, parks, embassies, high-rise buildings, major hotels, and bustling shopping centers, street shops, and restaurants. The major area here of interest to visitors is called **Kavaklidere**. This is where the top hotels, shops, and restaurants are found in the newer part of the city. Farther south is the **Çankaya** area with its many shops and restaurants.

**Atatürk Bulvari**, which runs north to south, connects Kavaklidere with the old city in the north.

Centered around the **Ulus** or **Samanpazari** (name used by Ankarites) area and the Citadel (*hisar*), the old city includes narrow and hilly streets and lanes, bazaars, shops, museums, mosques, and old houses. This area also boasts some excellent restaurants with lovely views of the city.

Most visitors focus their activities in and around the Kavaklidere, Çankaya, and Ulus areas. Indeed, the city's best hotels, restaurants, and shops are found in Kavaklidere and Çankaya neighborhoods. Most major sightseeing, as well as bazaar-style shopping, is found near the Citadel in Samanpazari (Ulus).

❑ Ankara has the feel of a youthful city with its many students, young professionals, chic boutiques, trendy restaurants, entertainment establishments and vibrant cultural and artistic life.

❑ Ankara includes both new and old sections as well as has a basic north-south orientation.

❑ Kavaklidere and Çankaya are the city's new major shopping areas.

❑ Most major sightseeing and bazaar-style shopping is found near the Citadel in Samanpazari (Ulus).

Driving in Ankara can be difficult, especially in the old city with its many narrow streets and limited parking facilities. Elsewhere in the city you often encounter confusing one-way streets and signage problems. Consequently, you may want to get around the city with taxis rather than hassle with the one-way streets, limited parking, and difficult signage. Going from Kavaklidere in the south to Ulus in the north by car takes about 20 minutes, depending on traffic conditions.

We recommend staying in the Kavaklidere area for both comfort and convenience. Major five-star hotels such as the Sheraton and Hilton are conveniently located in the middle of this major shopping, dining, and entertainment area. You can

easily walk from your hotel to the nearby shops and restaurants. In the evening this area becomes very crowded with
vehicles and pedestrians.

## SHOPPING ANKARA

While Ankara is by no means a shopper's paradise, it does offer
many nice items in a much less touristed environment than
most places in Turkey. In fact, shopping is one of Ankara's best
kept secrets largely overlooked by many tourists who tend to
quickly pass through Ankara. Since few tourists shop in Ankara,
prices and selections tend to be very good in Ankara because of
the city's alternative clientele. The major international shoppers
here tend to be embassy personnel who know where to find
quality items at bargain prices. As
a result, prices in Ankara for similar items found in Istanbul tend to
be less expensive and bargaining
less pronounced than in Istanbul.
Quality also tends to be very good
in Ankara given the demanding
tastes of Ankara's relatively sophisticated clientele.

❏ You may want to get around
the city with taxis rather
than hassle with the one-
way streets, limited parking,
and difficult signage.

❏ Shopping is one of Ankara's
best kept secrets largely
overlooked by many tourists
who tend to quickly pass
through this city.

You can easily spend two days
shopping Ankara for unique treasures. While shops in Ankara offer
many familiar items found elsewhere in Turkey, the city is especially noted for its quality antiques,
copper goods, rugs, handicrafts,
and art. You'll also find several
unique items in the shops of Ankara that are not readily available

❏ Prices in Ankara for similar
items found in Istanbul tend
to be less expensive and bargaining less pronounced
here than in Istanbul.

❏ Ankara is one of the best
places in Turkey to shop for
antiques and collectibles –
both Turkish and European.

in Istanbul, especially European antiques and collectibles left
behind by embassy personnel and which especially appeal to
Ankara's large expat community. In fact, Ankara is one of the
best places in Turkey to shop for antiques and collectibles –
both Turkish and European.

### SOUTHERN ANKARA

Assuming you are staying in the Kavaklidere area, you may
want to start your shopping adventure at the three-story
upscale **Karum Shopping Center** adjacent to the Sheraton
Hotel on Iran Caddesi Karum and Merkezi. Here you'll find

several quality clothing, accessory, and jewelry shops along with restaurants and pastry shops. **Vakko** (Tel. 468-3505), for example, has a very nice small men's and women's boutique in this shopping center. If you leave the shopping center at the Iran Caddesi entrance, turn right onto **Iran Caddesi** and head north which changes its name to **Tunali Hilmi Caddesi**. Here you'll find numerous upscale shops along both sides of the streets. The nearby Hilton Hotel, along the side street Tahran Caddesi (No. 12), has a small shopping arcade that includes branch shops of the Istanbul-based fine jeweler **Urart** (Tel. 426-0700) and art and antique dealer **Koleksiyon Auction House** (Tel. 467-7158). If you continue along the main street, Iran Caddesi/Tunali Hilmi Caddesi, you'll come to several clothing, leather, and jewelry shops as well as several restaurants, cafes, and fast food establishments. Look for **Derimod** (Iran Caddesi No. 13, Tel. 427-0270) for top quality leather coats, jackets, shoes, and handbags and **Beymen** (Iran Caddesi No. 7, Tel. 468-1242) for excellent quality and fashionable men's and women's clothing, shoes, and accessories. **Kugulu Pasaji** (Tunali Hilmi Caddesi 18) is a small three-story shopping mall specializing in gold and silver shops. One of the most unique shops in this area is **Çeşni** (Tunali Hilmi Caddesi No. 88 in the Ertuğ Pasaji, Tel./Fax 426-5787) with its wonderful collection of framed antique embroidery pieces, paintings, and ceramics. Somewhat difficult to locate on the second floor of a small shopping center, it's well worth finding this shop.

Further south of the Kavaklidere area is the more residential Çankaya area. The main and very long shopping street here is **Cinnah Caddesi**. Look for antique, carpet, home decorative, furniture, and art shops here. Our favorite here is **Atika** (Cinnah Caddesi No. 43/B, Tel. 438-5366) which offers good quality antiques, pottery, carpets, and contemporary art in its small two-level shop. Just off the main street, **Turkuvaz Sanat Galerisi** (Cinnah Caddesi, Kirkpinar Sokak No. 5/A, Tel. 439-1479, website: www.turkuvazart.com) includes art exhibitions of top Turkish painters. The **American Cultural Center** (Cinnah Caddesi No. 20, Tel. 426-2648) has frequent art exhibitions of local artists. **Bulvar Hali** (Cinnah Caddesi No. 20/A, Tel. 466-5355) offers a large selection of quality carpets from Turkey, especially the Adiyaman area in eastern Turkey, and from Iran, Nepal, and China. **Atakule Tower** includes a shopping mall.

Most other shopping in southern Ankara takes place along in **Kizilay** along Atatürk Bulvari. For example, look for **Candan Jeweller** (Buyuk Carsi No. 67/18 Atatürk Bulvari), popular with U.S. Embassy personnel, for a large selection of jewelry, including cartouches and Arabic necklaces. The elegant and fashionable **Vakko** department store (Atatürk Bulvari No. 113, Tel. 425-2285) is located just south of Kizilay in Bakanliklar.

## NORTHERN ANKARA AND COPPER ALLEY

Perched on top of a hill, Old Ankara in the Ulus or Samanpazari (haymarket) area is especially noted for its 7th century citadel, mosques, museums, and the Copper Alley, the American nickname for **Salman Sokak**. This is a fun place to shop. Indeed, you can easily spend a half day exploring Copper Alley and its adjacent shopping streets which overflow with copper goods, antiques, furniture, handicrafts, carpets, and food stuffs. An area that begs to be explored on foot and with lots of time on your hands, you're sure to find some unique gifts and treasures along the way. This is
the favorite shopping area for many local embassy personnel and their out-of-town friends. Tour groups also stop here briefly as they combine shopping with a visits to nearby museums and mosques.

Copper Alley was once the old city's major commercial and shopping district. Situated at the foot of the citadel walls and immediately to the south of the Museum of Anatolian Civilizations, this narrow and crowded street is lined with numerous small shops offering a wide range of goods for local residents – bedding, clothing, rubber boots, hardware, housewares, mouse traps, and copper pots – as well as antiques, wrought iron furniture, fabrics, carpets, and lanterns. You can spend a couple of hours just poking around the various shops along this street. Many of the shops also make products on their premises, especially copper pots and plates which you'll hear craftsmen incessantly pounding. Some of the most interesting shops here include: **Düven** (Salman Sokak Nos. 1/J and 11/E, Tel. 310-2420) for a wide selection of fabrics, pillows, carpets, clocks, candle holders, lights, and antique furniture; **Ferro Klasik** (Salman Sokak No. 6/B, Tel. 324-1176) for custom-made wrought iron furniture, lamps, candle holders, fireplace grilles and accessories, and hardware; **Erol Erzurumlu** (Salman Sokak No. 46, Tel. 310-6528) for a unique collection of old and new copper pots; and **Güzel Iş**

(Salman Sokak No. 12 ve Prinç Sokak, Tel. 324-1436) for copper pots, plates, and bowls.

But Salman Sokak is only one of several shopping streets in this interesting commercial and market area. Be sure to explore three adjacent streets: Can Sokak, Atpazari, and Atpazari Yokuşu. **Can Sokak** is really the main commercial street in this area. Several arts, crafts, antique, and carpet shops line both sides of this cobblestone street. Many are good sources for gift items and collections. Start at the foot of this street by visiting two shops: **Ulus Galeri** (Can Sokak No. 6/A, Tel. 311-3429) for a large selection of silver boxes, copper pots, knives, glassware, inlaid tables and chests, guns, ceramics, old copper and brass plates, bowls, and pipes; and **A & Z Bazaar** (Can Sokak No. 6/C, Tel. 310-1393) with its two floors of painted copper products, glass houkas (waterpipes), meerschaum pipes, handmade colored glass from Iran, Kütahya pottery, and old professional black and white photos taken by the owner, M. Atilla Torun. Other shops worth visiting here include: **Kartal Bakircilik** for copper pots, trays, and bowls; **Ekrem Torun** (Can Sokak No. 9/16, Tel. 324-3189) for two adjacent shops filled with European antiques, bronze statues, furniture, lamps, chandeliers, clocks, and mirrors; and **Adem Baba** (Can Sokak No. 11/E, Tel. 331-1288) for an excellent selection of antique furniture, paintings, glassware, silver serving pieces, French clocks, porcelain German stoves, carpets, and kilims (upstairs). The remaining shops along Can Sokak are primarily carpet and kilim shops. If you turn left at the end of this street, you'll be on Atpazari Caddesi and heading for the covered Spice Market. One of the best shops on this street is **Antikaci Yalçin** (Atpazari Caddesi No. 26/B, Tel. 309-2389) with its nice collection of paintings, Moroccan ceramic pots, Russian icons, furniture, and silver items from Iraq, and carpets (upstairs). If you turn left into a crowded lane that goes downhill, you'll pass several small shops selling hardware, spices, and sheepskins along Atpazari Yokuşu which also is known as "Hardware and Spice Alley." On the left look for **Idol Antik** (Atpazari Yokuşu No. 60, Tel. 311-1858) an attractive combination home decorative and carpet shop that also has a café on the top floor overlooking the street. Look for lamps, furniture, large candles, and carpets here.

## DEPARTMENT STORES AND MARKETS

As a relatively upscale shopping city, Ankara has several modern shopping malls. One of the most popular shopping centers is the three-level **Karum Iş Merkezi** (Iran Caddesi) which is located adjacent to the Sheraton Hotel in Kavaklidere. The 125-meter high-rise Atakule Tower (in Çankaya) offers shopping opportunities as well as a revolving restaurant, nightclubs, and an observation area. The **Gima** department store is located in Kizilay near the major intersection of Gazi Kemal Bulvari and Atatürk Bulvari.

Ankara also has several local markets which can be fun to explore. The largest one is located near Abdi Ipekçi Park in Sihhiye and is open on Wednesdays and Saturdays from dawn to dusk. **Ankara Hali** (in Ulus) is open daily. **Maltepe Pazari** (near the Maltepe Mosque) is open on Mondays. **Bahçelievler Pazari** (at 10 Sokak near Azerbaycan Caddesi in Bahçelievler) is open on Fridays.

---

## BEST OF THE BEST

While Ankara has many good quality art, antique, handicraft, home decorative, copper, and carpet shops, we found the following places to be particularly attractive.

### ANTIQUES

❏ **Atika:** *Cinnah Caddesi No. 43/B 06680 Çankaya, Tel. 438-5366.* Popular with embassy personnel, this eclectic antique and home decorative shop offers a limited but nice selection of old pottery, ceramic figures, Konya wood mortars, chests, carpets, and kilims. It also includes some new ceramic pieces. The lower level is primarily devoted to carpets and kilims, although you may find some nice chests and ceramic pots here. Since this shop does not pack and ship nor take credit cards, you'll need to take your purchases with you and pay cash.

❏ **Adem Baba:** *Can Sokak No. 11/E, Samanpazari, Tel. 331-1288.* Especially popular with embassy personnel, this well established antique and carpet shop offers a good collection of furniture, paintings, glassware, silver serving pieces, French clocks, and porcelain German stoves. The upstairs area includes carpets and kilims. This shop also operates a home decorative and furniture shop on Copper Alley, Düven (see below). A ceramic pot we found here for US$300 was selling for US$1,000 in a major antique shop in Istanbul.

❏ **Antikaci Yalçin:** *Atpazari Caddesi No. 26/B, Tel. 309-2389.* A very different shop for the area, Antikaci Yalçin includes an interesting selection of paintings, Moroccan ceramic pots, Russian icons, furniture, and antique silver from Iraq. The upper floor includes a good collection of carpets and kilims.

### CARPETS AND KILIMS

❏ **Hilmi's Carpet and Kilim:** *Denizciler Caddesi, Yapincak Sokak No. 8/A, Tel. 312-3463.* Popular with embassy personnel, this shop offers a good selection of carpets and kilims as well as grain bags and kilim pillow covers.

❏ **Gallery "Z":** *Atpazari Sokak No. 23, Tel. 312-2130.* English-speaking owners Fatma and Yetki Tuna offer one of the best selections of Santa kilims in Turkey. Good quality carpets and kilims as well as excellent service.

### EMBROIDERY AND PAINTINGS

❏ **Çeşni:** *Tunali Hilmi Caddesi, Ertug Pasaji 88/44, Kavaklidere, Tel./Fax 426-5787. E-mail: cesnituk@hotmail.com.* This small ceramics and textile shop is a real find in Ankara as well as

in all of Turkey. Located on the second floor of a nondescript shopping center (may be difficult to find, but do persist), the second room of this shop is jam-packed with numerous restored and framed pieces of antique Ottoman embroideries, many made of silk with gold and silver threads, which make lovely wall displays. They are part of the owner's (Mr. Alper Yurdemi) rare collection of over 800 old embroideries. Many are taken from royal garments, napkins, runners, tablecloths, pillows, and baby blankets. Since most of the old royal garments are beyond repair, he has preserved this textile and art form by creating hundreds of small to medium-sized framed displays of textile fragments. Indeed, you can own remnants of the old Ottoman Empire by purchasing these wonderful embroideries. Each has a unique story, with great symbolism, which Alper enthusiastically shares with his customers. The pieces are very reasonably priced – most cost US$30 to US$80 – considering they are already double-matted and framed. One of our favorite and inexpensive purchases in Turkey, our black and silver antique embroidered fragment from Çeşni is one of our precious gallery additions. For more information on Alper's collection and this collectible art form, contact Alper by email and ask him to email you a copy of an English-language article that appeared in the *Turkish Daily News* entitled "Tracing Turkey's Ottoman Legacy Through Embroidery." He'll send it to you as an email attachment. This is a good article for better understanding this art form as well as Çeşni.

## FURNITURE AND HOME DECORATIVE ITEMS

❑ **Düven:** *Salman Sokak Nos. 1/J and 11/E, Samanpazari, Tel. 310-2420.* Also owned by the nearby Adem Baba (see above under Antiques), this attractive combination home decorative, furniture, antique, and accessory shop includes a good selection of fabrics, pillows, carpets, clocks, candle holders, lights, and antique furniture.

❑ **Ferro Klasik:** *Salman Sokak No. 6/B, Samanpazari, Tel. 324-1176 or Fax 310-5228.* A very different shop for the neighborhood, this one produces attractively designed wrought iron patio furniture, lamps, candle holders, fireplace grilles and accessories, hardware, staircase railings, chandeliers, tables, doors, window bars, gates, and anything else you might think appropriate for this medium. This is an excellent source for custom-designed work. The shop includes a very large selection of items in two adjacent shops. However, be sure to pick up a copy of their catalog. They are experienced in shipping abroad.

## COPPER POTS

❑ **Erol Erzurumlu:** *Salman Sokak No. 46, Samanpazari, Tel. 310-6528.* This well established and popular shop includes a unique collection of antique copper pots, lights, and collapsible lanterns. The upstairs area contains carpets and kilims, along with many old and new copper pots.

## HANDICRAFTS

❑ **Dösim:** *Mithatpaşa Kültür Ülünleri Satiş Mağazasi, Mithat-paşa Caddesi No. 18, Tel. 309-4953.* This government-operated handicraft emporium includes a nice collection of copper, silver, and bronze reproductions, rugs, wood boxes, ceramics, jewelry, handbags, leather puppets, instruments, and music CDs. Includes a large book section, mainly in Turkish, on second floor.

## ACCOMMODATIONS

Ankara has two five-star hotels that are centrally located in the Kavaklidere area near the embassies. Both are very convenient for shopping, dining, and entertainment:

❑ **Sheraton Ankara Hotel and Towers:** *Noktali Sokak, Kavaklidere, 06700 Ankara, Turkey, Tel. (90-312) 468-5454, Fax (90-312) 467-1136, Toll-free from U.S. or Canada: (800) 325-3535. Website: www.sheraton.com.* Centrally located in downtown Ankara near businesses, government offices and embassies and a few minutes walk up the hill from the Hilton, the Sheraton's round tower's light-filled atrium lobby is a pleasant place to meet friends, and the mezzanine lounge features an art gallery. 307 guestrooms and suites are decorated in soft, muted colors and hung with local prints. 16 Smart Rooms are available. Guestrooms offer marble bathrooms and the level of luxury visitors expect from Sheraton. Tower Rooms and Club Rooms provide additional services and amenities. There are non-smoking rooms and Smart Rooms available. *Le Jardin Restaurant* is available for all-day dining and in the summer *La Jardin Terrace Grill* is also open. *L'angoletto* offers Italian cuisine and also serves on the terrace during the summer months. The *Vienna Café* and *Godiva Shop* offer tasty delicacies. The enclosed Karum shopping mall is just a few steps down the hill adjacent to the Sheraton. A jeweler, *Storck's Jewellery* is located on the lobby level. Health/Fitness Center (includes roof-top tennis court, two squash courts, heated outdoor swimming pool, sauna, jacuzzi and steam bath); Business Center; Conference/Banquet Facilities.

❑ **Ankara Hilton:** *Tahran Caddesi No. 12, Kavaklidere, 06700 Ankara, Turkey, Tel. (90-312) 468-2888, Fax (90-312) 468-0909, Toll-free from U.S. & Canada (800-445-8667). Website:*

*www.hilton.com. E-mail: ankhitwsal@hilton.com.* Located near the center of the city, close to businesses, government offices, and embassies, the Hilton (and the Sheraton, which is just a short walk up the hill) offers a convenient location and a brand name that visitors recognize. The 323 guestrooms and suites offer the amenities expected from Hilton including mini-bar, electronic door locks, laptop telephone connections, as well as non-smoking rooms and guestrooms for persons with disabilities. Executive Floors offer additional services and amenities including a separate lounge. Hhonors Floors. The *Greenhouse* is a casual dining venue serving both a la carte and buffet throughout the day, and offers a BBQ on the terrace in the summer. Try *Marco Polo* for fine continental dining or the *Lobby Lounge & Bar* for afternoon tea, cocktails and light snacks with live music in the evenings. Health Club; Business Center; Conference/ Banquet Facilities.

# RESTAURANTS

Ankara offers a good range of Turkish and international restaurants. Some of the best include:

❏ **Kale Washington:** *Doyran Sokak No. 5-7, Ulus/Samanpazari, Tel. 311-4344. Open daily, 12noon to 2pm and 6:30pm - 11pm.* If you take a taxi, tell the driver to take you to "Ankara Kalesi." Located near the arched entrance to the old fortress and set in an old Ottoman house surrounded by a garden, this popular restaurant serves excellent French, Turkish, and Russian cuisine with wonderful views of the city. Try the excellent Sac Kuvarma, a unique dish served in a flat copper dish consisting of braised tips of lamb sauteed with tomatoes, onions, and spices.

❏ **Mangla Ocakbasi:** *Kuloglu Sokak No. 29, Cankaya, Tel. 440-0959. Open daily, 12noon - 11pm.* Located near the Russian Eembassy, this noted restaurant serves southeastern-style Turkish cuisine. Especially famous for their large selection of mezes and grilled kebabs – chicken, beef, and lamb.

❏ **Marco Polo:** *Hilton Hotel, Tahran Caddesi No. 12 Kavaklidere, Tel. 468-2800. Open daily for dinner only.* One of Ankara's best continental fine dining restaurants. Serves an excellent range of international dishes, from steaks to seafood, in an elegant setting.

❑ **Amisos:** *Filisten Sokak No. 28, Gazi Osman Paşa, Tel. 446-6098. Open daily for both lunch and dinner.* Housed in a restored villa, this fine dining restaurant serves both Turkish and international cuisine. Try the seafood dishes. Includes live piano music. During the summer months, ask for a table outside in the garden area.

❑ **Haciç Arif Bey Kebabçisi:** *Güniz Sokak No. 48, Kavaklidere, Tel. 467-0067. Open daily, 12noon - 11pm.* Located in a two-story building with a garden, this traditional kebab house serves an excellent range of grilled meats. Also try their popular baklava.

❑ **La Jardin:** *Sheraton Ankara, Noktali Sokak, Kavaklidere, Tel. 468-5454.* Serves an excellent Turkish and international buffet accompanied by live piano and violin music. Sunday brunch (11:30am - 4pm) is especially popular.

❑ **Yakamoz Diplomat Fish Restaurant:** *Turan Güneş Bulvari No. 249, Sokak 77/7Oran, Tel. 439-5050. Open daily, 12noon to midnight.* Serves excellent fish dishes. Try the "diplomat specialties."

❑ **Schnitzel:** *Mega Residence Hotel, Tahran Caddesi No.5, Kavaklidere, Tel. 468-5400. Open daily, 12noon to 11pm.* Offers Austrian cuisine accompanied by an excellent wine list and live cigan music nightly. Dine on the popular patio during the summer.

❑ **Budak Alti Café:** *Budah Sokak No. 5, Gaziosmanpaşa, Tel. 427-8545. Open daily 9am - midnight.* Serves excellent Turkish dishes. Offers a very popular Sunday brunch. A favorite of diplomatic personnel who live and work in this area.

❑ **Urfali Haci Mehmet:** *Iran Caddesi No. 11/A, Kuğulu Park Karşisi Kavaklidere, Tel. 466-5904.* Centrally located in the city's upscale shopping district, this relatively inexpensive restaurant serves excellent kebabs. Includes both inside and outside (sidewalk) dining areas. Offers picture menus and good service.

❑ **Mest:** *Attar Sokak No. 10, Gaziosmanpasa (GOP), Tel. 468-0743. Open daily except Sunday, 12noon - midnight.* A favorite of embassy personnel, this restaurant serves excellent Italian and continental cuisine.

❑ **El Torito:** *Billlur Sokak No. 117, Kavaklidere, Tel. 468-6980. Open daily, 11:30am - 1am.* Located near the Hilton Hotel, this popular Tex Mex restaurant serves excellent dishes in a nice setting. A favorite of both Turks and foreigners.

## SEEING THE SITES

Ankara is a city of many museums and monuments, several of which honor Turkey's national hero and father of the Republic, Kemal Atatürk.

❑ **Anatolian Civilizations Museum (Ankara Anadolu Medeniyetleri Müesi):** *Hisarparki Sokak, Hisar-Ulus (near Ankara Castle), Tel. 324-3160. Open 8:30am - 12:30pm and 1:30 - 5:30pm. Closed on Mondays during the winter.* This is the major sightseeing attraction in Ankara for anyone interested in ancient Turkish history. Housed in two 15th century buildings – a caravanseri (overnight rest stop for caravans) and a bedesten (covered bazaar) – the museum includes an intriguing collection of Paleolithic, Neolithic, Hatti, Hittite, and Urartian artifacts. Includes a nice collection of pottery, cave paintings, bronzes, jewelry, and stone statues and panels displayed over two floors. Surrounded by lovely grounds and within walking distance of Copper Alley.

❑ **Atatürk's Mausoleum and Museum (Anitkabir):** *Anit Caddesi, Tandoğan, Tel. 231-7975. Open Tuesday through Sunday from 9am to 5pm (4pm in the winter).* Known as Anitkabir, this national shrine complex is built on a hill overlooking the city. A massive mausoleum of Turkey's great hero, Atatürk, it draws crowds from all over Turkey who come here to pay respects to the man who had such a tremendous impact on modern-day Turkey. Includes a small museum that houses artifacts of Atatürk, three of his cars, and information on the construction of the tomb.

❑ **Ethnographical Museum (Etnografya Müzesi):** *Turkocaği Sokak Sihhiye (above Opera Square), Tel. 311-3007. Open Tuesday to Sunday, 8:30am - 12:30pm and 1:30 - 5:30pm (5pm in winter).* Showcases a unique collection of artifacts from the Selçuk period. Includes musical instruments, weapons, tools, and tiles. Also displays Turkish costumes and embroidery as well as artifacts of the dervish sect.

If time permits and you enjoy museums, consider visiting the following museums:

❑ **Antatük's House Museum at Atatürk's Forest Farm:** *Gazi Mahallesi, Tel. 211-0170. Open Sunday, Tuesday, Wednesday, and Saturday, 9am - 12noon and 1:30 - 5:30pm.*

❑ **Atatürk Cultural Center Museum:** *Hipodrom, Ulus, Tel. 342-1010. Open daily, 9am - 5pm.*

❑ **Gordion Museum:** *Yassihoyuk Village, Polatli, Tel. 638-2188. Open Tuesday to Sunday, 8:30am - 5:30pm.*

❑ **Köşk Museum (Atatürk's House):** *Located on the grounds of the Presidential Palace, Çankaya Caddesi, Tel. 427-4330. Open Sundays, religious, and national holidays, 1:30 - 5pm.*

❑ **Meteorological Museum:** *Sanatoryum Caddesi, Kalaba, Tel. 359-7545. Open weekdays, 9am-noon and 1-5pm.*

❑ **Museum of Liberation (Independence War Museum):** *I TBMM, Cumhuriyet Caddesi, Ulus, Tel. 310-5361. Open Tuesday to Sunday, 9am - 5pm.*

❑ **Museum of the Republic:** *II TBMM Binasi, Tel. 311-0473. Open Tuesday to Sunday, 9am - 5pm.*

❑ **Natural History Museum:** *Grounds of the Mineral Research and Exploration Institute, Eskişehir Highway. Open daily, 9am - 5pm.*

❑ **Painting and Sculpture Museum:** *Next to the Ethnographical Museum above Opera Square, Tel. 310-3091. Open daily, 8:30am - 12:30pm and 1:30 - 5:30pm (closed Mondays in the winter).*

❑ **Railroad Museum:** *T.C.D.D. Ankara Gar (Railroad Station). Open Tuesday to Sunday, 8:30am - 12noon and 1:30 - 5:30pm.*

❑ **The Toy Museum:** *Faculty of Education Science, Ankara University, Tel. 431-8840, ext. 329. Open Wednesday and Friday, 10am - 5pm.*

Other interesting places to visit in Ankara include the following temples, mosques, monuments, and baths:

❑ **The Temple of Augustus and Rome:** *Next to Haci Bayram Mosque, Ulus.*

❑ **Haci Bayram Mosque (Haci Bayram Camii):** *Just off of Hükümet Caddesi, Ulus.*

❑ **Kocatepe Mosque (Kocatepe Camii):** *Via Olgunlar Sokağ, Kocatepe.* One of the world's largest mosques.

❑ **Lion's Den Mosque (Aslanhane Camii):** *Close to the entrance of the Citadel, near Kadife Sokak.*

❑ **Yeni Mosque (Cenah Ahmet Paşa Camii):** *East of the Citadel at Ulucanlar Caddesi and Çankiri Sokak.*

❑ **Jülyanüs Sütunu (Column of Julian):** *Hükümet Meydani, northeast of Ulus Meydani.*

## ENJOYING YOUR STAY

After shopping, dining, and sightseeing, Ankara still has a lot to offer visitors. Its relatively young, well educated, professional, and sophisticated population supports the **Presidential Symphony Orchestra**, the **State Opera and Ballet**, and many other artistic and cultural groups and activities.

Ankara's bar, pub, disco, and nightclub scenes tend to be concentrated in the Çankaya area which is also popular with diplomatic personnel. Many of these places stay open until 2, 3, or 4am. For a great view of the city at night, visit the **Atakule Ufo Café-Bar** (Atakule Çankaya, Tel. 440-8818, open until 3am) at the top of the Atakule Tower and the chic **Cabare** club on the second floor of the Atakule Tower. Ankara has its own **Hard Rock Cafe** (Simon Bolivar Caddesi, Duyu Sokok No. 2, Yildiz, Tel. 440-6006). Popular night spots include: **Club House Bar** (Sheraton Hotel and Towers, Kavaklidere, Tel. 468-5454); **Club So** (Turan Güneş Bulvari No. 274 Oran, Tel. 491-1250); **Home Club** (Esat Caddesi No. 37 Küçük Esat, Tel. 424-0400); and **Replik** (Çevre Sokak No. 7/B, Çankaya, Tel. 427-0300).

If you are visiting Ankara during March, April, or May, you may have an opportunity to join in the various arts and music festivals: **International Film Day** (March) and **Sevad Canap International Arts and Music Festival** (April and May).

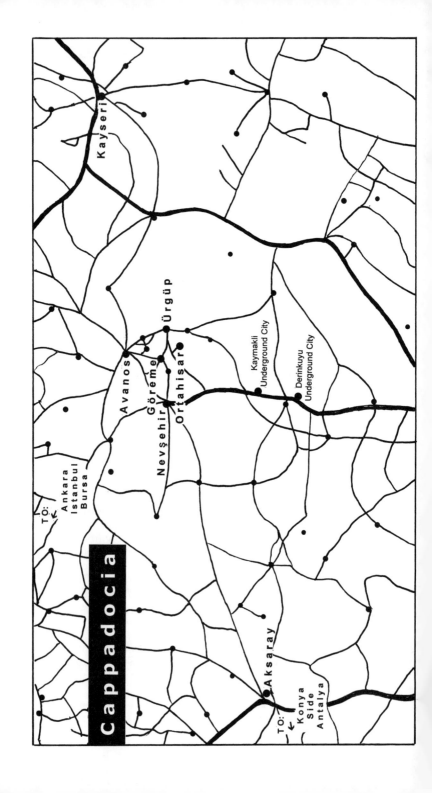

**Cappadocia**

Kayseri

Ürgüp

Avanos

Göreme

Ortahisar

Nevşehir

Kaymaklı Underground City

Derinkuyu Underground City

TO:
Ankara
Istanbul
Bursa

Aksaray

TO:
Konya
Side
Antalya

# 7

# Cappadocia and Konya

FEW WORDS EVER DO THIS PLACE JUSTICE. RE-presenting one of the world's most uniquely eroded volcanic landscapes, much of the area known as Cappadocia is characterized by a bizarre, surreal, and sensual landscape of "fairy chimneys" and stone phallic outcrops, strewn throughout valleys and punctuating hills, that look like they belong on another planet or in a child's play set. Within and beneath many of these chimneys lie centuries-old subterranean cities, cavernous fresco-filled monastic complexes of churches and chapels, and playful-looking homes, rooms, windows, and porticos. Best viewed in such places as Göreme and Zelve (churches, chapels, and homes), Ürgüp (hotels), and Kaymakli (underground cities), Cappadocia is a wonder to behold. It's also a surprisingly good place to shop for rugs, pottery, antiques, and handicrafts, especially in the towns of

Ürgüp (carpets, kilims, and antiques), Avanos (pottery, ceramics, and rugs), and Ortahisar (antiques and collectibles).

Whether you are exploring the chimneys and tunnels, shopping for local treasures, taking photos, or just absorbing the ambience, Cappadocia will undoubtedly become one of your most interesting and memorable travel experiences in Turkey. Viewed from the comfort of a hot air balloon or through slightly arduous, and later aching, climbing, this is simply a fabulous area to visit. Whatever you do, make sure you include Cappadocia in your travel and shopping plans. From five-star luxury travelers to backpackers, Cappadocia never disappoints with its endless treasures and pleasures.

## WELCOME TO CAPPADOCIA

Located within a three-hour drive southeast of Ankara, the area known as Cappadocia is some 220 kilometers east to west and 180 kilometers north to south. Within this area lie several small towns, settlements, historic sites, and wondrous landscapes that have become havens for travelers interested in exploring this region's many unique treasures and pleasures. The towns of Uçhisar, Göreme, Avanos, Ürgüp, Derinkuyu, Kaymakli, and Ihlara normally define the Cappadocia area. Hotel-rich Ürgüp, Göreme, Avanos, and Uçhisar are the major towns from which to explore the region, with Ürgüp and Göreme being the preferred locations because of their infrastructure of supporting services and activities.

❑ Cappadocia is characterized by a bizarre, surreal, and sensual landscape of "fairy chimneys" and stone phallic outcrops that look like they belong on another planet or in a child's play set.

❑ Cappadocia is a surprisingly good place to shop for rugs, pottery, antiques, and handicrafts in the towns of Ürgüp, Avanos, and Ortahisar.

❑ Plan your transportation carefully since most towns and sites are spread out, within 10 to 20 kilometers of each other.

❑ Wear a good pair of walking or climbing shoes – you'll be constantly climbing from one level to another.

Fascinating Cappadocia offers an abundance of evidence that this once was a very rich area of settlements and history. The eroded landscapes alone took millions of years to reach their present forms. Evidence of human settlements go back for thousands of years. The most recent monumental – both above and below ground – structures were created during the past 3,000 years. Understanding how this area evolved is of particular interest to history and geological buffs, but experiencing this area on the ground or in the air is exhilarating for most everyone who enjoys a good travel adventure.

There's much to see and do in Cappadocia to quickly occupy two days, if not a week, of time. A busy three-day visit may be ideal for first-time visitors who want to experience the highlights of this region.

In preparation for exploring this area, keep three realities in mind. First, because most towns and sites are spread out, within 10 to 20 kilometers of each other, you'll need to plan your transportation carefully. Renting a car, hiring a car and driver, or booking a local tour makes good sense for getting around this area quickly and conveniently. Second, be sure to wear a good pair of walking or climbing shoes. This is one of the few places we have visited where everything seems to be on different **levels**. From getting to your hotel room, or going from one room to another, or exploring cave rooms and underground tunnels, you're constantly climbing from one level to another. Your first day of exploring this area may result in exercising some muscles that haven't been used for some time. You'll know either immediately or the very next morning which muscles got the Cappadocia workout! Third, if you have a physical disability that prevents you from doing strenuous walking and climbing, you will probably miss many of Cappadocia's major attractions, including charming hotels, which are inaccessible to the disabled. Fourth, try to find an appealing central location from which to explore the area. Our personal favorite town to stay in is Ürgüp. Our second choice would be nearby Göreme. In addition to offering the best accommodations, these two towns also offer a good selection of restaurants, with Ürgüp having the decided edge on shopping and entertainment.

---

# THE BASICS

## GETTING THERE

While you can reach the Cappadocia area by plane through the gateway cities of Uçhisar and Kayseri, most visitors arrive by car or tour bus from Ankara, which is about a three-hour drive southeast to Uçhisar. Turkish Airlines flies twice a week into Uçhisar and twice daily into Kayseri. Uçhisar is about a 20-minute drive to Ürgüp, and Kayseri is nearly a one-and-a-half hour drive to Ürgüp. Regular bus services also connect Ankara to Uçhisar – roughly a six-hour trip.

## GETTING AROUND

Taxis, car rentals, and tour groups are well organized for exploring the Cappadocia area. For maximum freedom and flexibility,
rent a car or work a deal with a travel agency for a car and
driver to see the area. You'll find several car rental agencies in
Ürgüp to assist you with your local transportation needs.
Several tour agencies in Ürgüp also can arrange individual and
group tours of the area. One of the best agencies is **Argeus**,
which is also the local representative for Turkish Airlines:
Istiklal Caddesi No. 13, Tel. (0384) 341-4688, Fax (0384) 341-
4888; website: www.argeus.com.tr; e-mail: inform@argeus.com.
tr. Other tour agencies in the area include:

| | |
|---|---|
| ■ Alan Tur | Tel. 341-4325 |
| ■ Archalla Tur | Tel. 341-5069 |
| ■ Argenaud Escapades | Tel. 341-6255 |
| ■ Çiçek Tur | Tel. 341-2163 |
| ■ Dozami Tur | Tel. 341-4906 |
| ■ Eretne Tur | Tel. 341-5063 |
| ■ Erko Tur | Tel. 341-3252 |
| ■ Eytra-Tur | Tel. 341-6135 |
| ■ Kap-Tur | Tel. 341-5098 |
| ■ Magic Valley Tur | Tel. 341-2145 |
| ■ Ossiana Tur | Tel. 341-5063 |
| ■ Rock Valley Tur | Tel. 341-5061 |
| ■ Snow-Ball Tur | Tel. 341-5614 |
| ■ Stonepark Tur | Tel. 341-8897 |
| ■ Sun Set Tur | Tel. 341-8880 |
| ■ Yuki Tur | Tel. 341-6424 |
| ■ Yume Tur | Tel. 341-8515 |

Most international (Avis, Europcar, Hertz, Inter-rent) and local
car rental firms have offices near the main square in Ürgüp.
Also, check with the local **Tourist Information Office** in
Ürgüp for assistance: Kayseri Caddesi 37, Tel./Fax 341-4059.
Your hotel also should be able to recommend transportation
and tour alternatives, although some do get commissions for
referring you to their recommended sources.

For online information about Cappadocia, visit these useful
websites:

| | |
|---|---|
| ■ **Capadoce** | www.cappadoce.ouvaton.org |
| ■ **Cappadocia Online** | www.cappadociaonline.com |
| ■ **Cappadocia.gen** | www.cappadocia.gen.tr |
| ■ **Cappadocia.org** | www.cappadocia.org |

- **Cappadocia.net**      www.cappadocia.net
- **Tourism Turkey**     www.tourismturkey.org
- **The Turkey Guide**   www.turkeyguide.com

When visiting the Tourist Information Office in Ürgüp (across from the police station at Kayseri Caddesi 37), be sure to pick up a map of the area as well as the *Ürgüp Travel Guide* and other useful publications on the area.

---

## BALLOONING OVER CAPPADOCIA

One of the most exciting ways to experience the unique landscape and habitation of Cappadocia is to take a hot air balloon trip over the center of this area. Indeed, this is one of the most exhilarating balloon trips found anywhere in the world. Operated by the experienced company **Kapadokya Balloons Göreme**, which is owned and operated by the very competent and entertaining Swedish/English husband-wife team of Lars-Eric Möre and Kaili Kidner, this is a first-class operation from beginning to end. It delivers one of the best ballooning products we have ever experienced. In fact, Lars is an experienced pilot with more than  5,000 hours of balloon piloting experience, a perfect safety record, and specializes as a design engineer for record high-altitude burner systems (he also helped prepare Richard Branson for his record-breaking balloon successes). After being picked up at your hotel between 5:30am and 6am, you proceed to the company's head office in Göreme for coffee, tea, and cookies and to meet your fellow travelers and finalize payments. Boarding a comfortable Mercedes van, you follow Mercedes SUVs pulling small trailers that haul the ballooning equipment. Once arriving at a field just outside Göreme, the ballooning team off loads and begins assembling the equipment and inflating the balloon with large gas powered fans. Within 20 minutes the flame bursts, the balloon fills with air and becomes upright, and passengers climb into the sturdy 10-person baskets and off they go into the air, heading directly for the town of Göreme. Flying low over fairy chimney homes, hotels, and caves, and waving to local residents who have just gotten up at this early hour to greet the big balloons and their curious camera-clicking passengers, you quietly float over roof tops as your pilot skillfully maneuvers the balloon for even more exciting views of the town and outlying area. As the sun rises on a clear day, you get fabulous views of the horizon and valleys as you playfully fly between 2,000 and 3,000 feet outside the town of Göreme and then head for the town of Ürgüp where you can see all the interesting cave hotels carved from the rock cliffs and watch the uniformed children heading off for school. Comfortable, quiet, and serene, this balloon adventure is a wonderful way to see the unique landscape as well as peek into the start of daily lives on the ground. Followed by the ground crew that wheels its vans and SUVs into position for a landing in one of the open fields outside Ürgüp, your balloon eventually settles on one of the trailers (usually gets it right on target) and passengers climb out and wait for the crew to secure and pack the equipment as well as set up for the final stage of this trip – champagne, wine, and cake centered around one of the wicker baskets. The crew makes it a splendid and classy event by decorating the basket with leaves and flowers, setting up a small table with tablecloth, toasting the event with food and drink, and passing out free postcards featuring the balloon. They also set up a small gift shop where you can purchase memorabilia – caps, T-shirts, and books – of your ballooning trip in Cappadocia. Within 30 minutes everyone departs by van to their next destination, having started their morning with a truly exciting adventure. Everyone literally leaves on a high!

The cost of this trip is US$230 per person, which may initially seem pricey but is really good value for what you get. Emphasizing both safety and entertainment and with over 22 years of ballooning experience, this company really focuses on their customers. Fully licensed and insured, Kapadokya Balloons doesn't ask you to sign a tacky safety waver, because they already carry excess insurance on all passengers. Since this popular ballooning trip fills up quickly (they take over 3,000 passengers up during their 220- to 240-day season and usually fly two balloons each morning), be sure to make reservations well in advance of your arrival in Cappadocia by contacting:

Kapadokya Balloons Göreme
TR-50180 Nevşehir
Tel. (0384) 271-2442
Fax (0384) 271-2586
E-mail: fly@kapadokyaballoons.com
Website: www.kapadokyaballoons.com

Keep in mind that the ballooning season runs from April 1$^{st}$ to the end of November. From December to March, the flying team moves to France where they balloon the Alps during the winter – probably the world's most spectacular ballooning experience. If you enjoy your Cappadocia ballooning experience, you may want to consider making special arrangements with Lars and Kaili to join them in the Swiss Alps.

You will find a few copycat competitors offering cheaper ballooning trips in Cappadocia, but we have not heard anything positive to recommend their services. Our recommendation: Put yourself in the hands of experienced professionals who really know what they are doing – and love their work – Kapadokya Balloons. They may well be the highlight of your travel adventure to Turkey as well as your best ballooning adventure ever!

# GETTING TO KNOW YOU

Cappadocia is simply an intriguing area that begs to be explored in many different directions – north, south, east, and west as well as above ground, on the ground, and below ground! This whole area will certainly become one of the highlights of
visiting Turkey. It's a seemingly
"unreal" place that constantly
yields fascinating sights and
touches the imagination.

Cappadocia is especially famous and memorable for its unusual arid landscapes that often
resemble a moonscape of rocks,
cones, and eroded valleys and
habitats that have evolved and
adapted to this area. It's a photographer's delight and one of
the most interesting sights for
even the most jaded traveler. The landscape looks as if it had been turned over to a talented sculptor who literally fashioned it into a fanciful playground for grown-ups made out of colorful sand and clay.

Most visitors to Cappadocia immediately want to know how the geology of this area managed to develop in such an intriguing and magical manner. The theory and history go something like this. Several millennia ago three volcanic peaks – Erciyes, Hasan, and Melendiz – erupted and covered the area with several layers of ash and basalt. Over thousands of years, wind, rain, and earthquakes variously eroded the compressed layers of tufa (a soft porous rock) and disrupted the geology to eventually create the current distinctive landscape of colorful hills, valleys, cones, pillars, pyramids, and mushroom-shaped fairy chimneys often delicately balancing huge rock slabs.

The inhabited history of the area is still somewhat sketchy, although it does date from prehistoric times. There is evidence of Assyrian civilization during the early Bronze Age. The Hattis, Hittites, Phrygians, Persinas, Romans, Byzantines, Seljuks, and Ottomans all left their influence on the area. At various times the present-day towns of Nevşehir (Nissa) and Kayseri (Mazaca) served as capitals of local confederations. Somewhat of a backwater area for powerful kingdoms to the north and west, Cappadocia seemed to attract little long-term interest of the rich and powerful. Nonetheless, the area had long played an important role in the north-south and east-west trade routes, including the Silk Road. As a result, the area absorbed many different influences and frequently became a center for invasions and looting. The local population responded by adapting to their landscape – they retreated to the area's many caverns and grottos as well as carved numerous dwellings throughout the area, including subterranean cities complete with temples, wineries, fresh air, and food and water storage. Accordingly, today the area's main monuments consist of its natural geology and the habitats that local residents carved out of the cones, rocks, caverns, and grottoes both above and below ground.

It was during the Byzantine Empire that the local Christian population carved colorful churches, chapels, and monasteries out of the rock formations that now attract many visitors to this area. Indeed, more than 1,000 churches and chapels were believed to have been constructed. When threatened by Arab invaders, the local inhabitants went into hiding by ingenuously constructing underground cities which number over 100. Many of these carved dwellings include intricately designed and elaborated churches and chapels with artistic domes, columns, pillars, and vestibules. These unique structures, along with the area's many rock-hewn dwellings – from homes to hotels – can be viewed in several areas of Cappadocia:

- Göreme
- Uçhisar
- Çavuşin
- Ürgüp
- Mustafapaşa
- Tatlarin
- Açiksaray

Several underground cities attract visitors who are intrigued with the history, architecture, and stories these dwellings reveal:

- Bağlama
- Derinkuyu
- Dulkadirli
- Fertek
- Inlimurat
- Kayirli
- Kavlaktepe
- Kaymakli

- Konakli
- Kümbetalti
- Mazi
- Masiköy
- Mucur
- Özkonak
- Özlüce
- Tatlarin

Whether viewing Cappadocia from the air or ground, one thing is certain about this area: it's very spread out with lots of small settlements punctuating its already surreal landscape. With a car, driver, and/or good map, you should be able to find your way around this intriguing area with ease. Your basic problem will be deciding where to go, what to do, and how much time to spend in each place!

While the area and its landscape are a sightseer's delight, there's a lot more to Cappadocia than visiting carved dwellings and underground cities. Assuming your interests also include shopping, you are well advised to select one of our base towns (Ürgüp being our favorite and boasting the best tourist infrastructure) from which to explore the area for both sightseeing and shopping purposes as well as for attractive accommodations, dining, and entertainment.

## SHOPPING CAPPADOCIA

Shopping in Cappadocia is relatively pleasant and surprisingly rewarding for those who know what to buy and where to shop. You can easily spend two full days shopping its major towns. Unlike the many aggressive merchants found in İstanbul or Atalaya, most shopkeepers in Cappadocia are friendly and laid back, with many of them willing to spend time with visitors in educating them about their products. Not surprisingly, you may frequently encounter legendary Turkish hospitality while shopping in Cappadocia. Indeed, you'll find this willingness to spend time through presentations and answering questions to be one of the major strengths of shopping in Cappadocia and a good reason to expand your shopping time in this area. In fact, you'll

❑ You may frequently encounter legendary Turkish hospitality while shopping here.

❑ Cappadocia is especially famous for kilims.

❑ Avanos is the center for pottery and ceramics.

❑ Cappadocia is a rich agricultural region known for its wine production.

often find what should be a 10-minute visit to a shop quickly expands to a 60-minute visit involving lots of apple tea and conversation. In the process of shopping your way through Cappadocia, you'll learn a great deal about Turkish rugs, carpets, ceramics, pottery, antiques, and collectibles by visiting these friendly shops.

# WHAT TO BUY

Several towns in Cappadocia are especially famous for carpets, kilims, pottery, ceramics, antiques, collectibles, and handicrafts. Here's what you are most likely to find in this area.

### CARPETS AND KILIMS

Cappadocia is rightly famous for its excellent selection of kilims which can be acquired for very good prices compared to elsewhere in Turkey. Some shops also include carpets and kilims from the neighboring countries of Iran, Uzbekistan, Turkmenistan, and Afghanistan. Two of our favorite carpet shops are **Aksa Halicilik** (Belediye Sarayi Alti No. 38, Ürgüp, Tel. 341-4348) and **Avanos Cehri Hali** (Avanos, Tel. 511-4240). Both places spend a great deal of time with visitors in educating about Turkish carpets and kilims – definitely worth visiting just for the education alone!

### POTTERY AND CERAMICS

Cappadocia is a rich area for producing white clay ceramics and red clay pottery. The white clay comes from the mountains while the red clay is found along the banks of the Kizilirmak River. Avanos is the famous center for ceramic and pottery production. Several shops and factories here include demonstration areas, showrooms, and tours of their facilities. Many of the ceramic bowls and plates for sale are copies of famous museum pieces. Two of the best places to shop for locally produced ceramics and pottery include the unique and cavernous **Chez Galip** (center of Avanos, Tel. 511-4240) and the large ceramics factory and showroom **Kaya Seramik Evi** (Yeni Mah. Eski Nevşehir Yolu Üzeri No. 18, outside Avanos, Tel. 511-5755).

### ANTIQUES AND COLLECTIBLES

Several shops in the Cappadocia area specialize in old things from the Anatolia region as well as from neighboring countries, especially tribal jewelry from Uzbekistan, Turkmenistan, and Afghanistan. Look for old copper pots, plates, porcelain, weapons, instruments, jewelry, lamps, pocket watches, boxes, and furniture. Most such shops are found in Ürgüp and the small nearby town of Ortahisar. Some of the best shops here include: **Aziz Baba** (Kayseri Caddesi No. 28, Ürgüp, Tel. 341-2389); **Hediyelike Esya Saticisi** (Ortahisar, Tel. 343-3643); **Crazy Ali** (Ortahisar).

### HANDICRAFTS AND SOUVENIRS

Given the large number of tourists who support this area, expect to find numerous handicraft and souvenir shops that offer postcards, bookmarks, maps, evil eye key chains, T-shirts, ashtrays, coffee mugs, bags, leather goods, souvenir ceramics, and jewelry. For good quality arts and crafts, visit the local branch of **Dösim** (Tel. 271-2286) which is located just inside the entrance/exit gate of the Open Air Museum in Göreme.

### TRIBAL JEWELRY

Look for old tribal jewelry from neighboring countries of central Asia. While several antique and handicraft shops include jewelry, one of the best sources for such jewelry is our favorite antique shop in Cappadocia: **Aziz Baba** (Kayseri Caddesi No. 28, Ürgüp, Tel. 341-2389).

### WINE

Cappadocia is a rich agricultural region also known for its wine production. Indeed, it hosts an annual wine festival. To tour a famous local winery and taste and purchase the production, be sure to visit the **Turasan Winery** (Tel. 341-6570) which is located on the outskirts of Ürgüp.

# WHERE TO SHOP

Shopping in Cappadocia is concentrated in a few towns and around most major tourist sites. Catering primarily to tourists, most shops offer the typical range of carpets, kilims, ceramics, and handicrafts found elsewhere in Turkey. With a few exceptions, most shops offer similar quality items at competitive prices.

Almost every major tourist site has near its entrance numerous small restaurants and vendors offering a similar selection of souvenirs, from ceramic plates and inexpensive jewelry to T-shirts, books, and postcards. Many shops within the towns offer the same bewildering range of carpets, kilims, ceramics, and pottery. After awhile, you may be overwhelmed with so many look-alike shops. However, a few well established shops in three of the towns are well worth visiting.

## ÜRGÜP

If you have limited time to shop, you may want to focus on the small town of Ürgüp, which is the major administrative, shopping, hotel, dining, and entertainment center for Cappadocia but with a population under 500. Centrally located within Cappadocia – 750 kilometers from Istanbul, 300 kilometers form Ankara, 240 kilometers from Konya, and 650 kilometers from Antalya – it's our favorite place in the area. It's a delightful town which offers a full range of amenities for travelers, from hotels and restaurants to Internet cafes, a disco, and travel agencies. Especially noted for its many charming cave hotels, including upscale boutique properties such as the Yunak Evleri and the Cappadocia Cave Suites, the town is the best place to base yourself for exploring the surrounding area. In fact, there are more shops lining the streets of Ürgüp than any other community in the region.

Primarily specializing in ubiquitous rugs, antiques, and souvenirs, Ürgüp is a fun place to explore. Its main shopping street is **Kayseri Caddesi**. Here you'll also find the museum, tourist office, and police station. Be sure to visit the very helpful tourist office which has a map and brochures on the area. Several side streets also include shops. You can easily spend two to three hours browsing the many shops along these streets. However, if you sit through a few carpet demonstrations and accept all the drinks offered along the way, you can easily turn this shopping adventure into a full day familial affair.

Among the many shops found in Ürgüp, these two shops are well worth visiting for carpets and antiques:

❑ **Aksa Halicilik:** *Belediye Sarayi Alti No. 38, Ürgüp, Tel. 341-4348 or Fax 341-4888.* If you want to get a good education about rugs, and deal with a reputable dealer, this is the shop to visit. Muammer Sak has been selling carpets and kilims in this same location for more than 17 years. He also has a reputation for offering good quality at reasonable prices – qualities that are not always apparent when encountering Turkey's endless number of carpet and kilim shops. Nearly 90 percent of Muammer's rugs are old, or at least not new

(10 percent are new). Extremely knowledgeable about carpets and kilims, Muammer's approach to selling such items is especially appealing to many visitors – he first tries to identify your interests, needs, and budget and then spends a great deal of time explaining designs, colors, origins, and differences of the many carpets and kilims he offers in this shop. For example, you'll learn there are 15 different types of kilims in Cappadocia, the differences in weaving techniques, and why prices differ from one rug to another (age and quality differences). He'll even show you his large ugly duckling kilims (bad colors that appeal to no one) that sell for only US$250. In addition to carpets and kilims, this shop also has an interesting collection of tent bands, pillows, camel bags, and salt bags. The small Santa Claus rugs for US$10 (asking US$30 in Kas/Myra, along the Turquoise Coast, which is the home of St. Nicholas) make cute gift items for anyone who is into collecting Christmas memorabilia.

❑ **Aziz Baba:** *Kayseri Caddesi No. 28, Ürgüp, Tel. 341-2389. Website: www.turk-web.com/aziz. E-mail: rugs@lebazaardorient. com.* If you're in the market for antiques and collectibles, as well as unusual conversation, it doesn't get much better than this shop. The very affable owner, Aziz Güzelgöz, has operated here for nearly 30 years, and his shop shows it. Crammed to the rafters with a wide range of antiques and collectibles, you'll find a great deal of interesting items here: copper pots, Turkeman silver, Russian icons, rifles, bells,  jewelry from Turkmenistan and Afghanistan, pocket watches, tribal jewelry, old porcelain, Ottoman knives, bronze mortars, beads, instruments, coffee boxes, belts, and lanterns. He offers a good selection of jewelry, from tribal neck pieces to rings. Since Aziz is an accomplished musician, he may take out his string instrument and play you a Turkish tune. If not, ask him to do so.

Since wine is one of Cappadocia's major products, you may want to tour the popular winery in Ürgüp, **Turasan** (Tel. 341-

6570 or Fax 341-4872), which is located near the outskirts of town, on the right, as you pass by the major cave hotels on the road that leads to Göreme, Ortahisar, Avanos, and Uçhisar. This winery has been in operation since 1943.

## AVANOS

Located 13 kilometers northwest of Ürgüp and spread along the banks of the Kizilirmak (Red) River with charming old stone houses on its hillside, this town of nearly 12,000 inhabitants is justly famous for its pottery and ceramics factories, demonstration workshops, showrooms, and shops. Indeed, Avanos has been producing pottery from the red clay of its river for centuries. It reputedly has nearly 300 pottery factories operating at present. The town also includes many ubiquitous rug shops – just in case you need to see more examples of ostensibly old and new carpets and kilims – as well as many handicraft shops. In fact, during three days in August, Avanos celebrates the annual International Festival of Handicrafts with a lively pottery-making competition.

Shopping in Avanos is relatively educational and fun. The shopkeepers tend to be very friendly and invite visitors into their shops for demonstrations of the art of pottery making. Using the traditional hand (shaping) and foot (spinning the wheel) method for transforming the red clay into various pottery forms, some of the demonstration workshops invite visitors to try their hands and feet at the wheel. If you don't mind getting your hands, and possibly your clothes, dirty with red clay, this is one of those participatory handicraft activities that may be your shopping highlight in Cappadocia. Demonstrations by talented craftsmen are often amazing as they pull out a glob of red clay from a plastic bag and easily mold it with their wet hands into a beautifully shaped piece of pottery within three to five minutes. If only you could be so productive with your initial try at the wheel!

Most of Avanos's pottery production takes place outside the town in large factories which are often frequented by tour groups. While you may want to visit these production centers, the most interesting shopping takes place in the downtown shops. Once you arrive in Avanos, take the main street (Atatürk Caddesi) to the center of town. If you're traveling east along this street, you'll see a large statue of a potter on your left. Go two more blocks east and then turn left. Start your shopping adventure within 100 feet of making this turn. Here you'll see numerous shops on your left, right, and directly ahead. Three shops worth visiting include:

❑ **Chez Galip:** *P.O. Box 22, 50500 Avanos, Tel. 511-4240 or Fax 511-4543. Website: www.chez-galip.com. E-mail: info@chez-galipl.com or chzgalip@tr-net.net.tr.* It's difficult to miss this shop. If you don't find it, chances are it will find you as its more aggressive shop representatives stand in front of this colorful cave shop trying to persuade visitors to enter what you will soon discover to be one of the most unusual shops in town, if not all of Turkey. After a half hour of exploring this cavernous shop's nine cave rooms (watch your head for low entrances), as well as its handicraft shop across the street (Chez Sülo) and its nearby (five-minute walk west) carpet shop (Avanos Cehri Hali) – and learning the owner also owns a travel agency, tour company, horse riding company, and a huge pottery and ceramics factory on the outskirts of town (next to the cultural center which is 10 minutes away) and sponsors special workshops on pottery making and guitar playing and has been instrumental in developing the local cultural

center – you get the impression that Chez Galip owns the town or at least understands the economics of saturation marketing! This is both an enlightening and weird shop. It's enlightening for its many rooms and varieties of red clay pottery and beautiful white ceramics but weird for its strange hair museum. As soon as you enter the shop, you'll be in a basic demonstration workshop area where a potter will show how to quickly produce a red clay pot using a traditional foot wheel. You also will be invited to try your hand at making a pot. From here you enter into several other rooms that include many modern art and reproduction pieces which may or may not appeal to your design and color tastes. The "Special Collection" room includes beautiful white Iznik ceramics which are produced in their factory on the outskirts of town. But it's the freaking lady hair museum that really gets your attention and demonstrates Chez Galip's marketing kitsch. With over 15,000 locks of hair, each 6 to 12 inches in length, clipped from female visitors and attached to name cards hanging from the ceiling and walls of this cave, this museum room definitely speaks to you! The deal is that visitors shed their locks in exchange for a chance to win a free two-week trip to Cappadocia. Drawings for the winners supposedly take place 10 times a year. The winner here seems to be the lady hair museum, which claims to be listed in the *Guinness Book of World Records* for assembling this unique collection of hair. At some time during your tour, you will probably be invited to visit their carpet shop and pottery and ceramics factory. Most prices appearing on the items in this shop are for commission-seeking tour guides – if you pay the full amount you will be paying too much. A 30 to 50 percent discount on items would more accurately reflect their true value and the price you should pay. The best part of this shop is its "Special Collection" room which includes some really nice, and expensive, ceramics. If you plan to be in the Avanos area for several days or weeks, you may want to inquire about this shop's special courses on pottery making, guitar playing, and other arts, crafts, and skills.

As you leave this shop, be sure to cross the street to visit Chez Galip's handicraft and antique shop – **Chez Sülo**. This shop includes an interesting collection of jewelry, old Turkeman decorations, donkey and camel bags, bells, print blocks (not for sale since these are part of the owner's collection), pots, and textiles. You can easily spend a half hour to an hour exploring these two adjacent shops.

❑ **Chez Ali Baba:** *PTT Karşisi Firinbaşi Sokak, 50500 Avanos, Tel. 511-3166.* Located just in front of Chez Galip, this small pottery shop is just a teaser to get you to walk down the cobblestone walkway on your right (2 minutes) to its main demonstration showroom and shop. Here you initially will be offered a demonstration on how to make red clay pottery (it always looks so easy when demonstrated by a expert craftsman) before entering the shop's five cave rooms which are filled with uniquely designed pottery. The playful pots are designed as formal jackets with extended lapels and as animal figures (kangaroos, camels, and rams). Some are copies of interesting pieces found in the museum in Ankara.

❑ **Avanos Cehri Hali:** *P.O. Box 22, 50500 Avanos, Tel. 511-4240 or Fax 511-4543. Website: www.chez-galip.com. E-mail: info@chez-galipl.com or chzgalip@tr-net.net.tr.* Owned and operated by Chez Galip, this carpet and kilim shop includes a nice collection of old and new products from Turkey and nearby countries, especially some nice Afghan carpets. It also includes camel bags, salt bags, and donkey saddles that can be used as seats by creative home decorators. Includes a large demonstration area where salespeople unroll their treasures and explain why their rugs are so valuable, including several very old and worn rugs. Like most such shops, prices are determined through negotiations.

Located on the outskirts of town is one of the most interesting ceramics and pottery factories we encountered in Turkey. If you have a hard time finding it, be persistent since it's well worth the visit:

❑ **Kaya Seramik Evi:** *Yeni Mah. Eski Nevşehir Yolu Üzeri No. 18, Tel. 511-5755 or Fax 511-5091. Website: www.guraysera mik.com.tr.* Located two kilometers southwest of Avanos along the right side of the old Nevşehir Road, this expansive ceramics factory, demonstration workshop, and shop offers an excellent selection of white ceramics using Iznik and Ottoman designs. Its 12 rooms are carved out of a hill and function as cave rooms. Two lower level demonstration areas showcase the production of white ceramics and red clay pots, although 95 percent of this factory production is for white ceramics. The white ceramic demonstration area includes a very informative tour that shows how the ceramic plates are produced, fired, and hand painted with various de-signs, including several male and female artisans paint-ing designs (most plates are painted by artisans in near-

by villages). The demonstration also includes a dubious comparison of first and second quality ceramics complete with a dramatic alcohol and flame test applied to an example of first quality ceramics (this test usually produces the same results for second quality ceramics when you ask the demonstrator to actually flame the surface of a so-called inferior product!). The point of this demonstration is to emphasize the fact that a US$8 plate called "second quality" will probably cost you over US$100 if it's classified as "first quality." Not everyone can see the difference, even after flaming the plates, although you will see it at the cash register. Another major difference, which should be mentioned rather than this amateur flame test, is that top quality ceramic dishes can be used as serving dishes for hot foods. The inferior quality ceramics should never be used for such purposes because of their high lead content. Although this factory produces very few red clay pots, its pottery demonstration area affords visitors an opportunity to try their hands, and feet, at making their own creations. The real highlight of the tour are the various shop rooms which are divided into "Special" and "Regular" rooms. The really beautiful, and expensive, pieces are found in the "Special" room. Here you'll find gorgeous handmade ceramic plates, from large to small, adorning the walls and floors of the cave room. Huge ceramic plates three feet in diameter sell for more than US$3,000 (before bargaining). Many of the pieces are one-of-a-kind art pieces. Others are copies of museum pieces as found in the ubiquitous "catalog" – the *Iznik* ceramics book. The "Regular" room includes a wide selection of ceramics, as well as a small red clay pottery section, at different price ranges. Here you'll find plates, dishes, tiles, and pots. Since this factory and shop are set up for handling large tour groups, the prices tend to be all over the place, depending on whom you appear to be with and your negotiation skills. An initial quoted price may seem uncertain – not sure or may be given as a range, which is a strange pricing approach. In the end, the price will depend on whether or not you are with a tour group (as usual, guides get commissions), talk like a dealer, or bargain hard for a good discount. The first price quoted is not the one you want to pay – try the fifth price given after a friendly negotiation session and in the absence of a guide. If you are given a present after you made a purchase, you probably paid too much! Overall, this is one of the nicest and most informative ceramic factories and shops we encountered in Turkey.

## ORTAHISAR

Located only five kilometers from Ürgüp, the small and often overlooked town of Ortahisar is famous for its interesting fairy chimney castle. A challenging climb – 143 steps and 86 meters tall – at the very top visitors are rewarded with a panoramic view of the surrounding area. But one of the real travel-shopping rewards of Ortahisar are the antique shops at the base of the castle. Here you'll find four shops which are operated by two owners:

❑ **Crazy Ali:** *50650 Ortahisar, Ürgüp. No street address or phone number – just its presence!* This is the first shop on the left as you approach the chimney castle or citadel. The name of this antique and collectible shop hints of what you might encounter – Crazy Ali. Waiting for you in his beret, Crazy Ali is literally a real character. Seemingly more interested in reading his new-found love and literary creations – English language poetry – to his visitors than with selling all the interesting material things in this shop, Crazy Ali may treat you to one or two of his poems, even giving you an autographed copy of *All* or *Do You Know?* (actually, it's pretty good poetry for a shopkeeper amidst the fairy chimneys). If you're not too distracted by Crazy Ali, you might browse through his collection of antiques and memorabilia. He offers a  good collection of copper pots, old phonographs, pottery, chests, knives, lamps, guns, jewelry, coins, pocket watches, clocks, bells, lanterns, and other collectibles.

❑ **Hediyelik Eşya Saticisi:** *50650 Ortahisar, Ürgüp, Tel. 343-3643.* Just across the street from Crazy Ali, this inviting antique shop offers a wide range of interesting antiques and collectibles: print blocks, brass and copper pots, jewelry, guns, stone mortars, lanterns, wood boxes, coins, knives, oil lamps, candle holders, and phonographs. If you don't find anything here, move on to their two other antique shops which are located across the street from each other. These shops carry more furniture and other collectible items.

## GÖREME

The main streets of Göreme are lined with typical rug and souvenir shops, which may or may not appeal to your shopping senses. They are more oriented to busloads of day-trippers than to more long-term residents and serious shoppers. When you visit the Göreme Open Air Museum, be sure to stop at the small but nice government-operated **Dösim** (Tel. 271-2286) handicraft shop. It's located directly across from the ticket office, or near the exit (visit at the end of your tour), and is housed in a separate building along with a few money changers. Offering one of the better displays of handicrafts, this shop includes silver, jewelry, rugs, leather bags, brass pots, ceramics, wood boxes, glass pots, and meerschaum pipes. Within the Göreme Open Air Museum, just after the Dark Church and heading for the exit, you'll also find a small art shop which sells some interesting paintings and prints. The town itself has several carpet and kilim shops lining the main street.

## ACCOMMODATIONS

The communities in Cappadocia are so close to one another that it makes little difference where you stay in terms of proximity to visiting the many attractions in the area. Whether you chose to stay in Ürgüp, Göreme, Nevşehir, or Avanos, you can easily visit the attractions in any of the villages. Our suggestion is to select your accommodations based on the type of roof you want over your head. The unique attractions in Cappadocia are the many cave hotels which are disproportionately found in Ürgüp and Göreme. Many of these are literally carved out of the rock whereas others may be a combination of caves and additions built of rock to blend with the cave sections. By far the most upscale of the cave hotels is **Yunik Evleri** located in Ürgüp. A recent addition to the boutique cave hotel scene is **Cappadocia Cave Suites** in Göreme. Although there are other hotels than those built in caves for visitors who want traditional lodging, most are not considered luxury lodging.

❑ **Yunak Evleri:** *Yunak Mahallesi, 50400 Ürgüp, Cappadocia, Tel. (90-384) 341-6920 or Fax (90-384) 341-6924. Website: www.yunak.com. E-mail: yunak@yunak.com.* Ever wanted to sleep in a cave? Yunak Evleri carved into a white stone cliff opened in May 2000, offering a luxurious alternative to more commonplace accommodations. Built in the sixth century, the caves have been modernized into 17 rooms and suites with electrical lighting, handcrafted furniture, marble baths – one suite even has a jacuzzi. Each guestroom is configured differently. Some have many steps leading to the room or have levels within the rooms. If you have trouble with multi-level, specify this when making your reservation. The suite we had was very spacious. It had a bedroom separate from the living area which was huge with a step-up to the area with the seating which was formed by a large L-shaped banquette. We had a CD player but there is no TV in the guestrooms, although there is a large screen TV in the central lounge area. There is a central kitchen with refrigerator where guests are on an honor system for beverages. Breakfast is included and dinner is optional at about US$15 per person, served in a sunny third-story room in the main building. The dinner is home-cooked and was one of the best meals we had in all of Turkey.

❑ **Cappadocia Cave Suites:** *Gafferli Mah. Ünlü Sokak No. 19, Göreme/Nevşehir, Cappadocia, Tel. (0384) 271-3800 or Fax (0384) 271-2799. Website: www.ccscappadociacavesuites.com. E-mail: info@ccscappadociacavesuites.com. In the United States, Tel. 1-800-935-8875.* Opened in August 2001, this 17-room boutique cave hotel is the ultimate in luxury and a perfect getaway for honeymooners. Built into a hillside, it has more levels within the guestrooms than other cave hotels. It has a very homey, cozy atmosphere. Owned by Bora Özkök, a noted San Francisco-based tour operator who specializes in cultural tours to Turkey (www.boraozkok.com), this is lovely property overlooking the town. Each room has a distinctive design, incorporating many local arts and crafts, but all come complete with towel warmers in the bathrooms and televisions. All guestrooms have a small kitchen which includes a table, minibar, and tea and coffee making facilities. Some rooms have Internet connections and fireplaces. One of the unique features of this property is its two outdoor wine taps which provide self-service white and red wines – a very surprising and popular feature with its guests! Breakfast is included. Dinner is optional. Meals are served is a subterranean cave. The stairway, banister, and grille work on the entryway to the restaurant are very eye catching and attractive.

❑ **Esbelli Evi:** *Esbelli Sokak 8 (P.K. 2), 50400 Ürgüp, Cappadocia, Tel. (90-384) 341-3395 or Fax (90-384) 341-8848. Website: www.esbelli.com.tr. E-mail: esbelli@esbelli.com.* This is Cappadocia's original cave room hotel which opened nearly 12 years ago. A small and very friendly family-run property with only 10 rooms (seven are cave rooms), this cozy hotel has a decided family atmosphere that makes the visitor feel very much at home. Frequented by many Americans, the charming and relaxing property is perfect for anyone planing a lengthy stay in Cappadocia. Special free features include a washing machine for guests, Internet connection, mountain bikes, and beverages.

❑ **Elkep Evi:** *Eski turbn Oteli Arkasi (P.K. 70), 50400 Ürgüp, Cappadocia, Tel. (90-384) 341-6000 or Fax (90-384) 341-8089. Website: www.elkepevi.com. E-mail: elkepevi@superonline. com.* The cave hotel includes 16 rooms in three separate buildings each of which has its own kitchen. Each room is nicely appointed, including a special touch with dolls placed in wall niches. The dining area is in the building on the hill with the one large suite and a nice view of the surrounding area.

## RESTAURANTS

Don't expect fine dining or exceptional cuisine in small town and highly touristed Cappadocia. The various towns in this area have many small, basic, and inexpensive restaurants. Most hotels include breakfast with their bed and breakfast plans as well as serve other meals. Some include restaurants which are open to outside guests. If you're visiting Ürgüp, these two restaurants are very good choices:

❑ **Şömine Café and Restaurant:** *Ürgüp, Tel. 341-8442.* Located in the center of town, this large upstairs and roof-top restaurant is popular with expats and tourists who find a large selection of excellent local dishes on its multilingual menu. During cool evenings, a table next to the wonderful center room fireplace makes for cozy dining. The fish, kebab, and mixed grill dishes are all excellent – as are the desserts.

❑ **Yunak Evleri Restaurant:** *Yunak Mahallesi, Ürgüp, Tel. 341-6920.* As part of the exclusive Yunak Evleri cave hotel, this restaurant serves excellent home-cooked Turkish meals. It includes a lovely outdoor dining area during the regular season as well as indoor dining on cool nights. It has a set menu for about US$15 per person, but you need to make reservations and let the restaurant know your culinary preferences.

## SEEING THE SITES

Cappadocia is a sightseer's paradise, especially for those who are intrigued with the geology and architecture of the area. Indeed, you can spend a couple of weeks exploring this area and still feel you haven't covered everything. If you have limited time, you may want to concentrate on these major sights.

## GÖREME

❑ **Göreme Open Air Museum:** *Göreme, Tel. 271-2167. Open daily, 8am - 5pm. Admission US$3.50.* A World Heritage Site, this very large and compact Byzantine monastic complex of carved churches, chapels, and related dwellings with elaborate religious art in the form of frescos is a "must see" for all visitors to Cappadocia. The initial entrance fee of US$3.50 covers everything in this complex except the Dark Church and its frescos which has a separate US$7 admissions fee (it's a double-edged sword – you may be disappointed if you don't go as well as disappointed if you do go!). There are several churches and dwellings, many created nearly 1,000 years ago. Expect to do a great deal of walking and climbing to see the whole area. Somewhat frustrating to visit without a map (the gate only takes your money and gives you a paid receipt with no information on the area), signs are in both Turkish and English. Many of the churches in this complex have nicely restored 11th and 12th century frescos, although several frescos are damaged by graffiti. Some of the major churches and dwellings include the Nun's Convent, Sandal Church, Snake Church, Chapel of St. Barbara, Apple Church, and Chapel of St. Basil. The complex includes two shops – an **Art Gallery** just after the Dark Church, which includes prints and miniatures, and **Dösim**, a small government-operated shop with a nice selection of handicrafts (silver, jewelry, rugs, leather bags, brass pots, ceramics, wood boxes, meerschaum pipes). You'll also find moneychangers in the same building with Dösim.

## ÜRGÜP

❑ **Zelve Open Air Museum:** *In the Zelve Valley which is off the Ürgüp-Avanos road, Tel. 411-2525. Open daily, 8am - 5:30pm. Admission US$3.* Best explored with a guide and especially popular for its sunsets, this large complex of abandoned churches, dwellings, tunnels, and caves are situated in three valleys. A very unstable area, be careful where you walk and take a flashlight with you, since exploring this area often involves climbing through dangerous and dark places.

❑ **Valley of the Fairy Chimneys:** Located near the village of Aktepe on the road to Ürgüp, this area has one of the best collections of attractive stone cones, many of which are capped with stone slabs. A good place to take photos of these strange yet compelling geological formations.

ORTAHISAR

❑ **Castle:** *At the center of Ortahisar. Open 8am - 5pm. Admission US$1.50.* Since you will probably visit Ortahisar for its antique shops, you may want to climb the town's landmark structure, the 86-meter *kale*. A fortress during Byzantine times, it's now a tourist attraction. Visitors who climb its cavernous narrow and winding 143 steps are rewarded with a nice view of the town and surrounding countryside. Be sure to visit the wine cellar underneath the castle (ask the person in the ticket booth to open it for you).

While Cappadocia at one time boasted more than 100 underground cities, today over 20 of these intriguing places are open to the public. If you are claustrophobic, you may want to skip this adventure which will take you underground through narrow passageways to see how people centuries ago hid underground from invaders for up to six months at a time. The maze of passages can be disorienting but most of these places have good signage so you won't get lost. Two of the most popular underground cities include **Kaymakli** and **Derinkuyu**.

## ENJOYING YOUR STAY

Numerous opportunities are available to experience several other aspects of Cappadocia. In addition to ballooning over the area, which we discussed at the beginning the this chapter, various groups offer hiking and horseback riding tours and a variety of handicraft workshops. For horseback riding, contact Galip's Tour (Tel. 511-5758, Fax 511-4543, website: www.chez-gallip.com) which also owns the Chez-Galip pottery shop in Avanos. This same group sponsors pottery making, weaving, and musical instrument workshops.

Don't expect a great deal of nightlife in small town Cappadocia. Most evening entertainment is centered around hotels and restaurants as well as a few discos and bars in Ürgüp. Check with your hotel or Tourist Information Office for the latest information on local entertainment.

## DISCOVERING KONYA

If you're traveling by road between Cappadocia and Antalya, be sure to stop in Konya for a couple of hours. This interesting city is nearly halfway between the two areas. It offers some nice sightseeing and shopping breaks from this rather long six-hour road trip. While many tour groups overnight here, it's really not necessary to do so since an intense two to three hours in the city is all the time you need to spend in Konya.

## GETTING TO KNOW YOU

Located 160 kilometers south of Ankara and 120 kilometers southwest of Ürgüp (Cappadocia), this city of nearly 700,000 residents is home to one of Turkey's most famous religious sects – the Mevlâna whirling dervishes. Indeed, any trip to Konya requires an obligatory visit to the fascinating whirling dervish museum – the **Mevlâna Müzesi and Türbesi** (Mevlâna Museum and Tomb of Mevlâna Celaleddin) – which is one of Turkey's most visited and intriguing museums.

For visitors, Konya is all about the museum and tomb of the whirling dervishes. Dedicated to the founder and disciples of mystic Mevlâna Celaleddin, a 13th century poet and philosopher, the combination museum and tombs provide a glimpse into the importance of this religious sect to hundreds of individuals who worship each day at the impressive tombs covered with elaborately embroidered covers and white turbans. The massive tomb of Mevlâna Celaleddin, which lies beneath an impressive painted dome, ceiling, and walls, is almost startling for many visitors unaccustomed to such displays of grave site opulence. The museum section includes an interesting collection of religious books, carpets, silver, costumes, instruments, and caps. Just outside the tomb/museum is a second building on your left which includes a model display of whirling dervishes in a variety of settings. The museum shop, which we'll return to shortly, lies between these two buildings.

Overall, this is one of the most impressive museums and tombs we encountered in all of Turkey – a stop well worth making if you are in the Konya area. After visiting this place, you'll come away with a whole new view, and appreciation, of the history, meaning, and actions of the whirling dervishes. You may be tempted to buy a book, CD, video, painting, drawing, or even a huge 900-bead rosary as a momento of your short visit to Konya's holy whirling dervish site.

If you think those colorful and noisy whirling dervishes that perform for tourists and are portrayed in many paintings and drawings are nothing more than a fancy cultural dance and music troupe, think again. They are part of a mystical religious sect which has its origins and spiritual center in the old city of Konya. It's based on the philosophy that all human existence is about rotation.

## Shopping Konya

The main shopping area of interest to visitors is found in and around the whirling dervish museum. The streets surrounding the museum are lined with many rug and souvenir shops selling almost identical things. They offer the same products found in most other rug and souvenir shops set up for busloads of tourists in search of postcards, books, and other memorabilia and for those who may have a weak moment and purchase a rug. Several shops do offer a few unique items representative of the whirling dervishes, such as the huge rosaries that may take up half of your suitcase space.

If you're looking for whirling dervish memorabilia, consider shopping at the **museum shop on the grounds of Mevlâna Müzesi and Türbesi**. Located between the museum/tomb and cultural display buildings, this expansive small kiosk is jam-packed with books, videos, CDs, paintings, prints, cards, and postcards that spill out onto the sidewalk. Most everything here is related to the Mevlâna whirling dervishes. You may, for example, want to purchase a CD of whirling dervish music, especially the one currently playing at the kiosk. They cost about US$4.15 each. The paintings and prints of whirling dervishes are rather nice and prices appear reasonable. In fact, the identical framed three-panel painting we purchased here for US$40 cost $50 at the Antalya Museum in Antalya. You'll pay even more in the shops of Istanbul.

Several other shops can be found along the main street leading to the museum, **Mevlana Caddesi**. Two shops in particular are worth browsing for antiques, collectibles, carpets, and kilims:

❑ **Karavan:** *Mevlana Caddesi No. 19/B, Tel. 351-0425 or Fax 352-7842.* You can see immediately from the window display that this is a quality shop that probably offers some very unique treasures. Step inside and you'll discover your hunch is right on target. This richly appointed shop was once an old Turkish bath house. As you walk in, you'll see many intriguing antiques, handicrafts, and collectibles in the entry room immediately to your right and left – copper pots, print blocks, wood mortars, bird traps, phonographs, and doors as well as a large cart and nomad tent. As you step up to the next room to go further into this shop, you come to a huge carpet and kilim gallery that includes many old carpets. Like many other rug shops, the personnel here will invite you for a drink and a demonstration session for examining their carpet collection. Be aware at this point you are only a few steps away from a stairway that takes you to two lower levels where you will discover a unique collection of old dusty furniture, wood ceilings, windows, chests, and doors that still need restoration. These are collectors' and decorators' treasure rooms. If you see something of interest, the shop will restore it to your specification as well as ship to your destination. Operating for more than 25 years, Karavan wholesales to many dealers abroad, including nearly 25 dealers from the United States. Prices appear reasonable. The very personable owner, Hüseyin Kaplan, has a keen eye for collecting many rare antiques and is experienced in working with international visitors.

❑ **Galeri Selçuk:** *Mevlana Caddesi No. 53/D, Tel./Fax 351-5036.* Located several doors west of Karavan, this small shop includes numerous rugs as well as lots of small yet interesting antiques and collectibles in its two front display windows. The bell collection is especially attractive. The owner, Mustafa Temiz, does not speak English. Expect very little discounting here.

## STAYING OVER

If you decide to stay over in Konya, you may want to consider these three hotels which represent the best in the city:

❑ **Hotel Bera:** *Kemerli Caddesi No. 13, Konya. Tel. (0332) 238-1090 or Fax (0332) 238-1099. Website: www.bera.com.tr. E-mail: info@bera.com.tr.* Represents Konya's newest and best hotel.

❑ **Otel Özkaymak:** *Nalçacaci Caddesi, Konya, Tel. (0332) 233-8720 or Fax (0332)237-8729. Website: www.ozkaymak.com.tr. E-mail: konya@ozkaymak.com.tr.*

❑ **Otel Selçuk:** *Alaaddin Caddesi No. 4, Konya, Tel. (0332) 353-2525 or Fax (0332) 353-2529.*

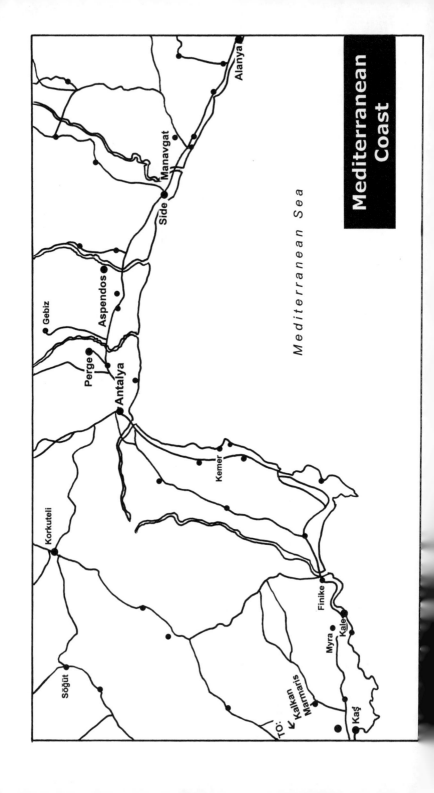

## 8

# Mediterranean Coast

T URKEY'S SUN-DRENCHED MEDITERRANEAN coast is located in the south and southwest sections of the country. Bordering Syria and facing the disputed Turk and Greek island of Cyprus in the south and the Greek island of Rhodes in the southwest, this is a lengthy, fascinating, and truly decadent area for travelers in search of Turkey's many seashore treasures and pleasures, from fabled ancient Roman ruins to festive resorts and glittering marinas in a picture-postcard setting of beaches, mountains, pine forests, quaint fishing villages, and relaxing cruises.

Also known as the Turkish Riviera and the Turquoise Coast, this area is to Turkey what the Riviera is to France and Italy – the country's playground for beaches, water sports, yachts, cruising, hotels, dining, shopping, sightseeing, and noisy late night bar carousing and entertainment. Sometimes tacky and often overrun with tourists, tour buses, cafes, and the same monotonous souvenir, rug, jewelry, leather, spice, and knock-off clothing and watch shops that provide some evidence you are indeed still in Turkey, nonetheless, this fun area of fascinating villages, towns, cities, and ancient ruins continues to draw large crowds of holiday makers. Miles and miles of beautiful coastal areas, with majestic mountains in the background, and glistening emerald waters punctuated with million-dollar yachts moored in pristine bays and crowded marinas make this area one of the great highlights of visiting Turkey.

If you enjoy visiting seaside resorts and the tourist culture and activities these places usually imply, then plan to spend several days along Turkey's Riviera. If you only want to sample the best of the best along the coast, with special emphasis on shopping, dining, accommodations, and yachting, we personally vote for Kaş and Kalkan and then head for Bodrum along the nearby southern Aegean coast. You'll most likely enjoy spending more time in these places than in other locations along the coast. Kaş, Kalkan, and Bodrum are in a class of their own. They also appeal to many expatriates who have permanently, or at least seasonally, settled in these pleasant communities.

❑ This area also is known as the Turkish Riviera and the Turquoise Coast.

❑ If you want to experience the best of the best along the coast, we personally vote for Kaş and Kalkan and then head for Bodrum on the Aegean.

❑ Day-trippers from nearby Greek islands crowd the aggressive tourist bazaars of Antalya and Marmaris.

❑ It's easiest to get around this area by rental car.

❑ Americans tend to stay two or three days in several locations whereas Europeans often stay one to two weeks in a single location.

# WELCOME TO THE TURKISH RIVIERA

The Mediterranean coast draws millions of visitors each year from Europe and the Americas who head directly for their favorite coastal resorts. If you're German, family oriented, budget conscious, or want to combine waterfront resort activities with snow skiing in nearby mountains, you may want to visit the German-speaking seaside resorts of Antalya and Side. More international and heady coastal destinations, with wonderful resort ambience, include Kaş, Kalkan, and Marmaris. Day-trippers from nearby Greek islands crowd the aggressive tourist bazaars of Antalya and Marmaris. In the midst of all these tourist-dependent seaside communities are a few shops of distinction worth exploring during your visit to these areas.

While by no means comparable to Istanbul, or even Ankara or Cappadocia, these communities do offer some rewarding shopping opportunities that go beyond the typical tourist kitsch found in so many seaside resorts.

Wherever you decide to visit along the Turkish Riviera, you'll discover many additional dimensions to this fascinating country. You'll leave the Mediterranean coast with a renewed sense that Turkey has some really great treasures and pleasures. Best of all for travel-shoppers, these seaside resorts offer lots of interesting shopping in the midst of miles of beachfront hotels, restaurants, and beaches.

# THE BASICS

## GETTING THERE

Getting to Turkey's south and southwestern Mediterranean coasts is relatively convenient. If you are driving around Turkey by car, most major towns and cities are within a one- to three-hour drive from each other. Like in other parts of Turkey, the roads here are very good, although heavy truck and bus traffic on many winding two-lane highways can be slow going at times.

If you choose to fly to this area, you'll find several regional airports located near the cities of Antalya and Dalaman (between Fethiye and Marmaris). Kaş and Kalkan are over 100 kilometers from the nearest (Dalaman) airport. These airports are serviced by regular flights from Istanbul and Ankara. Many visitors choose to rent a car immediately upon arrival since their destination may be some distance from the airport and because a car provides a great deal of flexibility to visit these areas.

If you arrive by cruise ship, chances are you will be coming into Antalya and Marmaris or Bodrum and Kuşadasi in the Aegean region. Most ships, however, stop in Kuşadasi because of the major tourist attraction in this area – the nearby Roman ruins of Ephesus. Like most port cities, shops and bazaars with aggressive merchants are conveniently located near the port entry point and offer a disproportionate amount of jewelry and souvenirs for such short-time visitors who are known to be impulsive shoppers who think they can get a great deal at these shops. Whatever you do, bargain hard in these places, just like you should do at the Grand Bazaar in Istanbul.

If you arrive by yacht, most major towns and cities have well organized marinas. Most of the cities and towns we cover here have extensive marinas and yacht clubs which also are serviced by upscale shops and shopping centers with boutiques and marine equipment shops. You'll find several of these cities to be yachters' paradises.

### GETTING AROUND

The easiest way to get around this area is by rental car. Many Americans will stay two to three days in several locations whereas European visitors often stay one to two weeks in a single location. Whatever your plans, a rental car should prove to be most convenient for getting around the area, and especially when going outside the cities and towns for sightseeing. In crowded cities with difficult one-way streets or blocked sections of town for pedestrians, such as Side, Antalya, and Marmaris, walking is a good approach. Taking mini-buses (*dolmuş*) is a good way to shuttle between your hotel and the central shopping area.

# SIDE, ASPENDOS, PERGE

If you are driving from Cappadocia or Konya on the way to Antalya, you'll initially pass through the ancient seaside town

of Side, which is approximately 80 kilometers east of Antalya. While the city traces its history to 4000 BC, it began to flourish as a trading port in the 2nd century BC. During the 2nd century AD numerous large buildings were constructed, including the huge and well-preserved Roman amphitheater which once held over 15,000 people. Side also is an important resort destination with beautiful beaches and numerous hotels, condos, restaurants, cafes, and shops. Especially popular with German and Scandinavian families, who stay here from one to three weeks at a time, Side is a very lively place for dining, drinking, shopping, and water sports. You'll quickly discover this is basically a German town – people address you in German, signs are in German, restaurants serve German dishes, everyone accepts payment in Euros, and beer flows plentifully. In fact, if you're not German and here for an extended family holiday, you may feel like an outsider.

If you don't stay in Side, you may want to spend two or

three hours here exploring the city's ruins and shopping along its main street, Liman Caddesi. In fact, the ruins and the main street are very close to one another. Just park your car in the lot adjacent to the amphitheater from which you can both visit the ruins (amphitheater and the temples of Apollo and Athens) and enjoy the local shopping and dining scene. This also is a good place to view the oceanfront and marina.

Most shops are found along Liman Caddesi and several side streets that run to the marina. For most visitors, this is a fun area that combines shopping with people watching, dining, drinking, and discos. It's a honky-tonk tourist area. Accordingly, you'll find numerous jewelry shops along with typical tourist handicraft and souvenir shops selling carpets, clothing, leather goods, T-shirts, Turkish delights, tea, and spices. Several shops offer knock-off name brand leather purses and bags.

If you're traveling from Side to Antalya, be sure to stop at **Aspendos** along the way. Located 45 kilometers northeast of Antalya, this is the site of the best preserved Roman amphitheater in Turkey. Built in 161-180 AD, this structure once held 15,000 spectators. Be sure to walk to the top of the hill behind the amphitheater for a good view of the surrounding structures and landscape. Today the amphitheater is used for concerts and theatrical performances. It includes two government-operated **Dösim** shops inside the amphitheater doors which offer a good selection of handcrafted items. The so-called ancient coins being offered by local touts are obvious fakes.

Located 18 kilometers east of Antalya is the ancient city of **Perge**. Established in the 12$^{th}$ and 13$^{th}$ centuries BC but flourished under the Romans during the 2$^{nd}$ and 3$^{rd}$ centuries BC, Perge is well worth visiting. It's a very interesting site with a long colonnaded street, large Roman and Hellenistic gates, city walls, Roman baths, agora (marketplace), mosaic sidewalks, and theater and stadium. Many of the impressive statues found in the Antalya Museum were taken from this site. You'll encounter many vendors selling small handcrafted items along the colonnaded street.

# ANTALYA

## GETTING TO KNOW YOU

Seaside Antalya is one of Turkey's major holiday resorts and convention centers. A city of over 1 million, it's especially noted for its award-winning marina (Antalya Kaleiçi Marina) and beautiful 13$^{th}$ century Seljuk-designed Fluted Minaret (Yivli

Minare) of the Yivli Minareli Mosque at the center of the city. Antalya also boasts an attractive Archaeological Museum, a convenient tramway, and numerous shops, bazaars, restaurants, and cafés that beckon visitors to spend their money. For an online introduction to this city, we recommend visiting these two useful websites:

- **Antalya Guide**         www.antalyaguide.org
- **Antalya Convention**    www.antalyaconvention.org

Antalya is a very compact and vibrant city for shoppers and diners who can concentrate their activities around the old historic district of **Kaleiçi**, which is located within the old city walls. This is the commercial center for the city and one of the most popular areas for visitors. The old stone Clock Tower (Saat Kulesi), which is at Kalekapisi Square – near the intersections of Cumhiriyet Caddesi and Atatürk Caddesi and the yacht harbor and marina – stands at the center of the city with the minaret, bay, and Taurus Mountains in the background. This is a very busy and crowded area with numerous jewelry, carpet, leather, handicraft, and souvenir shops lining the main and side streets. Here you'll encounter several aggressive vendors who try to persuade you to enter their shops, often with the not-so-subtle but always humorous line, *"Let me help you spend your money!"* They can be both persistent and pesky. At times you may feel you are running the gauntlet of merchants.

## SHOPPING ANTALYA

The Clock Tower is a good orientation point for shopping the city center. Just north of the Clock Tower is the city's small bazaar which is filled with jewelry stores. Immediately west of the bazaar is a pedestrian mall along Kasim Özalp Caddesi. East of the Clock Tower, along Cumhuriyet Caddesi and Atatürk Caddesi, are more jewelry stops. Indeed, this whole area seems to light up with jewelers. Adjacent to and south of the Clock Tower is a narrow winding street overflowing with small shops selling a wide variety of carpets, leather goods, art, tea, spices, and souvenirs galore – **Iskele Caddesi**. Follow this shopping lane to the end and you'll eventually come close to the harbor. While much of this street is the territory of aggressive carpet merchants, you'll find several interesting shops along the way selling ceramics, leather goods, fashion wear, copper and brass ware, art, tea, and spices. One of our favorites here is **Pikamo** for its unique and fashionable leather goods and ceramics:

❑ **Pikamo:** *Iskele Caddesi No. 20, Tel. 241-4879 or Fax 243-5800.* Offers one of the most unique and colorful collections of leather goods in Turkey – coats, purses, and wallets – with hand-painted designs of such noted abstract painters as Miro, Matisse, Picasso, and Kandinsky. In fact, the name Pikamo comes from combining two initials from the names of three major artists – <u>Pi</u>casso, <u>Ka</u>ndinsky, and <u>Mi</u>ro. Similar designs appear on a special collection of colorful hand-painted porcelain cups, plates, and saucers. The colors on the leather goods are guaranteed for 25 years. Also

includes cotton and wool jackets, scarves, and a special sale room with the previous season's leather goods. Most purses cost US$80 to US$120. The leather coats run US$210 to US$500. Pikamo has four other shops in Antalya as well as 28 shops in Germany and one shop each in Holland, Austria, Denmark, Sweden, Poland, Norway, and the United States.

Nearby, along Atatürk Caddesi, is **Capitol Leather** for a large selection of leather goods:

❑ **Capitol Leather Centre:** *Atatürk Caddesi No. 50, Tel. 248-6258 or Fax 242-0062.* This huge leather emporium includes two floors of leather goods – coats, jackets, purses, wallets, belts, briefcases, and luggage. Includes several noted Turkish leather lines – Tergan, Matras, Nobel – as well as knock-off labels. The lower level has a large collection of fashionable leather coats and jackets, including many interesting colors that are especially popular with their Russian and German clients – bright orange, green, red, yellow, and turquoise. Many of the wild colors and designs are fit for movie stars! Also look for mink and beaver fur coats and unique reversible leather jackets. The store will also do made-to-order leather goods which usually take two days to complete. Most items are subject to discounting which can run 30 percent. Capitol Leather Centre also owns a jewelry store which is located three shops away – **Capitol Jewellery** at Atatürk Caddesi No. 42 (Tel. 241-2436). It includes a good collection of gold, sapphire, ruby, and diamond jewelry.

### ACCOMMODATIONS

While Antalya offers a wide range of resort accommodations, the two best properties include:

❑ **Talya:** *Fevzi Çakmak Caddesi No. 30, 07100 Antalya, Tel. (90-242) 248-6800 or Fax (90-242) 241-5400. Website: www.tal ya.com.tr. E-mail: talyaotell@talya.com.tr.* Located near the city center on a cliff-top overlooking a stunning view of the turquoise Mediterranean and the Bey Mountains, the Talya Hotel is just a few minutes walk from the Old City. Talya Hotel offers five-star amenities and award-winning restaurants. Part of the local Divan Hotel Group, its 204 guest-rooms (standard, deluxe, and suites) all have balconies and overlook Antalya Bay. The rooms are relatively spacious and nicely furnished. Upgrade to a suite and in addition to more space you will find reproduction European furniture, gilded mirrors, and arrangements of local prints on the walls. However, as is frequently the case with establishments that are not part of international chains, if you arrive after the summer months you may find the air-conditioning for the entire building has been turned off – no matter what the temperature. The *Teras Restaurant* offers both Turkish and international cuisine and serves an excellent buffet breakfast and dinner – offering one of the widest selections of dishes that we encountered anywhere, and very good as well. Try the baklava if it is a dessert choice; it is one of the best we have had – anywhere. There is an a la carte menu available as well. You'll even forgive that there are a lot of tour groups that patronize this restaurant. In the evening there is live music, and a belly-dancer will appear at some point along with a photographer who will capture the moments when she dances close to or with diners on film. Photos can be purchased. *Pub Talya* serves snacks and grills and the *Piano Bar* serves a patisserie buffet as well as a variety of drinks. Breakfast or breakfast and dinner are often included in the price of the room, so ask when booking. Fitness Center (including Turkish Bath); Business Center; Internet Café; Convention Center with Conference/Banquet Facilities.

❑ **Sheraton Voyager:** *100 Yil Bulvari, Antalya 07050, Turkey, Tel. (90-242) 243-2432, Fax (90-242) 243-2462, Tel. (90-242) 243-2432, Fax (90-242) 243-2462. Website: www.shera ton.com/voyager. E-mail: reservations_voyager@sheraton.com.* Minutes away (by car) from the city center of Antalya, and overlooking the Mediterranean Sea, the soaring atrium lobby provides ample light and a spacious feel. The sound of the waterfall provides a soothing backdrop to the lobby area. All 395 guestrooms and suites are tastefully decorated and provide expected five-star amenities. Balconies allow guests to enjoy the sea breezes. Smart Rooms specifically designed for business travelers offer the convenience and comfort of an office within the room. *Panoramic Restaurant* serves international cuisine; *Maritime* offers a variety of seafood; *Tropic* is open for lunch; *Sundowner* serves Turkish pizza at lunch and *Islander* serves light lunch and snacks by the beach. A small shopping arcade includes a very nice jewelry shop, **Maya Jewellery** (Tel. 243-2432) which creates its own designs as well as carries a Michaela Frey line of jewelry. Internet Center; Health/Fitness Facilities (including a variety of baths, massages and steam treatments); Conference/Banquet Facilities.

### ENJOYING YOUR STAY

Being a beachfront resort, Antalya has a great deal to offer visitors who enjoy beaches and sailing. **Sailing excursions** can be booked directly with various boats moored at the marina. Good **beaches** can be found at several four- and five-star hotels as well as at Konyaalti (one and a half miles west of the city center), and Lara Beach (seven miles east of the city).

If you enjoy museums, don't miss the **Antalya Museum** (Antalay Müzesi, Tel. 241-4528) which is located one mile west of the Clock Tower on Kenan Evren Bulvan. This is one of the best museums in Turkey. It's jam-packed with artifacts and pottery as well as a large collection of statuary from Perge (2$^{nd}$ century AD), Christian icons from the 19$^{th}$ century, a fabulous room of stone sarcophagi (including one retrieved from the Brooklyn Museum which had been illegally excavated and transported to the United States in 1985), ethnography section, coins and jewelry, costumes, weapons, copper pots, ceramics, glass lamps, musical instruments, and carpets. A museum shop at the entrance includes a good collection of books, postcards, pictures, cards, mugs, oil lamps, jewelry, and ceramic plates.

# KALE AND MYRA

If you travel west of Antalya, we recommend taking the coastal road along the Turquoise Coast. This is a lovely drive through pine forested hills. In addition to encountering lots of tour buses, you'll witness a very rugged coastline with pebbly beaches, hot-house farming, and overbuilt towns with many abandoned or partially built flats (especially around Finike and Kumbeca).

Two small settlements along the way are worth visiting. If you enjoy Christmas, you'll want to stop in **Kale** (also known as Demre). This small town of approximately 300 inhabitants is famous for the Church of St. Nicholas and hot-house farming. Legend has it that one of the bishops in the 4th century AD, Bishop St. Nicholas, became known as Santa Claus. This is not forgotten with the small shops and street vendors in Kale who offer an interesting selection of St. Nicholas memorabilia, including Christmas tree ornaments made from gourds but painted as Santa Claus. Visiting the interesting old church and shopping for such items shouldn't take more than one hour – a good break from driving along the coast.

The nearby settlement of **Myra** – two kilometers from Kale – is the site of the famous Lycian tombs carved into the hills and another interesting Roman theater. The walkway to the viewing area is lined with numerous souvenir stalls selling a wide range of handcrafted items at often inflated prices. Be sure to bargain. We found the small Santa Claus rugs that sold for US$10 in Urügup (Cappadocia) going for US$30 here.

---

# KAŞ

This is easily one of our very favorite places along the Mediterranean coast. A small but very upscale resort destination with

lots of ambience, friendly people, and colorful bougainvillea and hibiscus growing along its cobblestone streets, the charming village of Kaş has a beautiful harbor setting with islands nearby. Its town square has several good shops and restaurants and adjacent streets include many quality jewelry, souvenir, carpet, antique, and ceramic shops. Catering to a much more discerning clientele than in the mass tourism destinations of Antalya and Side, the shops here tend to offer good quality products.

Be sure to visit Kaş between March and October. Because of the low season, nearly 95 percent of the shops close around

November 15th and reopen around March 15th.

Some of our favorite shops are found on the town square and along cobblestoned Uzunçarşi Gürsoy Sokak:

❑ **Silk Road:** *Uzunçarşi Gürsoy Sokak No. 1, Tel. 836-3980. E-mail: silkroadshop@hotmail.com.* This small corner shop offers a wide selection of antiques, handicrafts, jewelry, ceramics, textiles, and photographs from all over the world, but with special emphasis on Turkey and Central Asia. Includes a nice collection of Turkeman and Afghan jewelry, old locks from Iran and Turkmenistan, bells, and small collectibles. Like most shops in Kaş, this one closes during the winter months (beginning November 15th) when the owners travel to add to their unique collection. The very personable husband and wife team who own this shop also are professional photographers whose many mounted photos are for sale in a tiny adjoining room.

❑ **Turgueria:** *Uzunçarşi No. 21, Tel. 836-1631 or Fax 836-2894. Website: www.turgueria.com. E-mail: nauticakas@superonline.com.* Previously known as Nautica, this small but very nice shop includes a good collection of nautical instruments, knives, copper pots, watches, leather puppets (both Turkish and Indonesian), lights, paintings, prints, icons, locks, textiles, and much more.

❑ **Gallery Desen:** *Uzunçarşi No. 18, Tel. 836-2351.* This shop is jam-packed with copper pots, plates, and inlaid boxes. Includes many large and nice pieces, both old and new.

❑ **Galeria Seramik:** *PTT. Karşisi, Tel. 836-1018 or Fax 836-1242.* Located on the town square, this shop offers a nice collection of ceramics in the form of bowls, coasters, and tiles as well as jewelry, pipes, and silver. Open year around.

# KALKAN

Located 25 kilometers west of Kaş and 80 kilometers east of Fethiye, this former fishing hamlet is now a relatively upscale seaside holiday destination with lots of charm and ambience. It's especially popular with wealthy Turks. Built on a hillside and popular with yachtsmen, it claims to have the largest number of restaurants and bars per inhabitant or square meter on the Turkish coast. Maintaining its traditional quaint village architecture and restricting traffic to pedestrians only, the streets and lanes of Kalkan are fun to explore on foot. Just park at the top of the hill and walk along the cobblestone streets that descend into the village. Along the way you'll pass numerous tempting shops and restaurants and interesting pensions and hotels with roof-top terraces overlooking the village and attractive harbor. Its white buildings, purple bougainvillea, red hibiscus, stone streets, attractive marina, and sea views give Kalkan a very special ambience that makes this such a delightful place to visit.

You can easily spend a few hours exploring Kalkan's many shops which offer a good selection of carpets, kilims, copper items, jewelry, ceramics, leather goods, and assorted handicrafts and souvenirs. Customer service is not something that has taken hold in this village. Since this is a very laid back and

trusting community, you may find some shops open but with no one around to help you. Chances are the proprietor is visiting another shop, in a restaurant, or went home briefly. Just ask the shop next door or across the street for assistance. They should know when the shopkeeper will be back, or this person may actually fill in and help you with your purchase. When visiting this village, keep in mind that most shops, restaurants, and hotels close from November to March when only a trickle of tourists visit this area. For online information on Kalkan, including photos, be sure to visit this website:

www.kalkan.org.tr

Half the fun of visiting Kalkan is exploring the streets and lanes where you will discover many interesting shops. Some of our favorites here include:

❑ **Regard Jewellery:** *Yaliboyu Ham. Hasan Altan Caddesi No. 53, Tel. 844-3874 or Fax 844-3874. Website: www.kalkan.org. tr. E-mail: ceemjewellery@superonline.com.* In operation since 1987, this small shop produces nicely designed earrings, necklaces, and rings using diamonds, emeralds, and sapphires. Everything is designed and produced by the owner's wife in their Istanbul factory and studio.

❑ **Mina Art:** *Tel. 844-1002. No address, but located in the center of village, next door to Sakir Antik Galerie.* Offers a nice collection of contemporary glass and ceramics designed by an artist in Bodrum. The fish, cow, frog, dog, and shark themes are great for collectors and individuals in search of unique gift items.

❑ **Emin Bazaar:** *Tel. 844-2503, Yali Boyu Han.* Offers a large collection of old copper pots, plates, jewelry, bells, and carpets. A fun place for collectors in search of unique items.

❑ **Memik Antique Shop:** *Yali Boyu Mahalleşi, Tel. 844-2315.* Includes an attractive collection of copper plates, bowls, pots, lanterns, and inlaid boxes. Offers attractive hanging paper and copper lanterns.

❑ **Folk Art Gallery:** *Yali Boyu Mah No. 3, Tel. 844-3271.* Offers a good selection of both old and new rugs.

---

# MARMARIS

Located approximately 600 kilometers west of Antalya and 170 kilometers south of Bodrum, Marmaris lies at both the western end of the Mediterranean and the southern end of the Aegean Coast – literally where the Mediterranean and Aegean meet. Surrounded by pine-covered hills, with dramatic mountains in the background, the city is located on a beautiful fiord. Given its picturesque harbor setting, with a wide and curving palm tree-lined oceanfront boulevard, an old castle, charming neighborhoods, enticing bars and restaurants, appealing shopping, cosmopolitan atmosphere, and famous yachting culture, this is understandably one of Turkey's most famous seaside resorts. It's especially popular with cruise ships, day-trippers, and yachtsmen who are drawn to this sprawling city's attractive natural harbor and local treasures and pleasures. Marmaris's large private yacht marina, with its upscale shops and restaurants, lies adjacent to what often becomes transformed into a honky-tonk seaside resort overrun by tourists frequenting the city's many bars, restaurants, and souvenir shops. If you like a very active nightlife accented by bars with loud Western music, Marmaris will not disappoint you. Just go to **Bar Street** where you will find many bars and discos that stay open until 4am. Aside from the city's lovely harbor setting and its many cruising opportunities, there's nothing particularly compelling about Marmaris itself. It's a popular resort town for mass tourism.

People basically come here to party in the city or on the water – or both. Marmaris is a noted destination for the Blue Voyage, which is any cruise along the Turquoise Coast. You can charter a *gulet* (a large traditional Turkish-designed wooden yacht, 20-30 meters in length, with 5-10 cabins for up to 20 people) or other boats by the day or week to cruise the waters around the

Marmaris Peninsula. In fact, the peninsula is famous for its 12 ancient cities, some of which can be visited from the water, as well as several private beaches. Hydrofoils and other types of boats from the nearby Greek island of Rhodes (45 kilometers) bring day-trippers to the city for six or seven hours of shopping and dining. Indeed, shopping here takes on the character of a cruise ship center, much like Kuşadası to the north but on a much smaller scale.

For online information about Marmaris, visit these useful gateway websites:

- **About Marmaris**      www.aboutmarmaris.com
- **Marmaris Info**       www.marmarisinfo.com

The About Marmaris website also offers visitors a free shopping service – a "Personal Shopping Guide." For information on this service, including online reservations, visit this section of their information-rich website:

www.aboutmarmaris.com/marmaris-shopping/marmaris-shopping-guide.htm

Marmaris has three shopping areas: covered bazaar, main street (Kordon Caddesi/Atatürk Caddesi), and the upscale Netsel Shopping Center at the private marina. Most visitors interested in shopping, especially the day-trippers from Rhodes, head directly for the **covered bazaar** which is located across the street (Kordon Caddesi) from the marina and the statue of Atatürk. This is a very large bazaar filled with numerous shops and aggressive shopkeepers who primarily cater to the short-term (cruising) tourist trade: carpets, leather goods, jewelry, ceramics, tea, Turkish delights, and knock-off name brand clothes. The bazaar opens at 8:30am and closes sometime in the evening – depending on the traffic, which is usually sometime between 8pm and 9pm. The open-air Friday market offers lots of fun shopping, especially for fake goods.

Several jewelry and souvenir shops can be found along the main adjoining promenade streets of **Kordon Caddesi** and **Atatürk Caddesi**.

The upscale **Netsel Shopping Center** is attached to the private Marmaris International Yacht Club which is located east of the downtown area and castle. Just walk across the foot bridge that joins the oceanfront restaurant and yacht section of the city to the Netsel Marina. The small shopping center offers some of the best quality shopping in Marmaris. Here you'll find several nautical, resort wear, jewelry, and boutique shops catering to the marina's upscale clientele. **Lacoste, DKNY, Polo Garage**, and **Tommy Hilfiger** offer clothing and accessories. **Kuka Collection** presents a unique collection of Arabic calligraphy from the Koran, maps, and old photos. For marine gifts and silver items, check out **Evcim**. The shopping center also has several trendy restaurants and cafes overlooking the marina.

While Marmaris has numerous hotels and pensions for all tastes and budgets, the best hotel is the Grand Azur Hotel:

❑ **Grand Azur Hotel:** *Kenan Evren Bulvan, No. 13, 48700 Marmaris, Turkey, Tel. (90-252) 417-4050, Fax (90-252) 417-4060. Website: www.hotelgrandazur.com. E-mail: info@hotel grandazur.com.* This modern five-star hotel set on its own beach offers the best accommodation in Marmaris. The large circular marble lobby with its statue of Aphrodite offers no hint of one's being in Turkey. Even the Turkish carpets found in abundance in most hotels are absent. You realize how spread out the hotel is as you leave the lobby and make your way to your room. The 285 guestrooms are unexceptional but do offer the basic amenities of a five-star hotel. The pie-shaped rooms in the circular sections offer somewhat more space than those off the straight hallways. The main restaurant, *Palmiye I,* serves bountiful buffets. Two other restaurants with the imaginative names of *Gourmet Restaurant* for dinner, and *A la carte Restaurant* for all-day dining provide choices. *La Patisserie,* with its displays of colored glass on shelves, provides a pleasant area near the lobby with a choice of comfortable chairs or tables with chairs and serves pastries and snacks. The real draws here are the garden setting and the many water- related activities available – both for children (indoor jungle water park) and adults (indoor and outdoor pools, speedboats, jet skis, water skis, wind surfing, and diving programs). Health/Fitness Center; 2 Meeting Rooms/Banquet Facilities.

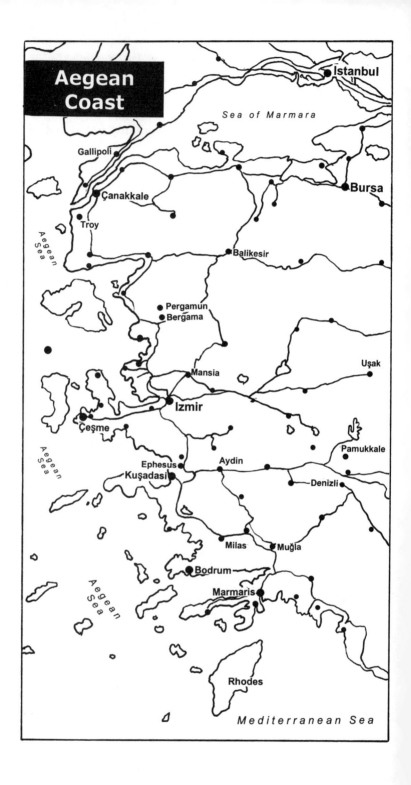

# Aegean Coast

Istanbul

*Sea of Marmara*

Gallipoli

Bursa

Çanakkale

Troy

*Aegean Sea*

Balikesir

Pergamun
Bergama

Mansia

Uşak

İzmir

Çeşme

*Aegean Sea*

Pamukkale

Ephesus
Kuşadasi

Aydin

Denizli

Milas

Muğla

Bodrum

Marmaris

*Aegean Sea*

Rhodes

*Mediterranean Sea*

# 9

# Aegean Coast

URKEY'S PICTURESQUE AEGEAN COAST OFFERS
even more seaside sun, shopping, sightseeing, and
dining opportunities. Pristine waters, sandy beaches,
old whitewashed Greek and Turkish villages, quaint
fishing villages, miles of olive and citrus groves and
pine-tree covered hills, crowded marinas with million-dollar
yachts, giant cruise ships making brief sightseeing and shopping
forays, ancient Roman and Greek ruins, and numerous seafood
restaurants distinguish this region from other areas in Turkey.

Extending north of Marmaris, the Aegean coastal area is an
attractive playground for millions of local and international
visitors who come here by sea, air, or road. Towns and cities
such as Bodrum, Kuşadasi, Çeşme, Izmir, and Çanakkale each
have their own compelling character that define much of this
region. Given the prominent role Ephesus plays in attracting

millions of tourists each year to Turkey by both land and sea, the Aegean coast has become Turkey's number one tourist destination. It's an area where you'll want to spend a week or more exploring its many treasures and pleasures.

## WELCOME TO THE AEGEAN REGION

Like much of the rest of Turkey, the Aegean Coast has a rich history, dating for more than 5,000 years, as exemplified in its many Roman and Greek ruins centered around the ancient cities of Ephesus and Pergamum and the forts and castles of Bodrum, Kuşadasi, and Izmir. It's also a great destination for seaside sun and fun with its many unspoilt beaches, picturesque bays, and numerous hotels, restaurants, shops, bars, and discos found in such places as Bodrum, Kuşadasi, Çeşme, Foça, Gümüldür, and Dikili.

❑ The Aegean coast has become Turkey's number one tourist destination.

❑ The Aegean coast has a rich history, dating from more than 5,000 years.

❑ Many people visiting this region book a one- to two-week cruise to explore this beautiful and intriguing coastal area.

The Aegean coastal region is usually divided into three sections – south, central, and north. The south Aegean encompasses Bodrum and Kuşadasi. The central Aegean encompasses Çeşme and Izmir. The north Aegean includes Pergamum, Troy, and Çanakkale on the Dardanelles. A heavily touristed area, the Aegean includes many small towns and villages that beg to be discovered by road or by sea. In fact, many people visiting this region book a one- to two-week cruise (the generic blue-voyage cruise) to explore this beautiful and intriguing coastal area.

## BODRUM

Located 170 kilometers north of Marmaris and 160 kilometers south of Kuşadasi and Ephesus, Bodrum was the birthplace of Heredotus and the site of Halicarnassus (1000 BC) which boasted one of the Seven Wonders of the Ancient World – the Mausoleum or Tomb of King Mausolus (4th century BC) from which the word "mausoleum" is derived. A lot has changed since that time.

## A PICTURE-POSTCARD SETTING

Present-day Bodrum seems to be everyone's favorite resort, including many expatriates and inspired artists who have settled here permanently. Indeed, it's Turkey's number one seaside resort, a picture-postcard resort town with an ambience resembling the French Riviera's St. Tropez in many ways. Beautiful, charming, and upscale, this city of white sugar-cubed (cuboid) flat-roofed buildings spreading over several hills and palm-lined streets is the favorite haunt for the rich and famous, whether from Turkey or other countries. Its two adjacent harbors, separated by a famous landmark medieval castle (Petronion or Castle of St. Peter), are jam-packed with million-dollar yachts and wooden gulets ready to take passengers to nearby islands or just cruise the beautiful blue waters (Blue Cruise) surrounding Bodrum. Its streets are

lined with pleasant outdoor restaurants, boutiques, bazaars, bars, and nightclubs that make this one of the most exciting cities along the Aegean Coast. Similar in some respects to Marmaris, but on a grander scale, Bodrum is where people come to relax, shop, dine, people watch, and party until early morning. It has a well-deserved reputation for being one of the more expensive places to visit in Turkey, which is generally reflected in the excellent quality of its infrastructure. Whatever you do, plan to spend a few days in Bodrum. It may well become one of your favorite destinations in all of Turkey.

While Bodrum used to be a very exclusive destination, in recent years it, too, has become a destination for mass tourism as more and more tour groups come here with busloads of clients to enjoy the city's seaside ambience. As a result, Bodrum often has the look and feel of many other crowded Mediterranean communities that have become popular tourist destinations.

## GETTING TO KNOW YOU

As you plan your trip to Bodrum, be sure to visit these two useful gateway websites for online information about the town and surrounding area:

- **Bodrum-Info**          www.bodrum-info.org
- **Bodrum Turkey**     www.bodrumturkey.com

Bodrum can be a challenge to get around in by car, especially since it has so many disorienting one-way streets. If you're driving into the town, you may have to get lost three or four times before figuring out where you're supposed to go. The main street into the center of town is **Cevat Şakir Caddesi**. If you take this street to the end, it goes into **Kale Caddesi**, the main tourist center for shopping, dining, and boating which literally comes between the Inner Harbour (Salmakis Bay) and the Outer Harbour (Kumbahçe Bay). Located just north of the Castle, **Kale Oniki Eylül Meydani** (12 September Square) or Iskele Meydani, the Caddesi runs into the town plaza that includes the tourist office, cafes, and boats waiting to take visitors on excursions. Immediately northwest of this area is the **Inner Harbour** with the Marina Yacht Club which is lined with stunning yachts. This area also includes an upscale shopping center, **Karada Marina** (Marina Shopping Center), that primarily offers name brand clothes, accessories, and jewelry. The Outer Harbour, which lies to the east of the Castle, includes a pedestrian-only waterfront walkway that stretches east along **Dr. Alim Bey Caddesi** and **Cumburiyet Caddesi**. This area also is known as Bodrum's "bar street" with its many bars, discos, nightclubs, restaurants, cafes, and shops facing the sea.

Shopping in Bodrum is largely confined to the downtown shops along Kale Caddesi. Here you'll find the ubiquitous carpet, brass, ceramic, leather, clothing, jewelry, and souvenir shops catering to the tourist trade. Some of our favorite shops here include:

❏ **Galeri Anatolia II**: *Kale Caddesi No. 1, Tel. 316-1939.* Operated by Ismail Açikel, the brother of the rug shop owner two doors away (Ercan Açikel at Galeri Anatolia I, 3), this is a very deceptive looking shop with no sign or name attached (we've named it Galeri Anatolia II because it's part of Galeri Anatolia I – the second shop – but the owner often refers to it as the "Gift Shop"). Located on a corner leading into the bazaar, it definitely looks like a tourist kitsch shop with all kinds of copper, wood, and glass tourist trinkets and souvenirs spilling out onto the walkway. Many visitors would normally skip this place altogether because it looks like a tourist shop, but selling kitsch to tourists is called "cash flow" – it pays the bills! The gold mine is inside the shop. The owner is an avid antique collector who has a much larger inventory of antiques in a depot 20 minutes away by car (he'll take you there if you're interested). The treasures here are plentiful, the quality is excellent, and the prices are very high. Our advice: step over the kitsch and go inside this tiny shop and start browsing from floor to ceiling. You may have to literally crawl your way to the real antique treasures. Look for a nice collection of old textile wood block prints, silver and lacquer boxes from Uzbekistan and Turkmenistan, Çanakkale ceramic wedding vases, copper pots, antique belts, coffee grinders, ink and pen sets, Konya wood mortars, and textiles. While the friendly owner is at times

difficult to communicate with in English, his enthusiasm often gets the message over loud and clear. You'll have to drive a hard bargain here to get much of a discount on his many unique antiques. Indeed, expect to pay a lot more in this small shop than you might in more upscale antique shops in Istanbul. But this shop has some beautiful antiques you won't find elsewhere.

❑ **Galeri Anatolia I:** *Kale Caddesi Nos. 1-3, Tel. 316-2468, 313-2982 or Fax 316-5797.* If you visit Bodrum, this is the place to shop for carpets, kilims, and embroidered tapestries. The very personable owner, Ercan Açikel, has been in business for nearly three decades. Known for his excellent selections, quality, and service, Ercan offers a good selection of fine textiles in this two-story shop. His friendly and low-key approach emphasizes the importance of educating visitors about his many selections. Expect to spend some time here learning about rugs and tapestries. Experienced in packing and shipping abroad.

❑ **Diamond:** *Kale Caddesi 37 and 37-B, Tel./Fax 316-4670 and 316-7457; Karada Marina C26, Tel./Fax 316-6452; and Cumhuriyet Caddesi 43, Tel./Fax 316-4564 (main store).* Consisting of four jewelry shops in Bodrum and a workshop and antique shop (Grand Bazaar) in Istanbul, Diamond offers an excellent collection of nicely designed jewelry. Many pieces are copies of jewelry by Chopard, Tiffany's, and Cartier. Three of its specialties are black pearls, black diamonds, and antique gold jewelry. Its beautiful 24-carat collection of gold jewelry are copies of pieces designed by Gurhan, the famous Golden Boy of Turkey, who used to work for this firm (now in New York City). The shops also include a few antique silver pieces. The most exclusive of the four shops is found at Karada Marina.

Bodrum also has two markets of interest to some visitors: a Tuesday cloth market and a Friday fruit and vegetable market.

### ACCOMMODATIONS

Given the upscale nature of Bodrum's clientele, it boasts some of the best resort accommodations in Turkey. These two unique properties in particular warrant special attention:

❑ **The Marmara Bodrum:** *PK 199, 48400 Bodrum, Turkey, Tel. (90-252) 313-8130 or Fax (90-252) 313-8131. Website: www.themarmarabodrum.com.* This is a gem – not to be missed. Whether looking beyond your balcony over the city to the sea beyond, swimming in the infinity pool, or luxuriating in the spa, you will find something to delight and amaze you at this unique boutique hotel filled with wonderful treasures from Turkey and beyond. It's a tasteful and eclectic designer's showcase. A member of the *Small Luxury Hotels of the World*, the Marmara Bodrum delights both first-time and repeat guests alike. Enter the reception lounge and you are greeted by a large *chofa* from Thailand; lamps whose bases are large terra cotta jars with lampshades seemingly suspended in thin air; and comfortable chairs overlooking a glass wall that affords views of the grounds. Perhaps the first suggestions of the whimsy you will encounter are the colorful balls that occupy the chairs. Walk around the public spaces and you see a marvelous collection of Turkish things from the beautifully mounted textiles to walls full of locks of various sizes and shapes or old wooden print blocks. Interesting items – old and new – from all over the world as well as the whimsical, come together to create charm, interest, and comfort.

The architecture is that of a fortress of stone on the outside; whereas from the inside the impression is one of lots of open space and sun-filled glass-walled spaces. Check out the lavatories on the main floor. The clear glass doors of the individual cubicles turn to frosted glass once you lock the door. 100 guestrooms and suites offer spacious closet space with plenty of hangers and drawers with plexiglas fronts so you can easily see what you placed inside. The in-room safe can be set with the combination of numbers you select or simply slide a credit card through the slot – just like at the grocery store – to set your lock and later to open it again. Just don't lose your credit card in the interim! Regular rooms feature a window between the wall next to the tub/shower in the bathroom and the sleeping area beyond. There is a blind that can be lowered for privacy but with the blind up you can bathe while admiring the view out over the balcony to the sea.

Since Bodrum has a reputation as a "party town," the nightly turn-down service includes Alka-Seltzer, rather than a chocolate, on the pillow. Each of the five suites has a whirlpool tub in the bath. The largest suite has a jacuzzi. All the suites, as well as corner guestrooms have sofa-beds that can provide additional sleeping space for a family. Each guestroom has its own balcony or if on the ground floor – a patio. *Tuti Restaurant* serves breakfast, lunch, and dinner and offers international selections as well as local specialties. In nice weather the restaurant area flows out onto the terrace around the pool and overlooking the city. The *Pool*

*Bar/Lounge Bar* serve lunch and snacks. Pets are accepted, but check ahead. Business Center Services; Fitness Center includes Turkish Bath, Sauna, Jacuzzi, and a large range of massage treatments; an infinity swimming pool and a lap pool; squash courts; flotation tank; Meeting Rooms/Banquet Facilities for small groups.

❑ **Lavanta Hotel:** *Yalikavak - Bodrum, 48430 Turkey, Tel. (90-252) 385-2167 or Fax: (90-252) 385-2290. Website: http://lavanta.com/services.html. Closes from November 1 to April 15.* Located 11 miles outside of Bodrum near the village of Yalikavak, Lavanta is a small homespun hotel owned and operated by a charming couple, Tosun and Maria Merey. Selected by "Best Small Hotels of Turkey," it is only open in the summer months – approximately April thru late October. Lavanta is a quiet, homey retreat set on a tranquil hillside surrounded by olive groves and fields of fragrant herbs. All guestrooms – eight rooms and 12 suites – have views of the distant Bay of Yalikavak and are individually decorated with antiques and crafts collected by the owners. Guestrooms have expected amenities – mini-bar, satellite TV, hair dryer, safety deposit box, and robes. Internet access is available for guests. A bottle of wine and basket of fresh fruit welcome guests to their room on arrival. Many of the vegetables served at Lavanta are grown in their on-site garden and they keep chickens for fresh eggs, bake some of their bread, and have a wine cellar. Breakfast is included with the room, and guests may choose to have light snacks for lunch or dinner on premises at additional cost. Although classified as a small hotel, Lavanta has much of the feel of a bed and breakfast.

### ENJOYING YOUR STAY

There's a lot to see and do in and around Bodrum to justify several days here. Be sure to visit these worthwhile sites:

❑ **Castle of St. Peter (Petronion):** *Kale Caddesi, Tel. 316-2516. Open Tuesday to Sunday, 8:30am to 12noon and 1-5pm. Admission US$4.* Perched between two harbors, this well-preserved 15th century medieval castle stands at the center of the city. You can visit various towers, rooms, and court-yards which display interesting collections of artifacts. The Museum of Underwater Archaeology is of special interest with its many artifacts recovered from shipwrecks along the Aegean Coast. The castle affords excellent view of the town and harbors.

❑ **Mausoleum of Halicarnassus:** *Turgut Reis Caddesi. Open Tuesday to Sunday, 8am - 12noon and 1-5pm. Admission US$2.00.* If you are an ancient history buff, this site will have a great deal of meaning for you. Completed in 350 BC, this was once the site of the famous Wonder of the Ancient World, the huge marble tomb of King Mausolus of Caris. The structure collapsed in an earthquake of 1522. Many of the stones were used in the reconstruction of the castle. Today only a foundation, parts of pillars, and lots of rocks stand next to a model of the structure. The model and draw-ings bring to life the enormity of this once grand structure.

❑ **Theater:** Located just north of the Mausoleum on the southern slope of Göktepe hill, this is one of the oldest pre-Hellenic theaters in Anatolia. It is gradually being restored.

If you're interested in cruising the Aegean coast for a few days, you should arrange a **Blue Cruise** before you arrive in Bodrum. Most travel agents can make such arrangements. Several such agencies are identified on the two gateway websites we identified above for Bodrum. If you arrive in Bodrum without such prior arrangements, visit the Tourist Information Office, travel agencies, and cruise operators that are found near each other on Oniki Eylül Meydani (12 September Square).

Bodrum is especially famous for its lively and sophisticated nightlife of bars, discos, and nightclubs that cater to all tastes and budgets. In fact, many people prefer Bodrum over Istanbul for the best nightlife in Turkey. Bars usually open by midday and stay open until early in the morning. Most discos and nightclubs, which have cover charges, get started around 10-11pm and close around 3-4am. Bodrum's "Bar Street" consists of Dr. Alim Bey Caddesi that also becomes Cumhuriyet Caddesi. Some of the most unusual and popular places include **Halikarnas Disco** (Cumhuriyet Caddesi No. 178, Tel. 316-8000); **Hadigari** (Dr. Alim Bey Caddesi, Tel. 313-1960); **Bebek Bar** (Cumhuriyet Caddesi No. 53, Tel. 316-5302); and **Mavi Bar** (Cumhuriyet Caddesi No. 175, Tel. 316-3932).

# KUŞADASI

Located 150 kilometers north of Bodrum and 95 kilometers south of Izmir, Kuşadasi is the gateway city to the nearby Roman ruins of Ephesus (Efes), the ancient cities of Miletus, Priene, and Didyma, and to the popular travertine pools of Pamukkale. Lacking a regional airport (Izmir's Adnan Menderes Airport 100 kilometers away is the closest), all visitors arrive here by either ship or road.

## PRIMARILY SIGHTSEEING AND SHOPPING

Depending on the season, several cruise ships may dock at the waterfront or drop anchor in the harbor in a single day. Passengers disembark, board tour buses, and head for Ephesus which is only a 30-minute drive away. After two hours at Ephesus, they return to Kuşadasi, spend some time shopping, and return to their ship and then sail on to their next destination. This short cruise ship arrival-visit-departure routine has left a definite impact on the character and quality of tourism in Kuşadasi – everyone expects most tourists to be here this morning and gone this evening, with only a few hours available for shopping and sightseeing in the city. Hotels and restaurants benefit little from this traffic since passengers already have their accommodations and meals taken care of on board.

Most tour groups that arrive by bus spend one night in Kuşadasi. While they may have more time to shop in the bazaars and shops, in the eyes of most shopkeepers, they are similar to cruise ship shoppers – individuals with limited shopping time.

Independent travelers with a few days to spend in and around Kuşadasi will find numerous travel agencies offering a variety of interesting tours of the surrounding area, with special emphasis on Ephesus and Pamukkale as well as on the ancient cities of Miletus, Priene, and Didyma. Most such tours cost US$25 to US$40 per person.

## WELCOME TO THE CRUISE SHIP BAZAAR

As Turkey's most popular destination for cruise ships, Kuşadasi takes the honors for having one of the largest concentrations of bazaars and tourist shops which primarily service passengers disembarking from their cruise ships on their way to and from nearby Roman ruins of Ephesus. The shops here are all too familiar – jewelry, leather, clothing, rug, souvenir, tea and spice, music, and knock-off watches – and the competition is extremely fierce because of the oversaturation of such shops.

❑ Kuşadasi is the gateway city to the nearby Roman ruins of Ephesus (Efes).

❑ The short cruise ship arrival-visit-departure routine has left a definite impact on the character of tourism in Kuşadasi

❑ Shopkeepers tend to be very aggressive.

❑ Bargained prices can range from 20 to 60 percent off the initial asking price.

Since both cruise ship and tour bus visitors are all short-termers who will most likely never return to Kuşadasi again, merchants only have one shot at their pocketbooks.

Not surprisingly, given the nature of both the clientele and the competition, the shopkeepers tend to be very aggressive in attempting to persuade these potential customers to visit their shops and buy quickly. Indeed, you'll find an entertaining range of sales techniques to get you to make fast buying decisions, from emboldened to low key. Most shopkeepers speak English, German, or French, and they tend to be very personable, inviting you into their shops for a drink and a high-pressured sales presentation – they get to the basics quickly by offering you a "good price" which reflects a variety of daily specials for people like you (end of season, first customer of the day, cruise ship, end of day). Whatever the pitch, make sure you really want what you're looking at and bargain hard for everything. Prices will be all over the place. The good news is that since similar products are found in many different shops – competition is very intense because of the over-saturated market – you can quickly compare prices by going from one shop to another. Bargained prices can range from 20 to 60 percent off the initial asking price. So sharpen your bargaining skills and be prepared to walk out of a shop as part of your hard-nosed approach to bargaining.

Kuşadasi's major shopping area is centered on the shipping docks which are directly across the street from the Club Caravanśrail (Hotel Kervansaray at Atatürk Bulvari No. 2) in the center of the city. Here you will see numerous covered bazaars and street shops that go off into several different directions. There's no single best approach to this area. Just start walking and you'll eventually cover most of the area. The area has a disproportionate number of jewelry, carpet, leather, souvenir, spice, and knock-off (counterfeit) clothing and watch shops.

While many shops offer the same or similar items, a few jewelry shops worth exploring in Kuşadasi's bazaar include: **Fancy Jewellery** (Barbaros Hayrettin Paşa Bulvari No. 45, Tel. 613-4297); **Facet Jewellery** (Barbaros Hayrettin Paşa Bulvari No. 37, Tel. 614-1169); and **JeweleX** (Barbaros Hayrettin Paşa Bulvari No. 7, Tel. 614-1945). The latter two shops include a nice selection of 22-carat gold Trabzon (finely woven), jewelry. **Caravanśrail Hali** (Atatürk Bulvari No. 2, Tel. 614-3110) on the ground floor of the Hotel Kervansaray, includes a large collection of rugs and kilims displayed in a charming setting – the 300-year old Ottoman caravanserai. They also include an outdoor demonstration area showing the spinning of silk cocoons and the weaving of rugs.

### ACCOMMODATIONS

Since so many visitors to Kuşadasi arrive by cruise ship and thus already have on-board accommodations, the city has a limited number of quality properties. The best hotel in the city is the charming and elegant family-run Hotel Kismet:

❑ **Hotel Kismet:** *Akyar Mevkil 09400, Kuşadasi, Aydin, Turkey, Yel. (90-256) 618-1290 or Fax (90-256) 618-1295. Website: www.kismet.com.tr. E-mail: kismet@efes.net.tr.* Founded by the granddaughter of the last Ottoman sultan, the list of celebrities and heads of state who have been guests here is endless. It can be fun to look at the photographs of celebrities mounted in the lobby and note which ones stayed in the suite you are occupying. Hotel Kismet sits on a peninsula that juts into the Aegean Sea overlooking the marina and harbor. The gardens overlooking the turquoise sea are filled with pine and palm trees, the glorious color of bougainvillea and the scent of jasmine. With seating arranged for small groups in conversation, the gardens are a lovely place to sit. The lounge area off the reception area is enclosed by a wall of glass that affords views of the sea from the comfort of air conditioning in summer and heating in cooler months. The 107 guestrooms, three suites, and 12 deluxe rooms all have balconies with views of the sea and the expected in-room amenities. There is no doubt that Kismet offers the most luxury to be found in Kuşadasi; however, some rooms appear a bit worn and refurbishment would put the finishing touch on an otherwise splendid hotel. The setting is lovely, amenities in place, the warmth of a family in evidence. It exudes Old World charm. Lunch and dinner are served at the *Terrace Restaurant* where an international buffet or an a la carte menu featuring Turkish and Ottoman specialties are options. The *Lobby Bar* and *Marina Bar* offer views of the harbor. Internet available; Fitness Center; Water Sports; Meeting Facilities for up to 80 participants.

## ENJOYING YOUR STAY

Most visitors use this city as their base for sightseeing around the area. You'll find numerous travel agencies in the downtown area offering similar half- and full-day tours to a variety of destinations around Kuşadasi: Ephesus, Pamukkale, Priene-Miletus-Didyma, Bodrum, Dalyan, and the Greek island of Samos. Many of these agencies also will arrange boat trips, jeep safaris to the National Park, horseback riding into the mountains, and visits to villages as well as evening cultural shows (folk and belly dancing).

The highlight of any visit to Kuşadasi is a trip to the ancient nearby city of **Ephesus**, which is located 75 kilometers south of Izmir and 30 kilometers north of Kuşadasi. A very wealthy city, it was once the commercial center of the ancient world. Only a half hour drive from Kuşadasi, Ephesus is Turkey's most popular sightseeing attraction, drawing up to 3,000 visitors a day. It's also one of the most crowded sites. If you've not encountered many tourists elsewhere in Turkey, you definitely will in Ephesus. Depending on how many cruise ships arrive in a single day, you may feel overwhelmed by the hundreds of tourists that arrive here by tour bus, especially in the mornings. To avoid the crowds, plan to visit Ephesus early or late in the day. By 10am this place can be one big traffic jam. Be sure to wear a comfortable pair of shoes and bring your imagination since much of Ephesus consists of former structures that are now piles of collapsed columns and walls. One of the world's most impressive and well-preserved ancient sites, the highlights of Ephesus include the theater, Marble Avenue, Library of Celsus, Street of Kuretes, Temple of Hadrian, and the Ephesus Museum. Depending on how much you wish to see – much of the area consists of piles of rocks – you can easily cover Ephesus in one to two hours or spend a half day or more exploring the area. You can hire a guide near the entrance to the site.

---

# ÇEŞME

Located 80 kilometers west of Izmir on a peninsula, the quaint town of Çeşme is a surprise to many visitors. Standing at the most westerly tip of Turkey, this is an ancient area with more than 3,000 years of history. From the moment you get on to the impressive six-lane toll road (built for the NATO war effort in Kosovo), which connects Izmir to Çeşme, until you explore the charming downtown area of small shops lining the cobblestone main street that originates at the waterfront, Çeşme has the look and feel of an upscale community with lots of character. Indeed, it is noted as one of Turkey's exclusive seaside communities offering beautiful sandy beaches (they actually have sand rather than irritating pebbles) and good shopping and restaurants. Many independent travelers, as well as wealthy Turkish residents and Greek visitors, prefer Çeşme to Turkey's other mass tourist destinations along the Mediterranean Sea. Best of all, Çeşme is a very friendly and laid-back community where you are more likely to be treated as a guest rather than a tourist. In addition to shopping, you can visit its landmark 700-year old Genovese Castle, explore beaches, and visit the intriguing nearby village of **Alaçati** which still retains its Greek character.

## SHOPPING ÇEŞME

It's very easy to navigate Çeşme given its small size. The main street, **Inkilap Caddesi**, cuts through the center of town and functions as its main shopping street. You can easily cover both sides of this street in a couple of hours, more or less.

While Çeşme's shopping district is relatively small, it offers several good jewelry, leather, and rug shops for a few hours of concentrated shopping. The merchants here tend to be very friendly and laid back – unlike their aggressive counterparts in the cruise ship and mass tourism centers. Most of these shops are located along the main street within a two- to five-minute walk of each other. Some of our favorite shops include:

### CARPETS

❑ **Motif Gallery:** *Inkilap Caddesi No. 40, Tel./Fax 712-6273 or Tel. 712-7543. E-mail: hayimakyuz@superonline.com.* Located along the main street of Çeşme, this is one of our favorite carpet and kilim shops in Turkey. Operated by the very engaging and personable economist Hayim Akyüz, who

speaks impeccable English and whose family has been in the textile business for decades, this two-story shop and gallery is filled with excellent quality old and new Turkish carpets and kilims as well as tapestries from Turkmenistan. Hayim, a noted community leader, is extremely knowledgeable about textiles and spends a great deal of time with visitors in explaining the differences in quality, colors, and designs. He works with many international clients who have become long-term customers. There's no expectation of bargaining here since the shop offers excellent prices and good value. Experienced in packing and international shipping.

### JEWELRY

❑ **Eleganz:** *Inkilap Caddesi No. 87/A, Tel. 342-0881.* This small jewelry shop has its own workshop from which it designs its own attractive line of jewelry, especially rings, necklaces, and bracelets.

❑ **33 Jewelry:** *Inkilap Caddesi No. 87/A, Tel. 712-6918 or Fax 712-6785.* This innovative shop offers a nice selection of rings, diamonds, watches, and pins. Several of its clever pendant designs literally open up into other designs. Produces reversible diamond rings that become ruby rings.

❑ **Safran:** *Inkilap Caddesi No. 58/A, Tel. 712-9014 or Fax 712-7350.* Offers a nice selection of rings and diamond necklaces.

❑ **Taşci:** *Altinyunus Oteli, Tel. 723-51-15 or Fax 723-2250.* Located in the lobby of the Altin Yunus Hotel, this small shop offers a very nice selection of uniquely designed jewelry, with special emphasis on Tahitian black pearls.

LEATHER

❑ **Acar Leather Collection:** *Inkilap Caddesi No. 85, Tel. 712-6249 or Fax 712-9981.* Includes a good selection of nicely designed leather coats and jackets for both men and women. Include four shops along this main street.

❑ **Star Leather:** *Inkilap Caddesi No. 63, Tel. 712-6661.* Located across the street from the Motif Gallery, this shop offers both men and women a large selection of leather coats, jackets, vests, skirts, pants, caps, and suede shirts. Most everything here is produced in İzmir.

ACCOMMODATIONS

The Çeşme Peninsula includes numerous hotels. The two top properties in this area include:

❑ **Sheraton Çeşme:** *Şifne Caddesi No. 35, Llica, Çeşme 35940, Turkey, Tel. (90-232) 723-1240, Fax (90-232) 723-1856, or Toll-free in U.S. or Canada, 800-325-3535. E-mail: reservation @sheratoncesme.com.* The newest luxury accommodations in Çeşme, the Sheraton is positioned on a sandy beachfront. The lobby is filled with neutral beige marble and accented by columns, murals, and a geometric articulated ceiling. All 373 guestrooms and suites have a view and are elegantly appointed and equipped with the latest amenities. Deluxe suites are spacious and have a 550-meter terrace and a private swimming pool. Exclusive Floor guests may enjoy breakfast on their own floor. Flavors from all over the world meet at the Sheraton Çeşme. Californian specialties are served at the *Espace Grill. Cafézita* offers Italian cuisine, and an eclectic a la carte menu is offered by *Manzara Restaurant.* The *Palm Court Lobby Lounge* is a relaxing place to sit and sip a beverage. Thermal Water Pools/Massage Treatments; Business Center; Conference/Banquet Facilities. Includes a branch of the Sponza jewelry store which is headquartered in Izmir.

❏ **Altin Yunus:** *Çeşme Turistik Tesisler A. Ş., 35948, Çeşme-Izmir, Turkey, Tel. (90-232) 723-1250 or Fax (90-232) 723-2252. Website: www.altinyunus.com.tr. E-mail: infoaltinyunus.com.tr.* Altin Yunus in Çeşme, between Izmir and Ephesus, claims to have been the first holiday village in Turkey. Established in 1975, with 353 guestrooms, 63 marina rooms, 44 studios, 44 cabanas, eight suites, and five flats, Altin Yunus provides choices to suit many preferences. If you want a resort feel, you may wish to select a marina or cabana room. Guestrooms have expected amenities and are furnished with the look of an American mid-range chain hotel. There are several restaurants, though some are only open 'in season' and the largest services many tour groups with an extensive buffet. Tour groups and families are very much in evidence here. *Magnolia 'a la carte' Restaurant & Bar* serves international cuisine as does *Bacchus Restaurant & Bar*. *Captain Café* offers Italian specialties and fast food. *Petunia Restaurant* presents a selection from various world cuisines. *Pinar Sea Food Restaurant* offers fish and other seafood specialties. Sports Activities; Conference/Banquet Facilities.

---

# IZMIR

Often referred to as "Beautiful Izmir" and the "Pearl of the Aegean," Izmir is Turkey's second largest port (after Istanbul) and its third largest city (2.5 million people). Primarily built on commerce, industry, and trade, Izmir is a very cosmopolitan city worth visiting for a day or two. While it's not a major tourist destination, it does offer a few treasures and pleasures to warrant a short visit on your way to other attractions along the Aegean coast.

Located 560 kilometers southwest of Istanbul and 90 kilometers north of Kuşadasi, Izmir has a very appealing oceanfront setting. It's situated along an expansive and sweeping circular bay with a palm-lined promenade and wide boulevards at its center with picturesque hills and mountains in the background. Its mild climate, including refreshing sea breezes during the hot summer months, make this a very pleasant city to visit year-round.

While Izmir is a very important business city, it's also a noted art and culture center. It boasts several museums and theaters and is home to Turkey's famous Ege (Aegean) Philharmonic Orchestra. Izmir also hosts an International Arts Festival (June/July) and an International Fair (August/September).

Izmir also is a good base from which to visit nearby tourist attractions, especially Ephesus, Kuşadasi, the ancient city of Pergamum (Bergama), and the Çeşme Peninsula. However, many visitors to Izmir stay in Ephesus or the Çeşme Peninsula from where they then visit Izmir on a day trip. We prefer staying in the city for a couple of days since a day-trip cannot do justice to this often under-rated city.

For travel-shoppers, Izmir offers some interesting shopping opportunities in its bazaars, neighborhoods, and shopping malls. While by no means a competitor to Istanbul or Ankara, nonetheless, Izmir has enough good quality shopping to keep you treasure hunting for at least a day or two.

## GETTING TO KNOW YOU

Like so many other cities on the Aegean, Izmir has a long and interesting history. It has been a melting pot for numerous cultures and peoples. For centuries, until it changed its name to Izmir in 1923, this city was known as Smyrna. Established in the third millennium B.C., the city variously fell under the influence and control of the Hittites, Ionians, Lydians, Persians, Romans, Byzantines, Seljuks, Greeks, and Ottomans. Most recently, it played an important role in establishing the Republic of Turkey. Indeed, this is where the Turkish Army, led by Atatürk, defeated the much despised occupying Greeks (1918-1922) on September 9, 1922.

While large and often paralyzed by traffic, Izmir is still a relatively easy city to get oriented to and around in once you understand its traffic circles, boulevards, and one-way streets. It's best to orient yourself to the city by way of the waterfront. The main street fronting on the waterfront is **Atatürk Caddesi** which also is known by local residents as Birinci Kordon or First Cordon. Immediately to the west and parallel to Atatürk Caddesi is **Cumhuriyet Bulvari** or the Second Cordon (Ikinci Kordon). At the southern end of these two streets is the district of **Konak** which is the busy center of the city. It includes the Konak Square with the city's large and symbolic clock tower (Saat Kulesi), a waterfront park, tourist office, popular bazaar, and numerous hotels and restaurants. The main street here,

❑ Izmir is a very cosmopolitan city primarily built on commerce, industry, and trade.

❑ Izmir also is a noted art and culture center.

❑ This city has a long history of being a melting pot for numerous cultures and peoples.

❑ The Konak area includes two popular bazaars.

❑ The Alsancak area is Izmir's upscale shopping and dining district.

**Anafartalar Caddesi**, leads to the city's attractively restored old covered bazaar, **Kizlarağasi Hani**, which caters to tourists. The nearby **Kemeralti Market** area primarily appeals to locals with its many clothing, household goods, and jewelry shops.

Less than one-half kilometer north of Konak Square is the city's second major square, **Cumhuriyet Meydani**. which faces the waterfront. Immediately south east of the square, along Gazi Osmanpaşa Bulvari, you'll find the city's major four- and five-star hotels, as well as many travel agencies, rental car companies, and office buildings. Just northeast of this square in the district of **Alsancak** you'll find the city's major upscale shopping neighborhood.

### SHOPPING IZMIR

The most interesting shopping in Izmir is found in three areas: (1) Konak area with its two bazaars around **Anafartalar Caddesi**; (2) the area in and around the Izmir Hilton Hotel, along **Gazi Osmanpaşa Bulvari** (immediately southeast of Cumhuriyet Square); and (3) the Alsancak area northeast of Cumhuriyet Square, especially along **Sokak 1382, Pleyne Bulvari**, and **M. Enverbey Caddesi** and their adjacent pedestrian streets. Farther north of the city you'll find the upscale shopping area of **Karsiyaka**.

### KONAK AREA BAZAARS

Located in the heart of the city are two bazaars well worth exploring. The larger one is in the **Kemeralti Market** with its numerous lanes and aggressive salespeople. Unlike other bazaars, which tend to be organized into specialty areas, this one is relatively spread out and somewhat chaotic. The major specialty section here is the gold and jewelry market area (try **Sehrazat**, 928 Sokak No. 64, Tel. 484-3476). This bazaar primarily caters to local residents who come here to purchase household goods, from clothes to foodstuffs. However, you will find a few copper and antique shops in the area. The bazaar does include several leather and carpet shops whose aggressive salespeople will pester anyone who looks like a tourist. They all seem to have that wonderful "uncle" who will give you a good price on great quality leather goods and carpets. You may want to walk fast through this bazaar. While interesting to see, this is not a particularly attractive place to shop for quality goods.

The nearby old covered bazaar, **Kizlarağasi Hani**, located next to the mosque, is housed in a restored (1995) old market building which was originally constructed in 1744. It's open

Monday through Saturday (closed Sunday) from 9am to 7pm. Numerous shops here primarily cater to tourists who are interested in antiques, collectibles, carpets, leather goods, jewelry, embroidery, paintings, and handicrafts. It includes an adjacent food court with lots of bead merchants. Some of the most interesting shops here include: **Boutique Anatolia** (Kizlarağasi Hani, 871 Sokak No. 19/55, Tel. 446-0641, Fax 259-5031, website: www.boutiqueanatolia.com) for nice quality country antiques and textiles; **Yertan** (Kizlarağasi Hani, 871 Sokak No. 19/65, Tel. 489-8464) for a unique collection of handmade purses, embroidery, silver, and jewelry with Ottoman designs; and **Arsena Turizm** (Kizlarağasi Hani, 871 Sokak No. 69, Tel. 446-2936) for camel bone boxes and miniature paintings, inlaid picture frames and knives, water pipes, copper pots, dolls, and meershaum pipes. Also look for **Galeri Anatolia** (Kizlarağasi Hani, 871 Sokak No. 21/42-43, Tel./Fax 441-8306) for rugs and a few paintings and antiques and **Evvelzaman Antika** (Kizlarağasi Hani, 871 Sokak No. 19/35, Tel. 445-9806) for antiques and collectibles (i.e., lots of junk).

### IZMIR HILTON HOTEL AREA

Located at Gazi Osmanpaşa Bulvari No. 7, just southeast of Cumhuriyet Square, is the five-star Izmir Hilton Hotel with an attached shopping center and nearby street shops. While the shopping center has fallen on hard times – much of it is now vacant – you'll still find some good jewelry, carpet, and leather shops here. Just off the hotel lobby is **Sponza** (Tel. 425-8576) for excellent quality jewelry. The adjacent shopping center includes **Borg** and **Taştabanoğlu** for jewelry and **Anatolia** for carpets. **Taştabanoğlu** also has an arts and crafts shop on the 9th floor of the hotel, just outside the Colonnade Restaurant.

Across the street from the Izmir Hilton Hotel is **Topaki** (1385 Sokak No. 3/Z2, Yaniasir İş Merkezi, Tel./Fax 446-5981, website: www.topkapicarpets.com), a small but nice carpet, kilim, and Anatolian handicraft shop. Experienced in working with the American military in Turkey and shipping, the shop offers unique gift items in the form of small carpets designed as American flags and Santa Claus.

### ALSANCAK AREA

The Alsancak area is Izmir's upscale shopping and dining district – the best of the best of lifestyle shopping in Izmir. Indeed, this area is to Izmir what Nişantaşi is to Istanbul. Located a half kilometer northeast of Cumhuriyet Square, this is a pleasant and trendy neighborhood shopping area bordered by 1382 Sokak, Pleyne Bulvari, and M. Enverbey Caddesi. These streets are lined with boutiques, cafes, and restaurants. Several additional shopping streets connect to these main shopping streets. As you approach this area, you may want to first stop at a carpet shop along Cumhuriyet Bulvari – **Motif Hali** (Cumhuriyet Bulvari No. 159/D, Tel. 421-1436 or Fax 421-3976). This two-story shop includes a very good collection of carpets and kilims, some with modern designs and woven in Nepal. From here you can walk across the street and enter the main shopping area at **1382 Sokak** (Gül Sokak). This street is lined with many excellent quality shoe, fabric, home furnishing, clothing, and leather boutiques. A local branch of Istanbul-based **Matras** (1382 Sokak No. 12, Tel. 422-1979) offers top quality and fashionable leather purses, briefcases, coats, jackets, luggage, wallets, and belts. At the intersection of Pleyne Bulvari, turn left and you'll come to a very interesting costume jewelry shop which carries its own unique jewelry designs along with hair handbags from France and an interesting collection of watches with colored bands – **Beril** (Pleyne Bulvari No. 32/C, Tel. 421-2733). When you come to the intersection with M. Enverbey Caddesi, turn left and you'll pass several outdoor cafes and restaurants as well as one of our favorite shops in Izmir and Turkey on this delightful tree-lined street – **Derishow** (M. Enverbey Caddesi No. 10, Tel. 422-2025). Based in Istanbul, this combination fashion boutique and home decor shop includes a wonderful selection of leather fashion as well as a very attractive "home collection" consisting of ceramics, lamps, candle holders, and trays.

## BEST OF THE BEST

❑ **Derishow:** *M. Enverbey Caddesi No. 10, Alsancak, Tel. 422-2025.* This is a two-in-one shop – a fashionable leather and clothes boutique and a home decor shop. As noted in Chapter 4 on Istanbul, Derishow is one of Turkey's leading fashion designers. The owners have recently opened a new home decor shop called Mimarca. The lamps, ceramics, trays, metal bowls, candle holders, serving trays, and utensils come from their Mimarca operation.

❑ **Motif Hali:** *Cumhuriyet Bulvari No. 159/D, Tel. 421-1436 or Fax 421-3976.* This carpet and kilim shop is operated by a partner to the owner of Motif Gallery in Çeşme. It includes an excellent selection of carpets and kilims from Turkey and other countries. Offers both traditional and modern designs.

As a wholesaler of rugs primarily selling to the local market, this shop tends to offer good prices.

❑ **Boutique Anatolia:** *Kizlaragasi Hani, 871 Sokak No. 19/55, Konak, Tel. 446-0641 or Fax 259-5031. Website: www.boutique anatolia.com.* This is a very small but extremely nice and well focused shop. Specializing in country antiques and textiles from the villages of Anatolia, it also includes embroideries from Uzbekistan. The shop is filled to the ceiling and overflows outside the door with all kinds of unique and tempting treasures – lamps, jewelry, bells, wood coffee roasters, copper yogurt and water pots, keys, locks, and old wooden chests. The website presents their full product line which is difficult to display in their tiny bazaar shop.

❑ **Yertan:** *Kizlaragasi Hani, 871 Sokak No. 19/65, Konak, Tel. 489-8464.* This small shop also is very focused. It specializes in producing small purses made of silk, embroidery, silver, and jewelry – all with unique Ottoman designs.

❑ **Mustafa and Füsun Ünlü:** *Izmir, Tel./Fax (90-232) 231-3008. By appointment only.* Artisans and husband/wife team Mustafa and Füsun Ünlü have single-handedly revived the famous Ottoman art of "Tel Kakma," embroidered silks with finely woven ribbons of hammered silver and gold thread. The Ünlüs' painstaking, fabulous creations are fit for a sultan, if not other royalty. Many of their clients are, indeed, royalty. Prices for their exquisite creations start at US$15,000 and go up.

❑ **Topkapi:** *1385 Sokak No. 3/Z2, Yaniasir Iş Merkezi, Tel./Fax 446-5981. Website: www.topkapicarpets.com).* Located across the street from the Izmir Hilton Hotel, this small shop offers a good collection of carpets, kilims, and Anatolian handicrafts at reasonable prices. The owners regularly work with American military personnel stationed in Turkey. They are very experienced in packing and shipping, using the services of a company next door. Look for small carpets designed as American flags and Santa Claus.

❑ **Sponza:** *Izmir Hilton Hotel lobby, Gazi Osmanpaşa Bulvari No. 7, Tel. 425-8576. Also has a shop at the Efes Hotel, Gazi Osmanpaşa Bulvari 1.* Izmir is the headquarters for the Sponza chain of jewelry stores throughout Turkey which began in Izmir in 1906. The owner, Enzo Sponza, is often found in this shop. Sponza offers gorgeous pins, necklaces, and rings using diamonds, opals, and emeralds. Many of the designs are copies of major international jewelers, but they also do many original designs. However, the ostensibly friendly and knowledgeable owner has a bad attitude toward Americans – doesn't like them as customers because they are picky. Our advice: It's good to play American here since many of the pieces are expensive!

## ACCOMMODATIONS

If you plan to stay in Izmir, the best hotel in the city in terms of facilities and service is the Hilton Izmir:

❏ **Hilton Izmir:** *Gazi Osmanpaşa Bulvari No. 7, 35210 Izmir, Turkey, Tel. (90-232) 441-6060, Fax (90-232) 441-2277 or toll-free in U.S. or Canada 800-321-3232.* Located in the central city, this five-star hotel really does earn its stars. At 34 floors it towers above the rest of the city and is the tallest building on the Aegean coast. Convenient to Izmir's new convention center as well as the city center. The lobby is small but efficient and also comfortable if you seek out the lounge area located next to the Italian restaurant, *La dolce Vita*, on the ground floor. 381 guestrooms, including 43 Executive rooms and five deluxe suites, offer services and amenities expected of Hilton guests. Guestrooms and suites are nicely decorated, although the complaint has been heard that it could be a Hilton anywhere in the world. Although a piece of pottery or a painting in the room with Turkish roots would add a nice touch, if you have been traveling for long outside the major cities you may welcome a real five-star property where what you expect is what you get. Executive Floor rooms have tea/coffee making facilities, iron and ironing board, in-room safe, a CD player and video player, and laptop PCs are available to Executive Floor guests free of charge. *Windows on the Bay* offers a stunning panorama of the bay and city from the 31$^{st}$ floor. The international cuisine it serves is excellent, beautifully presented, and the service on the spot but unobtrusive. Live music is featured as well. The *Colonnade Restaurant* on the 9$^{th}$ floor serves breakfast and buffets, and the authentic Italian restaurant, *La Dolce Vita*, on the ground floor offers an extensive choice of pastas and caters to hotel guests and local patrons alike. It is also a great spot to enjoy morning coffee or afternoon tea. The only negative is that the indoor (only) swimming pool and massage rooms appeared "worn" and not up to the standards evident in the rest of the hotel. There is a shopping center attached to the hotel, but many of the shops were empty at the time of our visit. Health/Fitness Facilities; Business Center; Conference/Banquet Facilities.

## RESTAURANTS

Izmir is especially famous for its many waterfront seafood restaurants. Many of the best restaurants are found in the Alsancak area. The following restaurants are well worth considering when planning your dining agenda:

❑ **Windows on the Bay:** *Hilton Izmir, Gazi Osmanpaşa Bulvari No. 7, Tel. 441-6060.* Don't miss this one. It was one of our best dining experiences in Turkey. This is Izmir's only true fine dining restaurant. Located on the 31st floor, it offers a nice view of the city and harbor below. The striped chairs and large tables are set in a very pretty and romantic dining room with lots of ambience. Like the rest of the Hilton, this restaurant offers exceptional service. The food is excellent, especially the seafood mixed grill. Live but unobtrusive piano music.

❑ **Altinkapi:** *1444 Sokak No. 9, Alsancak. Tel. 422-5687.* Considered by many locals to be the best place for kebabs in Izmir.

❑ **Kemal'in Yeri:** *1453 Sokak No. 20/A, Alsancak, Tel. 422-3190.* A favorite seafood restaurant with reasonable prices.

❑ **Deniz:** *Atatürk Caddesi No. 188, Alsancak, Tel. 422-0601.* Facing the oceanfront, this popular seafood restaurant is located on the ground floor of the Izmir Palas Hotel. Deniz is especially noted for its delicious grilled swordfish kebab (kiliç şiş).

## ENJOYING YOUR STAY

Izmir offers a few museums, historical sites, mosques, and parks worth exploring if you have time. Some of the most popular places to visit include:

❑ **Archaeology Museum:** *Cumhuriyet Bulveri, Bahribaba Park (south of Konak Square). Tel. 484-8324. Open Tuesday to Sunday, 9am-noon and 1-5pm.* Showcases famous ancient statues (Poseidon and Demeter from the Agora) as well as ceramics, pottery, and glass.

❏ **Ethnographic Museum:** *Next to the Archaeology Museum. Tel. 484-8324. Open Tuesday to Sunday, 9am-noon and 1-5pm.* Presents an interesting collection of Turkish folk arts. Includes collections of carpets, costumes, ceramics, and much more.

❏ **Atatürk Museum:** *Atatürk Caddesi. Open Tuesday to Sunday, 9am-noon and 1-5pm.* Located in an old house used by Atatürk, the museum includes photos of Atatürk and some of his personal items.

❏ **Agora:** *Namazgah, Anafartalar Caddesi (at the foot of Kadifekale Hill near 816 Sokak). Open daily 8:30am to 5:30pm.* The interesting ruins of the old Roman market. Includes impressive columns, statues, and remnants of foundations.

---

# ÇANAKKALE, TROY, AND BERGAMA

The region north of Izmir, which connects Asian and European Turkey at Çanakkale along the Dardanelle Straits, is known for its ancient sites, quaint fishing villages, and holiday resorts. Referred to as the North Aegean, this area is especially popular with visitors interested in history and archaeological sites or getting to and from Istanbul and Izmir. Travel-shoppers will most likely find little of interest here.

## ÇANAKKALE

Located approximately 310 kilometers north of Izmir and 320 kilometers southwest of Istanbul, Çanakkale is strategically located at the narrow (1,200 meter) entrance to the Çanakkale Straits (Dardanelles). Historically it policed sea traffic plying the straits that connect Europe with Asia as well as the Sea of Marmara with the Aegean Sea. Many invading armies from ancient times have passed this way to conquer many areas of present-day Turkey. During World War I, Çanakkale became the site for Winston Churchill's ill-fated Gallipoli campaign that resulted in the deaths of more than 50,000 Allied troops and perhaps as many at 200,000 Turks (some accounts estimate the total Allied and Turk deaths to be closer to 500,000). From this great battlefield rose Turkey's great hero, Atatürk, who as Lieutenant-Colonel Mustafa Kemal, led the bloody resistance against the advancing Allies. This important nine-month battle, which turned the tide in World War I, is memorialized in 31 manicured cemeteries on the north side of the Dardanelles. Accordingly, Çanakkale serves as the base from which to visit one of the most important battle sites of the 20th century.

There's not much to see and do in Çanakkale. It's a small nondescript town that operates a ferry service connecting the northern and southern banks of the Dardanelles. If you're planning to drive from Izmir to Istanbul or visa versa, you may want to cross at Çanakkale, and if it is late in the day, stay overnight here. In fact, if you're coming from Izmir and plan to visit Bergama (Pergamum) and Troy along the way, Çanakkale will probably be your last stop for the day.

Most activities in Çanakkale radiate from the ferry terminal which begins operating at 7am. Ferries depart every hour and take about 30 minutes to cross to Eceabat and Kilitbahir on the European side. A relatively well maintained city, Çanakkale's downtown area can be easily covered on foot within an hour. Its single pedestrian-only street includes several jewelry and clothing shops of marginal interest to visitors. Most shopping in Çanakkale focuses on relatively uninteresting local consumer goods. Unlike many other cities, Çanakkale does not have a covered market.

If you are staying overnight in Çanakkale, the best hotel town is the Hotel Akol:

❑ **Hotel Akol:** *Kordon Boyu, 17100, Çanakkale, Turkey, Tel. (90-286) 217-9456 or Fax (90-286) 217-2897. E-mail: hotelakol@ hotelakol.com.tr.* The only four-star rated hotel in Çanakkale, the Akol does offer many four-star amenities – just don't let your expectations get too high. Like most "up-country" hotels, refurbishment occurs after, rather than before, it is apparent it is needed. The lobby is clad in marble and has lots of seating space. The 136 guestrooms and two suites all have balconies and expected basic amenities including a mini-bar and a hair dryer in the bath. There is no in-room safe. The twin beds and small table with two chairs in the regular rooms remind one of a budget chain motel in the U.S., but it is the best available here. Most guests stay one night as they wait for the morning ferry to take them across the Dardanelles Strait as they return to Istanbul. There are two restaurants and they are prepared to handle conferences and tour groups. The restaurants provide a choice of buffet or an a la carte menu. There is a panoramic roof bar. Swimming Pool; Seminar Halls/Banquet Facilities.

## TROY

The ancient site of Troy – the subject of Homer's *The Illiad* and the legend of the Trojan Wars and the Trojan Horse – is located approximately 20 kilometers south of Çanakkale. This site is best appreciated with an imagination since there isn't much to see other than a small museum, lots of rocks from ongoing excavations, and a large reproduction wooden Trojan horse visitors seem compelled to climb into for photo opportunities. Most of the surrounding area has been under excavation since the site was first uncovered in 1871 by the controversial amateur archaeologist Heinrich Schliemann. Subsequent diggings have uncovered the layering of nine distinct civilizations. Whether any of these layers can be associated with the civilization of Homer's *The Iliad* is still questionable. Nonetheless, it's always nice to imagine such a significant site, even though you may be doing so from the belly of the big brown wooden horse! You won't need more than one hour to visit this site.

## BERGAMA AND PERGAMUM

Located 250 kilometers south of Çanakkale and eight kilometers from the bustling town of Bergama, the ancient ruins of Pergamum (also known as Pergamon) constitute one of the best archaeological sites in Turkey. Located at the top of a hill overlooking the town and valley, Pergamum's famous acropolis includes an impressive library, theater, and gymnasium, an Agora, the temples of Trajan and Dionysus, and the altar of Zeus. Visiting this site will probably take a couple of hours, given the steep drive up and down the hill and the many interesting sites within the acropolis. Several tourist shops at the entrance to this area offer lots of overpriced carpets and souvenirs (the bookmarks offered here sell for four times what we paid elsewhere in Turkey!). However, at the very foot of the hill, just before you begin the ascent, are small shops of greater interest to tourists.

The town of Bergama includes an interesting **Archaeological Museum** (Hükümet Caddesi, Tel. 633-1096, open daily from April to October, 8:30am - 5pm, and open Tuesday to Sunday from November to March, 8am - 5:30pm) with numerous statues and artifacts from Pergamum. It also has a covered bazaar with many copper shops and small jewelry stores.

# Index

## ISTANBUL

## BURSA, IZNIK, AND BEYOND

**MEDITERRANEAN
COAST**

# The Authors

WINSTON CHURCHILL PUT IT BEST – *"My needs are very simple – I simply want the best of everything."* Indeed, his attitude on life is well and alive amongst many of today's travelers. With limited time, careful budgeting, and a sense of adventure, many people seek both quality and value as they search for the best of the best.

**Ron and Caryl Krannich**, Ph.Ds, discovered this fact of travel life nearly 20 years ago when they were living and working in Thailand as consultants with the Office of the Prime Minister. Former university professors and specialists on Southeast Asia, they discovered what they really loved to do – shop for quality arts, antiques, and home decorative items – was not well represented in most travel guides that primarily focused on sightseeing, hotels, and restaurants. While some guidebooks included a small section on shopping, they only listed types of products and names and addresses of a few shops, many of questionable quality. And budget guides simply avoided quality shopping altogether, as if shopping was a travel sin!

The Krannichs knew there was much more to travel than what was represented in most travel guides. Avid collectors of Asian, South Pacific, Middle Eastern, and Latin American arts, antiques, and home decorative items, they learned long ago that one of the best ways to experience another culture and meet its talented artists and craftspeople was by shopping for local products. Not only would they learn a great deal about the culture and society, they also acquired some wonderful products, met many interesting and talented individuals, and helped support the continuing development of local arts and crafts.

But they quickly learned shopping in many countries was very different from shopping in North America and Europe. In the West, merchants nicely display items, identify prices, and periodically run sales. At the same time, shoppers in the West can easily do comparative shopping, watch for sales, and trust quality and delivery; they even have consumer protection! Americans and Europeans in other parts of the world face a shopping culture based on different principles. Like a fish out of water, they make many mistakes: don't know how to bargain, avoid purchasing large items because they don't understand shipping, and are frequent victims of scams and rip-offs, especially in the case of gems and jewelry. To shop a country right, travelers need to know how to find quality products, bargain for the best prices, avoid scams, and ship their purchases with ease. What they most need is a combination travel and how-to book that focuses on the best of the best.

In 1987 the Krannichs inaugurated their first shopping guide to Asia – *Shopping in Exotic Places* – a guide to quality shopping in Hong Kong, South Korea, Thailand, Indonesia, and Singapore. Receiving rave reviews from leading travel publications and professionals, the book quickly found an enthusiastic audience amongst other avid travel-shoppers. It broke new ground as a combination travel and how-to book. No longer would shopping be confined to just naming products and identifying names and addresses of shops. It also included advice on how to pack for a shopping trip (take two suitcases, one filled with bubble-wrap), comparative shopping, bargaining skills, and shopping rules. Shopping was serious stuff requiring serious treatment of the subject by individuals who understood what they were doing. The Krannichs subsequently expanded the series to include separate volumes on Hong Kong, Thailand, Indonesia, Singapore and Malaysia, Australia and Papua New Guinea, the South Pacific, and the Caribbean.

Beginning in 1996, the series took on a new look as well as an expanded focus. Known as the *Impact Guides* and appropriately titled *The Treasures and Pleasures of . . . Best of the Best*, new editions covered Hong Kong, Thailand, Indonesia, Singapore, Malaysia, Paris and the French Riviera, and the

Caribbean. In 1997 and 1999 new volumes appeared on Italy, Hong Kong, and China. New volumes for 2000-2002 included India, Australia, Thailand, Hong Kong, Singapore, Bali, Egypt, Brazil (Rio and São Paulo), Vietnam, Cambodia, Mexico, and Southern Africa.

The *Impact Guides* now serve as the major content for a travel website appropriately called *i*ShopAroundTheWorld:

www.ishoparoundtheworld.com

While the primary focus remains shopping for quality products, the books and website also include useful information on the best hotels, restaurants, and sightseeing. As the authors note, *"Our users are discerning travelers who seek the best of the best. They are looking for a very special travel experience which is not well represented in other travel guides."*

The Krannichs' passion for traveling and shopping is well represented in their home which is uniquely designed around their Asian, South Pacific, Middle East, North African, and Latin American art collections and which has been featured on CNN and in the *New York Times. "We're fortunate in being able to create a living environment which pulls together so many wonderful travel memories and quality products,"* say the Krannichs. *"We learned long ago to seek out quality products and buy the best we could afford at the time. Quality lasts and is appreciated for years to come. Many of our readers share our passion for quality shopping abroad."* Their books also are popular with designers, antique dealers, and importers who use them to source products and suppliers.

While the *Impact Guides* keep the Krannichs busy traveling to exotic places, their travel series is an avocation rather than a vocation. The Krannichs also are noted authors of more than 35 career books (see page iv), some of which deal with how to find international and travel jobs. The Krannichs also operate one of the world's largest career resource centers. Their works are available in most bookstores or through the publisher's online bookstore: www.impactpublications.com.

If you have any questions or comments for the authors, please direct them to:

Ron and Caryl Krannich
IMPACT PUBLICATIONS
9104 Manassas Drive, Suite N
Manassas Park, VA 20111-5211 USA
Fax 703-335-9486
E-mail: krannich@impactpublications.com

# Feedback and Recommendations

WE WELCOME FEEDBACK AND RECOMMEN-dations from our readers and users. If you have encountered a particular shop or travel experience, either good or bad, that you feel should be included in future editions of this book or on www.ishoparoundtheworld.com, please send your comments by e-mail, fax, or mail to:

Ron and Caryl Krannich
IMPACT PUBLICATIONS
9104 Manassas Drive, Suite N
Manassas Park, VA 20111-5211 USA
Fax 703-335-9486
E-mail: krannich@impactpublications.com

_____

_____

_____

_____

_____

_____

_____

# More Treasures
# and Pleasures

THE FOLLOWING TRAVEL GUIDES CAN BE OR-
dered directly from the publisher. Complete this form (or
list the titles), include your name and address, enclose
payment, and send your order to:

IMPACT PUBLICATIONS
9104 Manassas Drive, Suite N
Manassas Park, VA 20111-5211 (USA)
Tel. 1-800-361-1055 (orders only)
703-361-7300 (information) Fax 703-335-9486
E-mail: info@impactpublications.com
Online bookstores: www.impactpublications.com or
www.ishoparoundtheworld.com

All prices are in U.S. dollars. Orders from individuals should be
prepaid by check, moneyorder, or credit card (Visa, Master-
Card, American Express, and Discover). We accept credit card
orders by telephone, fax, email, and online. If your order must
be shipped outside the United States, please include an additional US$2.00 per title for surface mail or the appropriate air
mail rate for books weighting 24 ounces each. Orders usually
ship within 48 hours. For more information on the authors,
travel resources, and international shopping, visit www.impact
publications.com and www.ishoparoundtheworld.com.

| Qty. | TITLES | Price | TOTAL |
|------|--------|-------|-------|
| __ | Air Traveler's Survival Guide | $14.95 | _____ |
| __ | Stone Gods, Wooden Elephants (fiction) | $14.95 | _____ |
| __ | The Traveling Woman | $14.95 | _____ |
| __ | Travel Planning on the Internet | $19.95 | _____ |
| __ | Treasures and Pleasures of Australia | $17.95 | _____ |
| __ | Treasures and Pleasures of the Caribbean | $16.95 | _____ |
| __ | Treasures and Pleasures of China | $14.95 | _____ |
| __ | Treasures and Pleasures of Egypt | $16.95 | _____ |
| __ | Treasures and Pleasures of Hong Kong | $16.95 | _____ |